Rhetoric is once again becoming valued as an essential element in the exploration of the ancient world. The present volume is part of a general renaissance in the study of rhetoric and bears testimony to a discipline undergoing rapid and exciting change. It draws together established and newer scholars in the field to produce a probing and innovative analysis of the role played by rhetoric in Roman culture. Utilizing a variety of critical approaches and methodologies, these scholars examine not only the role of rhetoric in Roman society but also the relationship between rhetoric and Rome's major literary genres. *Roman Eloquence* emphasizes the theory and practice of rhetoric in a variety of social, political and literary contexts. In addition to demonstrating rhetoric's critical significance for Roman culture, the studies reveal the important role played by rhetoric in the formation of the various genres of literature. This accessible and critically up-to-date volume will be of interest to classicists, literary theorists and anyone concerned with the origins, development and influence of Roman rhetorical theory and practice.

William J. Dominik is Associate Professor (Reader) of Classics at the University of Natal, South Africa, and the editor of the classical journal *Scholia*. He has published a number of books and articles on Roman literature and rhetoric.

ROMAN ELOQUENCE

Rhetoric in Society and Literature

Edited by
William J. Dominik

London and New York

First published 1997
by Routledge
11 New Fetter Lane, London EC4P 4EE

Simultaneously published in the USA and Canada
by Routledge
29 West 35th Street, New York, NY 10001

Typeset in Garamond by
Ponting–Green Publishing Services, Chesham, Buckinghamshire
Printed and bound in Great Britain by
T.J. International Ltd, Padstow, Cornwall

British Library Cataloguing in Publication Data
A catalogue record for this book is available from
the British Library

Library of Congress Cataloging in Publication Data
Roman eloquence: rhetoric in society and literature / edited by
William J. Dominik
p.   cm.
Includes bibliographical references and index.
1. Latin literature–History and criticism–Theory etc.
2. Rome–Social life and customs.
3. Literature and society–Rome.
4. Rhetoric, Ancient.
I. Dominik William, J.
PA6019.R66   1997
808'.00937–dc21   96–52767

ISBN 0–415–12544–8 (hbk)
ISBN 0–415–12545–6 (pbk)

Contents

CONTENTS

Part III Rhetoric and genre

Notes on contributors

Susanna Morton Braund is Professor of Latin at Royal Holloway, University of London. She is the author or editor of numerous publications on Roman satire and other aspects of Latin literature, including *Beyond Anger: A Study of Juvenal's Third Book of Satires* (1988), *Satire and Society in Ancient Rome* (ed.) (1989), *Roman Verse Satire* (1992), *Lucan's Civil War* (tr.) (1992), *The Roman Satirists and Their Masks* (1996), *Juvenal: Satires Book 1* (ed.) (1996), and *The Passions in Roman Thought and Literature* (co-ed.) (1997).

Gualtiero Calboli is Professor of Latin and Chair of the Department of Classical and Medieval Philology at the University of Bologna. Among his many books are *Studi Grammaticali* (1962), *A Commentary on Rhetorica ad Herennium* (1969), *M. Porci Catonis Oratio pro Rhodiensibus* (1978), *Papers on Grammar I–IV* (1980–94), *Subordination and Other Topics in Latin* (ed.) (1989), *Latin Vulgaire-Latin Tardif* (ed.) (1990), and *Über das Lateinische, Vom Indogermanischen zu den Romanischen Sprachen* (1997).

Robert W. Cape, Jr is Assistant Professor of Classics and Director of Gender Studies, Austin College. He is completing a commentary on Cicero's orations *Against Catiline* and writing a book on oratory and society in the Roman Republic.

Catherine Connors is Assistant Professor in the Department of Classics, University of Washington, Seattle. She has published articles on Petronius and on Roman epic. She is the author of *Petronius the Poet: Verse and Literary Tradition in the Satyricon* (forthcoming).

William J. Dominik is Associate Professor (Reader) of Classics at the University of Natal and editor of the classical journal *Scholia*.

His publications on Roman literature include *The Mythic Voice of Statius* (1994) and *Speech and Rhetoric in Statius' Thebaid* (1994). He is presently co-editing *Concordantia in Sidonii Apollinaris Epistulas* and *The Roman Satirists. Lucilius to Juvenal: An Anthology.*

Elaine Fantham, Giger Professor of Latin at Princeton University since 1986, is a British and Canadian citizen educated at Oxford University. Before coming to Princeton she taught for eighteen years at the University of Toronto. Her publications include *Comparative Studies in Republican Latin Imagery* (1972), *Seneca's Troades* (ed.) (1982), *Lucan: De Bello Civili II* (ed.) (1992), *Women in the Classical World* (co-author) (1994), and *Roman Literary Culture* (1996).

Joseph Farrell is Associate Professor of Classical Studies at the University of Pennsylvania. He is the author of *Vergil's Georgics and the Traditions of Ancient Epic: The Art of Allusion in Literary History* (1991) and of *Latin Language and Latin Culture* (forthcoming). He is also director of The Vergil Project, an interactive, hypertextual edition and commentary on the works of Vergil available via the World Wide Web.

Sander M. Goldberg is Professor of Classics at the University of California, Los Angeles. He is the author of *The Making of Menander's Comedy* (1980), *Understanding Terence* (1986), and *Epic in Republican Rome* (1995). From 1990–1995 he was the editor of the *Transactions of the American Philological Association*.

Joseph J. Hughes is Associate Professor of Foreign Languages (Classics) at Southwest Missouri State University. He has published a number of articles on Roman rhetoric.

John T. Kirby chairs the Program in Comparative Literature at Purdue University, where he founded the Program in Classical Studies. Educated at the University of North Carolina at Chapel Hill and St Benet's Hall, Oxford, he specializes in rhetorical and poetic theory. He is the author of *The Rhetoric of Cicero's Pro Cluentio* (1990) and editor of *The Comparative Reader* and *Landmark Essays on Ciceronian Rhetoric* (both forthcoming).

Neil O'Sullivan is a Senior Lecturer in the Department of Classics and Ancient History at the University of Western Australia and has been co-editor of *Antichthon* since 1993. His publications include *Alcidamas, Aristophanes and the Beginnings of Greek Stylistic Theory* (1992).

NOTES ON CONTRIBUTORS

Amy Richlin is Professor of Classics and Gender Studies at the University of Southern California. She is the author of *The Garden of Priapus* (1983; rev. 1992), editor of *Pornography and Representation in Greece and Rome* (1992), and co-editor of *Feminist Theory and the Classics* (1993). She is now working on a book on constructions of masculinity in the Roman rhetorical schools.

Michele Valerie Ronnick is Associate Professor of Classics in the Department of Classics, Greek and Latin at Wayne State University. She is the author of *Paradoxa Stoicorum: A Commentary, an Interpretation, and a Study of Its Influence* (1991) and of numerous articles on Latin literature and the classical tradition.

Peter Toohey is Associate Professor in the Department of Classics and Ancient History at the University of New England. He is the author of *Reading Epic: An Introduction to the Ancient Narratives* (1992), *Epic Lessons: An Introduction to Ancient Didactic Poetry* (1996), and co-editor of *Inventing Ancient Culture: Historicism, Periodization and the Ancient World* (1997).

Preface

Rhetoric is one of civilization's oldest and most persistent art forms. Introduced in the early part of the second century BCE into Rome, one of the foundational cultures of the modern world, it eventually established itself as the cornerstone of Roman education, literature and oratory. The present volume not only examines the origins, development and theory of Roman rhetoric but also its practice, role and influence in antiquity. A few important studies on Roman rhetoric as a cultural phenomenon have appeared in recent years, but the majority of books in the field are outdated. There is to date no single text on Roman rhetoric that examines its role in society and its relationship to various literary genres; hence this collection of essays, which attempts to address a clear gap in the existing scholarship on the subject. In fact, some of the topics and genres discussed have received little detailed critical attention, while the background material presented in some of the chapters is given for the sake of providing the context for the innovative work that follows. This volume forms a companion to *Persuasion: Greek Rhetoric in Action*, published by Routledge in 1994, which deals with the influence and exploitation of Greek rhetoric in ancient times and modern reactions to it.

Roman Eloquence has fourteen chapters, each focusing on particular aspects concerned with the function and exploitation of rhetoric. The introductory chapter deals with the development of Roman rhetoric from the beginning and outlines the contributions of each of the essays, while the subsequent chapters explore the function of rhetoric in Roman society, the transitions and tensions between various movements of rhetoric, between the adherents of different styles, and the relationship between rhetoric and various literary genres. Other chapters on a variety of topics could have been included, but any book must entail choices; owing to the constraints of space, these unfortunately had to be omitted in the planning stage.

Rhetoric is sometimes perceived as an obstacle rather than as a bridge to understanding, as Jorge Luis Borges has remarked. This volume is designed to make Roman rhetoric more understandable and accessible to students, teachers and scholars of classics, rhetoric, communication, English, philosophy, and speech and drama, as well as the informed general public interested in these areas. Scholars working specifically in the field of Roman rhetoric will also find new and interesting material within these covers. Quotations in Latin and Greek are generally accompanied by translations for readers without knowledge of these languages, and transliterated Greek is preferred to the original Greek characters.

My debts are many. Ian Worthington suggested this volume but withdrew from the project due to other commitments. Susanna Morton Braund, Elaine Fantham, John Kirby, Bernhard Kytzler and Peter Toohey offered sound advice and were supportive at various stages. I wish to thank Routledge, particularly Richard Stoneman, Senior Editor, for agreeing to publish the book in the first instance and for permitting me to make necessary changes to the original proposal; Barbara Duke, Desk Editor, for taking the book through the editing and production process; and Penny Nettle, freelance copyeditor, for preparing the final manuscript for publication. Special thanks are also due to Ann Delany, who assisted in the editing process and in finalizing the index, and to Segun Ige, who helped to compile the index. I would also like to acknowledge the support of the University of Natal for my research. Finally, I dedicate this book to the memory of my young children, Tristan and Chantelle, recently deceased.

W.J.D.
University of Natal
Durban, South Africa
April 1997

Abbreviations

ANCIENT AUTHORS AND WORKS

Abbreviations of ancient authors and works are those listed in the following works:

Hammond, N. G. L. and Scullard, H. H. (eds) (1970) *The Oxford Classical Dictionary*. 2nd edn. Oxford.
Souter, A., Wyllie, J. M., and Glare, P. G. W. *et al.* (eds) (1968–82) *Oxford Latin Dictionary*. Oxford.
Liddell, H. G., Scott, R. and Jones, H. S. (eds) (1940) *A Greek–English Lexicon*. 9th edn. Oxford.

In addition, note the following modern works:

RE   Pauly, A. and Wissowa, G. *et al.* (eds) (1893–1980) *Real Encyclopädie der klassischen Altertumswissenschaft*. Stuttgart.
FGrH Jacoby, F. (ed.) (1923–) *Fragmente der griechischen Historiker*. Leiden.

Part I

THEORIES, TRANSITIONS AND TENSIONS

1

Introduction: the Roman
Suada

Gualtiero Calboli and William J. Dominik

Suada appears as early as Ennius in a reference to Marcus Cornelius Cethegus as 'the marrow of Persuasion' (*Ann.* 308).[1] The passage is explained by Cicero (*Brut.* 59):

> Πειθώ, the Greek expression, which it is the duty of the orator to effect, Ennius termed 'Suada', the marrow of which he claimed Cethegus was; so that he said our orator was the marrow of that goddess which, Eupolis wrote, forever sat on the lips of Pericles.

This passage demonstrates that *Suada* (connected with *suavis*, 'sweet', 'pleasant') is the Roman counterpart of the Greek *Peithô* (connected with *peithein*, 'persuade', and *pithanos*, 'persuasive'). The oldest form of persuasion was the goddess Peitho, who was linked with Aphrodite. There is no mention in Cicero of the sexual element to be found in the original form of Peitho, but it is uncertain whether this is due to the actual absence of such an element, which is more probably the case, or upon Cicero's prudish attitude towards this subject. The story of Phryne, however, is enough to confirm that a sexual element was always present in Peitho's action and could emerge at the first opportunity.[2] When it was apparent that Phryne, a ministrant of Aphrodite, was about to be condemned on a capital charge of impiety, she (or her advocate Hyperides) revealed her breasts so as to invoke the pity of the judges, whereupon they refrained from putting her to death (Ath. 590d–e; Alciphr. 4.4; Quint. *Inst.* 2.15.9).

Ludwig Voigt draws attention not only to Peitho's connection with Aphrodite but also to the presence of this goddess in poetry and rhetoric.[3] In Aeschylus' *Agamemnon* Peitho is identified as the daughter of Ate and 'overpowers a man by persuading him that he

3

is obliged to do what it is not right for him to do, and at the same time talks him out of his resistance' (385–98).[4] In Aeschylus' *Choephoroi*, Peitho is called 'the deceiver' (726). The same expression occurs in Sophocles and Euripides,[5] prompting Voigt's comparison between Euripides' *Hecuba* ('Persuasion, the only tyrant for men', 816) and Gorgias' *Helen* ('speech is a great master', 8),[6] even though this comparison is only valid if one interprets the force of persuasion as consisting in *logos* ('speech'). In Aristophanes' *Frogs* there is a single verse that confirms this connection: 'Persuasion has no shrine but eloquent speech' (1391). Since this line appears in Euripides' *Antigone* (fr. 170),[7] it may have been known to the early Roman poets of tragedy. Certainly the act of persuasion, which occurs in Greek comedy, was known by the Roman comic poets (e.g., Men. *Epitr.* 379–80: 'Dear Persuasion, be my ally and render the words that I speak victorious'; Plaut. *Cist.* 566: 'I was already bringing her to me through my persuasion').

The presence of Greek rhetoric in Rome and its growing influence in the second century BCE is apparent from the expulsion of rhetoricians from Rome in 161 BCE (Suet. *Gramm.* 25). The widespread use of rhetoric began with the great political trials when the introduction of prosecution on the popular level gave rise to much litigation.[8] At this time rhetoric appears as it was in its original form, namely a legal instrument whose first aim was to persuade, but even from the outset it was concerned with more than just persuasion.

Apart from these first traces of Roman interest in rhetoric, it was not until the beginning of the first century BCE that the first truly Roman examples of rhetoric emerged – three handbooks of rhetoric, of which the first were left incomplete. The first manual was composed by the orator Marcus Antonius between 102 and 92 BCE, the year of the censors' castigation of the *rhetores Latini*'; only a short fragment survives of this work (cf. Cic. *De Or.* Z. IOG; Quint. *Iust.* 3.6. 45).[9] The earliest extant rhetorical treatise is Cicero's *De Inventione*, probably written in 88–7 BCE.[10] Between 86 and 82 BCE the *Rhetorica ad Herennium* (of unknown authorship), the first complete rhetorical treatise in Latin to survive, was composed. Antonius' manual, Cicero's *De Inventione*, and the *Rhetorica ad Herennium* suggest that rhetoric had arrived at Rome in the form of a comprehensive system (*technê*). These treatises followed Anaximenes' *Rhetorica ad Alexandrum*, the sole surviving pre-Aristotelian manual of rhetoric, Aristotle's *Rhetorica*, and the work of Hermagoras of Temnos. While the *Rhetorica ad Herennium* and the *De Inventione* are derived from scholastic activity and from similar Greek sources that probably developed on the island of Rhodes, the lost treatise of Antonius was derived from his oratorical activity and also from the Peripatetic and Academic philosophy he studied in Athens.[11]

Much Roman rhetorical doctrine was influenced by Greek philosophy,[12] as is evident from Antonius' doctrine of *status* (the determination of the issue under dispute) and from the *Rhetorica ad Herennium*. Plato and the Sophists had enlarged the discussion about rhetoric by considering the use of rhetoric beyond the law court. At the end of the *Phaedrus* Plato undertakes to distinguish between good and bad rhetoric (259e) and expresses his understanding of good rhetoric as corresponding to the practice of philosophy (261a; cf. *Plt.* 303d–311c) and 'dialectic' (*Phdr.* 276e–277a; cf. 265b–266c).[13] According to Plato, this rhetoric was not the type employed by Sophists in his time. Plato's critique of rhetoric in the *Phaedrus* (257d–277d) and in the earlier *Gorgias* (449a–480d) is derived not only from his polemic against the Sophists and democrats, who had condemned Socrates, but also from his belief in the supremacy of philosophy (*Plt.* 303d–311c). In suggesting that good rhetoric corresponds to 'dialectic', Plato takes into account that rhetoric ought to entail dialectic and that a good rhetorician and orator must have a sound knowledge of psychology (*Phdr.* 269e–272b). Aristotle, a pupil of Plato, went further than his master in the re-evaluation of rhetoric. One of Plato's main arguments against rhetoric was its ability to work both for and against something or somebody. In Polus' discussion with Socrates (Pl. *Grg.* 466a ff.), this was just a way of demonstrating the immorality of rhetoric. In the *Rhetorica*, however, Aristotle expresses an appreciation of the ability to speak for and against a position (1355a29–38). This favourable attitude towards rhetoric remains unchanged throughout the rest of the *Rhetorica*.[14] After Plato, Aristotle, Theophrastus (the successor of Aristotle), and Hermagoras (an influential Hellenistic rhetorician), Greek rhetoricians began to formulate a system of rhetoric that went far beyond that of the simple handbook.

What is the difference between Athenian and Roman rhetoric? Elaine Fantham accepts the account of the Athenian popular assembly as it appears in Aristophanes' *Acharnians*, where everyone could speak (45ff.), even if only the great personalities were given the opportunity to be appreciated.[15] At any rate, popular government had its decision-making power in the Athenian assembly, whereas political power in republican Rome was concentrated in the senate, the seat of the central government. Unlike the Athenian assembly, in which all male ordinary citizens could participate, all rhetorical activity in this restricted council at Rome took place among small élite groups of senators.

At first glance, the situation in the judicial field appears to be not very different from the political one. Lawyers were usually senators and former magistrates and, as patrons of clients, were involved in criminal cases.[16] In fact, Roman society was dominated by the bond between *patroni* and *clientes*, and the legal and judicial activities of patrons were crucial to this link. In this situation the need to persuade through public speeches does not seem to have been as important in Rome as in democratic Athens. In order to escape from a situation dominated by a senatorial and aristocratic élite, it was necessary to remove the courts from the power of the senators and to popularize the law. For this reason, it was only after the Gracchi that formal rhetoric entered Roman society.[17] In a similar way judicial activity began to become popularized by becoming a written system, a process that seems to have begun with the *De Usurpationibus* by Claudius Caecus (censor in 312 BCE) and was continued by Mucius Scaevola and Sulpicius Rufus into the first century BCE.[18]

Although the Roman rhetoricians were banned in 161 BCE, this does not mean that a distinguished speaker like Cato was ignorant of Greek rhetoric or uninterested in teaching his sons rhetorical principles. Quintilian says only that 'Marcus Cato was the first Roman, as far as I know, to handle this topic' (*Inst.* 3.1.19). However, this probably refers to ethical or more general principles, judging by two extant fragments of Cato's rhetorical work:[19] *orator est ... vir bonus, dicendi peritus* ('The orator is a good man who is skilled in speaking', Cato *Libri ad M. Filium*);[20] *rem tene, verba sequentur* ('Grasp the subject matter; the words will follow', *Libri ad M. Filium*).[21] Rhetoric that could be handled by anyone who had a reasonable education became available in handbooks and was taught to patricians and plebeians alike by famous rhetoricians such as Diophanes of Mytilene and Menelaus of Marathus, teachers of Tiberius Gracchus and Gaius Gracchus respectively. But even the first manuals of rhetoric are full of inconsistencies, uncertainties and cautious remarks. In fact, Marcus Antonius did not finish his work (Quint. *Inst.* 3.1.19); nor did Cicero, who even repudiated his early *commentariola* (short treatises) in his later work (*De Or.* 1.2.5). The author of the *Rhetorica ad Herennium*, perhaps a certain Cornificius, otherwise unknown,[22] states that he is writing his work for his friend and relation Gaius Herennius (1.1.1; 4.56.69).

In 92 BCE another ban was imposed on Roman rhetoricians. This ban not only had a cultural basis but also a political one, since it came from one of the leaders of a group of senators, Licinius Crassus, and was designed in part to prevent the path to political and social advancement from being widened. Cicero's response to this ban thirty-seven years later in 55 BCE appears in the *De Oratore*, a work that is full of the rich philosophical and cultural content of Greek rhetoric. However, the rhetoric of precise, manual rules did not end with this work. Cicero himself later returned to this subject perhaps some time in the late 50s BCE in his *Partitiones Oratoriae*; he also placed great emphasis on stylistic and linguistic matters in his polemic against the Atticists, particularly in the *Brutus* and *Orator*, written in 46 BCE. More than a century later (in 94 or early 95 CE) Quintilian wrote and published the *Institutio Oratoria*, the most comprehensive manual of Graeco-Roman rhetoric produced up to its time.

From its origins rhetoric in Rome was connected with literature and poetry, a connection that was later strengthened by Cicero and others. In the process of exploring this connection between rhetoric and literature, the present volume goes far beyond the mere discussion of rhetorical models for the production of written text and speeches. The following specially commissioned, critically and methodologically distinct essays fall into three parts: Theories, transitions and tensions; Rhetoric and society; and Rhetoric and genre. Part I (chapters 2–4) explores the theory and practice of rhetoric, tensions between Greek and Roman, classical and post-classical, and in the process offers an overview of some of the major Roman practitioners of rhetoric. John Kirby's contribution on Ciceronian rhetoric is divided into two sections. After situating Cicero and Roman rhetoric generally against the Greek background and providing an overview of Cicero's major rhetorical treatises, Kirby then examines Cicero's practice of rhetoric by focusing on the *exordium* of the *Pro Milone* to uncover and theorize about aspects of his rhetoric that do not surface in his own theoretical writings. He demonstrates that in the published version of this oration we have an excellent example of the heights that Roman rhetoric was capable of attaining under a figure such as Cicero, with his vast knowledge of word-patterns and ability to manipulate the rules of rhetoric.

At a time when the word 'canon' is much used by scholars in the sense of an authoritative or select list of texts on a particular subject,

Neil O'Sullivan's study on the term and concept is timely. In his analysis of the ancient discussions of the so-called 'canon' of Attic orators, he maintains that the term as well as the concept are anachronistic in the context of ancient literary studies; furthermore, the select lists of recommended writers that existed were polemical rather than authoritative, and their existence cannot be demonstrated before the beginnings of Atticism. Although the authorship of the canon of the ten Attic orators and other lists of writers is uncertain, as are the origins of the Atticist movement, Caecilius of Calacte, an Augustan critic of the first century BCE, seems to have played a part in the drawing up of these lists and in the contemporary origins of Atticism. The precise nature of Caecilius' contributions cannot be determined, but O'Sullivan propounds his importance to this movement and to ancient literature.

The writings of the imperial period are replete with references to and discussions about style. In the final essay of Part I, William Dominik examines a few of the more important passages on style from the works of Quintilian, Seneca and Tacitus. Dominik's purpose is to appraise their purpose and intent within the context of their authors' works and the ancient debate on style generally in the first century CE. Since Quintilian's polemic against Seneca has heavily influenced ancient and modern scholarship, this passage raises the question as to what stylistic model Quintilian was promoting in his judgment of Seneca. Seneca's discussion of style in his *Epistles* and Marcus Aper's defence of postclassical rhetoric in Tacitus' *Dialogus* help to place Quintilian's criticism of Seneca and his style in its rhetorical, literary and historical contexts. While Quintilian disparaged the postclassical style as exemplified by Seneca, Aper argued that this style reflected the changed social and political circumstances of the early imperial period and therefore was a form of expression particularly suited to the contemporary age.

Part II (chapters 5–7) explores the ways in which rhetoric and society interacted in antiquity, focusing broadly on the areas of culture, agriculture, gender, politics and law. Catherine Connors examines how Roman rhetoricians use representations of rusticity, theatricality, nature (e.g., grass, thickets, flowers), agriculture (e.g., fruitful fields) and geography (e.g., Attica and Asia) to describe oratorical techniques. She argues that these representations reinforce the cultural institutions that introduced Greek rhetoric into Rome and adapted it for use by the urban élite. At the same time, Connors points out how the importation of Greek rhetoric into Rome is played down by 'naturalizing' it in terms of native agricultural practice. Nature and the processes of growth are compared in rhetorical treatises with the training of an orator and the acquisition of rhetorical expertise. This use of rustic and agricultural representations to describe rhetorical practice substantiates Connors' essential thesis that speaking about nature is a way of speaking about culture.

The relationship between gender and rhetoric has recently become the focus of increasing scholarly attention. In her fascinating discussion of this subject, Amy Richlin considers how the Roman forum as gendered space contributed to the formation of masculinity for adolescent Roman males, who were apprenticed to adult male speakers; although the feminine assumed an important role in the forum, women were excluded from this public arena. Roman theorists connected oratorical style with gender: the correct style was virile; effeminacy defined one of the undesirable styles. A particularly risky area was *actio* (the speaker's manner of delivery, including his movement and voice), which was associated with the effeminate oratorical style. Roman orators also associated Asianism with effeminacy on account of its eastern origins. In the process of illustrating the exclusively male posturings of institutionalized rhetoric at Rome, Richlin unmasks the male hegemonic structure of Roman culture itself.

To the Greeks and Romans the aim of rhetoric was to make public speech effective. But there were differences in the practice of oratory in Greece and at Rome. The last essay in Part II is by Elaine Fantham, who commences her discussion by distinguishing the occasions of formal rhetoric at Rome from those of Athenian public life. Using Cicero as example and source, she proceeds to outline the pattern of political speeches in assembly and senate, of judicial speeches (criminal and civil), and of expository rhetoric, and shows how speeches of similar content may belong to different contexts. Finally, she distinguishes the changing pattern of public oratory at Rome from the middle republic of Cato to the late republic of Cicero and the early principate in the time of Pliny and Tacitus.

Part III (chapters 8–14) considers the ways in which rhetoric and literature interacted and the relationship of rhetoric to the major literary genres. The first two chapters deal with epic, Rome's primary verse-form, and satire, Rome's own creation. Joseph Farrell considers the different understandings of rhetoric that have emerged in the process of examining its role in Roman epic. He maintains that rhetoric, far from being merely an extrinsic system of rules for speech-making that has somehow worked its way into epic, is not only intrinsic to this genre but also is part of a more extensive system of communication that operates in other genres and structures. Farrell's approach is intended to counter the belief among some scholars that Roman epic, especially that of the postclassical period, is too rhetorical and therefore unpoetic. Farrell examines some of the approaches of scholars who have explored the relationship between epic and rhetoric and calls for a different approach based on a broader conception of rhetoric. Susanna Morton Braund's study shows how rhetorical theory and practice permeated Roman satire from the beginning and especially how the schools of declamation influenced Juvenal's choice of a highly rhetorical idiom for his satire. Braund observes not only that rhetoric shapes the treatment of satire's themes, but also that the Roman audience's knowledge of rhetoric enabled it to appreciate the satirist's twists and parodies; above all, satire reproduces the contestatory function of rhetoric in Roman society by its staging of conflict.

The next two chapters explore the relation between rhetoric and the dramatic arts. In explaining the changes that overtook Roman tragedy from the late republic until the age of Nero, Goldberg argues that declamation proved to be a beneficial influence by countering tragedy's tendency – most pronounced in Cicero's day – toward spectacle by reasserting the primacy of language; he adduces scenes from Seneca's *Thyestes* and *Phaedra* to illustrate this phenomenon and its sources. Joseph Hughes' contribution presents an overview of the interaction between comedy and rhetoric from roughly 200 BCE to 100 CE. The application of rhetoric in the comedies of Plautus and Terence is examined, as is the use of comedic diction, characterization, and plot structures in the oratory of Crassus and Cicero. Hughes also examines references to comedy in Roman rhetoric with reference to Cicero's practice of borrowing from comedy.

The final three chapters treat didactic poetry, historiography and philosophy. Peter Toohey maintains that Ovid in the *Ars Amatoria* fixes the persona – which persuasion requires – at three levels. The didactic addressee may be urged to assume the persuasory persona of the orator, as may the didactic narrator. Ovid may also assert a persona or ethos for his poem as a didactic and seductive medium by emphasizing its ludic role, an idea akin to his conception of love. Robert Cape's essay focuses on the relationship between Roman historiography and the practical art of rhetoric as stated by Antonius in Cicero's *De Oratore*. Evidence from the early historians, especially Cato and Coelius Antipater, and close attention to Antonius' argument clarify Cicero's reasons for discussing historiography in a volume on rhetoric. Cape argues that Cicero's theory about the stylistic relationship between oratory and history, which is closely tied to his view of the social function of oratory in the late Roman republic, is maintained by later historians, although the function of oratory necessitated a change in style. In the final contribution of the volume, Michele Ronnick shows how Fronto frequently makes his point with the vocabulary and imagery of traditional Roman culture. His letters use elements of architectonic rhetoric built upon the philosophical and moral values that underlie Cato's seminal dictum of an orator as a *vir bonus, dicendi peritus* ('a good man skilled in speaking'). Ronnick also traces Graeco-Roman attitudes toward philosophy and rhetoric and briefly considers the opposition between the two fields.

Rhetoric has been viewed merely as a catalogue or system of rules for language, associated with falseness and dishonesty, particularly artful misrepresentation and deception, and regarded as a superficial art concerned with the exercise of linguistic tricks. The present volume is intended to move the study of rhetoric away from such narrow applications and prejudicial associations. All of the following essays, despite their different critical approaches and methodologies, demonstrate that Roman rhetoric is best viewed as part of a larger cultural process, that is, not just as a system of rules applicable to spoken and written language but as a fundamental component in the exploration of Roman society and literature. For rhetoric, like any other field of activity, is constructed socially, politically and cognitively in ways that reflect, express and extend – through its rules, structures, processes and values – the culture that produces it. And the Roman use of rhetoric – as evident in its diverse forms – lies at the very heart of Rome's major cultural and literary forms.[23]

NOTES

1 Skutsch 1985: 96.
2 Kowalski 1947: 50–62.
3 *RE* 19.1937: 195–202.
4 Fraenkel 1962: 201.
5 On Peitho in Greek tragedy, see Buxton 1982; Bers 1994: 184–91.
6 *RE* 19.1937: 204; see also Untersteiner 1949: 98.
7 Nauck 1964: 408.

8   David 1992: 281–320, esp. 286.
9   Calboli 1972.
10 This is the most likely date of the *De Inventione*, since Cicero devoted himself entirely to the study of philosophy under the instruction of Philon of Larissa, head of the Academy, after the philosopher came to Rome in 88 BCE.
11 Montefusco 1986: 200–4.
12 See Montefusco 1986: 37–46, 197–203, particularly in regard to the central doctrine of *status*.
13 For this considerable change in meaning, see Cassin 1990.
14 See Grimaldi 1980: 29.
15 See p. 111.
16 For material about Roman lawyers, see Bauman 1983; 1985; 1989. For the relationship between the *patronus* and his *clientes* and the attendant political and civil implications, see David 1992.
17 For rhetoric in Rome before the Gracchi, see Calboli 1982.
18 Bauman 1983: 224ff., 312–82, 412–28; 1985: 4–15; Schiavone 1987: 25–136; Bretone 1992: 107–209.
19 Calboli 1978: 11–39.
20 Jordan 1860: 80 no. 1.
21 Jordan 1860: 80 no. 2.
22 Calboli 1993: 2–8.
23 We thank Susanna Morton Braund and John Kirby for their helpful comments on an earlier version of this introduction.

2

Ciceronian rhetoric: theory and practice

John T. Kirby

Let me begin with a word about the title I have chosen. The word 'rhetoric' is commonly used in both a stricter sense, that is, having to do with *theory about* (or *the study of*) discourse, and a looser, that is, as synonymous with discourse itself, or 'oratory'. In the brief space allotted to me here, I shall attempt to say something about Cicero's rhetoric in both senses. As for the term 'Ciceronian', I should say that I mean 'of Cicero' in the strictest sense; it is far beyond the scope of this collection to chart the course of the Ciceronian tradition in Renaissance (and later) rhetorics.

THEORY

Cicero himself was a voluminous writer on the topic of rhetoric, beginning with the *De Inventione Rhetorica* and spanning the rest of his adult life, to the late *Orator* in 46 BCE. It is important to remember that, in this lifelong enterprise, he was the heir of a cultural phenomenon that was firmly entrenched, elaborately institutionalized, and minutely codifed. Horace wrote, *Graecia capta ferum victorem cepit et artis / intulit agresti Latio* ('Captive Greece captured her fierce captor, and introduced the arts to hayseed Latium', *Epist.* 2.1.156–7);[1] and in no area of human endeavour was this truer than in that of rhetoric. Well before Aristotle began to work on his monumental *Rhetoric* – of which more below – the Greeks, and especially those in and around Athens, were absorbed (not to say obsessed) with the phenomenon of persuasive language, with its formalization in oratory, and with its theoretical abstraction in what came to be called *rhêtorikê*. Indeed this group of cultural practices stands fair to be considered one of the greatest achievements and

13

legacies of the Greek-speaking peoples – on a par with the invention of democracy, with whose development and practice it is intimately, even organically, involved.[2]

Having absorbed so much else, then, from Greek culture, it was inevitable that, when the Romans came to repudiate monarchy in favour of a *res publica*, they should also absorb and institute a Hellenic model of oratory – and, with it, a philhellenic approach to rhetorical theory. This is evident both from the pitifully sparse fragmentary remains of the pre-Ciceronian orators[3] and from theoretical works such as the *De Inventione Rhetorica* and its cousin-german, the *Rhetorica ad Herennium*.[4] The greatest rhetorical genius of the Greeks, to generalize somewhat, was theory; that of the Romans, practice. Moreover, short of a drastic cultural shift, for which there was no evident impetus, it would at any rate have been virtually impossible for the Romans to turn quite away from the Greek model of rhetoric that was presented to them.

Consequently, in turning to Roman writers on rhetoric, we must not be surprised to find them fortifying the Hellenic edifice rather than tearing it down and laying radically new foundations. This is true primarily of Cicero himself, in whose own lifetime that edifice was still being explored. The youthful *De Inventione Rhetorica*, of which he later wrote disparagingly, cannot be dated exactly – his own reference to the time of composition, namely when he was *puer aut adulescentulus* ('a boy or just coming into adolescence', *De Or.* 1.5) is not particularly precise. But in any case it shows that at the time of its composition (say, tentatively, around 91–88 BCE)[5] Cicero's rhetorical training must have been derived partly from the teachings of Hermagoras, a Greek of the second century BCE, himself influenced by Stoicism, and partly from the Peripatetic tradition – the latter, especially, in the doctrine of the syllogism, and the former in that of stasis theory. As the *Rhetorica ad Herennium* shows, these are likely to have been typical influences in Roman rhetorical education at this time. Cicero was well-connected in educated circles, even at an early age, and met not only prominent Roman orators but probably also visiting Greek rhetoricians and philosophers, such as Menedemus, Philo, and Apollonius Molon.[6] From these or other such teachers he may have made his first acquaintance with the Aristotelian *Synagôgê Tekhnôn*, a compendium or summary (unfortunately now lost) of earlier Greek rhetorical treatises (*Inv. Rhet.* 2.6–7):

And indeed Aristotle brought together into one place the ancient writers of the art, all the way back from Tisias, the earliest and the inventor [of rhetoric]. Aristotle arranged clearly and individually the great teachings of each, which had been carefully collected, and diligently unravelled the knotty parts; in fact he so far surpassed the original writers in sweetness and succinctness that no one [now] learns their precepts from their own books: rather, anyone who wants to know what they teach turns instead to this [book], as to a much more convenient expositor. And indeed Aristotle himself published for us both himself and his predecessors, so that we might learn about him and the others from himself. Moreover, those who came after him, although they spent the greatest part of their energies on philosophy, just as he whose teachings they followed had done, nonetheless left us quite a few precepts of discourse.

At the same time he received instruction in what was undeniably the greatest opposing tradition of Greek rhetorical training, the Isocratean (*Inv. Rhet.* 2.7–8):

And from another fount there also flowed other teachers of oratory, who likewise helped extensively in public speaking (if artifice can be said to be of any help). For there lived at the same time as Aristotle the great and noble *rhetor*[7] Isocrates, whose own handbook [*artem*], while it is generally agreed that there was one, I have not found. But I have found many teachings on the subject by his students and by those who continued in that tradition.

By his own testimony, then, Cicero had read widely in the Greek authorities on rhetoric by the time he was twenty years old or so.

In 79 BCE he left Rome for a two-year stint, travelling first to Greece to study philosophy, then to Asia Minor and the island of Rhodes to study rhetoric under Greek and Levantine teachers – Menippus of Stratonicea, Dionysius of Magnesia, Aeschylus of Cnidus, Xenocles of Adramyttium, Demetrius of Syria, and again Apollonius Molon (*Brut.* 315–16). Much of his training there must have been in the form of declamation-exercises, as was then customary, but it is possible that Molon's tutelage was more specifically tailored to Cicero's needs. One would give a great deal to know what specific theoretical works Molon and others recommended for Cicero's reading at this time.

But this same period was to bring a significant windfall to Rome: in around 84, Sulla, returning from Greece, brought with him the library of Aristotle.[8] This will have included the *Rhetoric* and other writings on language and communication, which Cicero evidently had not seen before that time, but to which he eventually gained access. It very likely also included some of Aristotle's dialogues – also among our grievous losses from antiquity – which served, in some capacity, as models for the writing of the *De Oratore*:[9] in an important letter to Lentulus Spinther (*Fam.* 1.9), Cicero says that the *De Oratore* is written *Aristotelio more* ('in the Aristotelian manner') and that in it he has contrived to synthesize both the Aristotelian and the Isocratean traditions (*omnem antiquorum et Aristoteliam et Isocratiam rationem oratoriam complectuntur*). The former remark seems to refer to form, the latter to content: that is, the form of the dialogue is Aristotelian rather than Platonic, in that the interlocutors hold forth at length rather than engaging in what Plato calls *brakhylogia*, the quick give-and-take so vital to the Socratic elenchus. As for the content, it is above all in the *De Oratore* that Cicero shows the influence of Aristotle's *Rhetoric*: we now find, in book 2, a fundamental shift from the (originally sophistic) approach to invention based on the *moria logou*, or parts of the oration, to the tripartite Aristotelian schema of ethos/pathos/logos – *ethos*, the perceived good character of the *rhetor* as he speaks; *pathos*, the emotional response of the audience to the discourse; and *logos*, the use of logical inference (whether inductive or deductive) in the discourse itself.[10]

Several aspects of the *De Oratore* distinguish it from the typical rhetorical handbook. First and most obvious, there is the dialogue-format, which in itself has several important effects: because the discursive presentation is conversational, it will lend itself more naturally to broad discussion of ideas than to dense, list-like enumeration.[11] Because, *as dialogue*, it presents a multiplicity of subjectivities in the various speakers, it avoids the monologic presentation of the treatise. Because, too, the speakers are Romans, the Greek legacy is now overlaid by something important and new: the sense that the reader is now being presented with rhetorical theory that feels uniquely Roman.

The distinction between verisimilitude and veridicality is sometimes difficult to discern, and the historicity of the *De Oratore* has been called into question.[12] But as George Kennedy points out, Cicero is at pains to stress that the opinions expressed by the interlocutors in the dialogue are consonant with those held by the

16

historical people.[13] Moreover, despite the fact that he was 'not part of the actual conversation' (*nos enim . . . ipsi sermoni non inter-fuissemus*, 3.11), he knew the speakers – Crassus and Antonius in particular – well enough to be able to represent them accurately in both style and substance. All of this leaves us with the conviction that, if such a conversation ever occurred, it would have gone something very like what we read in the *De Oratore*. The question it cannot answer – and nothing can – is, 'But *did* it ever occur?' Which brings us back to the important, if basic, fact that the ultimate source and guiding genius behind the whole work is of course Cicero himself. In this massive dialogue he attained to a breadth and depth of rhetorical originality that he equalled in one other place only: the corpus of his collected speeches.

There remain two other major rhetorical treatises of Cicero to mention,[14] both apparently dating from 46 BCE, and both dedicated to Marcus Brutus: the *Brutus* and the *Orator*. The *Brutus* is a remarkable piece in a number of ways, different perhaps from every other work of Cicero. Like the *De Oratore* it is a dialogue, but here Cicero figures (with Titus Pomponius Atticus) as a principal inter-locutor. The major substance of the dialogue is to trace the history of eloquence in Rome and in Greece before it. Among the Greeks, Demosthenes and Isocrates are particularly valorized. The development of Roman eloquence is charted on an evolutionary course from its early efflorescence in Cornelius Cethegus and the elder Cato, moving toward its full flowering in Antonius, Crassus, Caesar, Calvus, Hortensius, and – of course – Cicero. Far from being a disinterested history of eloquence, however, the *Brutus* is in fact a carefully crafted investigation of the Atticist-Asianist controversy, and a justification of what the unsympathetic might call Cicero's own Asianist practices (cf. Quint. *Inst.* 12.10.12; Tac. *Dial.* 18). What emerges is a redefinition of what constitutes Atticism (*Brut.* 285–91) so that it closely resembles the Ciceronian style.

The *Orator* is likewise an apologia for the Ciceronian style in the face of Atticist criticism. Thus, while it touches on such topics as the genres of oratory and the parts of rhetoric, it concentrates above all on matters of rhetorical style – the three levels of style (plain/middle/grand) and their uses. In fact it is here that he makes an important theoretical innovation: he connects these three with the three *officia oratoris* ('functions of the orator') as outlined in *De Oratore* 2.115: to teach, to charm, and to move, respectively.[15] He also offers a very detailed treatment of composition (i.e., how individual words are put together in a sentence), particularly the difficult topic of prose-rhythm (168–236).

PRACTICE

Cicero was certainly important for his inscription and codification of the current wisdom about rhetorical theory; and he himself advanced knowledge in the field in a number of ways. He, however, like all of us, was culturally and temporally bound, and the body of rhetorical theory to which he was heir had its inevitable limitations. If humanity survives another two thousand years, the same will doubtless be said of our situation. Nonetheless we now have interests and concerns in rhetoric that Cicero could not have imagined from his vantage-point in history.

Moreover, in Cicero's published orations we are able to discern aspects of his rhetorical strategies and tactics that (for whatever reason) he never discusses in the theoretical works. Close attention to the form and content of a Ciceronian oration reveals considerable and valuable information about the way he actually went about achieving his rhetorical goals. Our fullest understanding of 'Cicero-nian rhetoric' as that is most broadly conceived, then, can only come to fruition after careful scrutiny of the extant corpus of his speeches, for it is here that we are able in some wise to take the measure of his creative powers. Many volumes could be written in close analysis of his speeches; again, space forbids such dilation here. But as a single splendid example of his rhetorical genius as evinced in practice, I direct my reader's attention to one of his most celebrated orations, the *Pro Milone*.

On the day of Titus Annius Milo's trial, we are told, Cicero was so afraid of the violent tendencies of Clodius' followers that he was carried to the forum in an enclosed litter. He may or may not in fact have been frightened; but one thing is certain, that he understood the rhetorical value of this extravagant gesture. In any case, this dramatic arrival by Cicero in the forum certainly made a statement, and one that set the stage for the things he was going to say. It is on the *exordium* of the speech that I want to concentrate here, paying attention to two devices in particular, *parallelism* and *paradox*. Far from being mere stylistic fillips, these strategies are crucial in providing Cicero with the notional categories that shape his argument overall.[16]

Terminology

By 'parallelism' I intend something other than what is ordinarily meant by that word – several things in fact. The term, as commonly used, obfuscates rather than clarifies, and – more importantly – does not account for the intricacies of language that we find, for example, in Cicero. Consequently I subdivide the topic of parallelism under two headings: (1) *structural* (or *syntactic*) parallelism, the close juxtaposition of compared or contrasted verbal forms or syntactic structures, and (2) *thematic* (or *conceptual*) parallelism, the close juxtaposition of compared or contrasted ideas. Typically structural parallelism will be used to draw attention to thematic parallelism that is being highlighted in the discourse.

Each of these categories can be broken down into two sub-categories, *conjunctive* and *disjunctive*. Conjunctive parallelism, of course, relies on the notion of joining or juxtaposition; disjunctive, on that of separation. Common strategies for signalling conjunctive parallelism include the use of particles such as 'both ... and' (*et ... et*), 'either ... or' (*aut ... aut, vel ... vel*), and the like. The commonest method of signalling disjunction is the pair 'not ... but' (*non ... sed*). Using this terminology, we can say that the word 'parallelism', as most commonly used, refers to what I would call *conjunctive syntactic parallelism*.

Although all these sub-categories of parallelism appear in this *exordium*, two of them are particularly important to the presentation of its arguments: *disjunctive thematic parallelism* and *disjunctive structural parallelism*. These two, especially the latter, are generally referred to as *antithesis*.[17] In its thematic and structural guises, antithesis works closely with paradox to give the *exordium* its characteristic shape, as we shall see.

Parallelism

The first sentence, stripped of all its levels of hypotaxis, reveals one basic antithetical theme: *fear* versus *courage*. The syntax of *etsi ... tamen* ('although ... nonetheless') sets us up for this (*Mil.* 1):

Etsi vereor, iudices, ne turpe sit pro fortissimo viro dicere incipientem timere minimeque deceat, cum T. Annius ipse magis de rei publicae salute quam de sua perturbetur, me ad eius causam parem animi magnitudinem adferre non posse, tamen haec novi iudici: nova forma terret oculos qui, quocumque inciderunt, veterem consuetudinem fori et pristinum morem iudiciorum requirunt.

Although I fear, gentlemen of the jury, that it is disgraceful for one who is beginning the defence of an extremely courageous man to exhibit fear, and that it is particularly unbecoming (seeing as Titus Annius himself shows more concern for our country's *salus* [safety, welfare, salvation] than for his own) that I am not able to muster the same intrepid spirit as he has when I speak on his behalf; nonetheless, the unfamiliar aspect of this unfamiliar tribunal exercises an alarming effect on me. Wherever my eyes turn, they look in vain for the customary sights of the forum and the traditional procedure of the courts.[18]

Within this superstructure are several nested levels of subordination and several other structural and thematic antitheses:

* Milo versus Cicero (Milo is fearless, Cicero is fearful)
* public versus private *salus* (Milo cares more about the public *salus* than about his own)
* *novi iudici nova forma* versus *vetus consuetudo*.

This last one is the conceptual link with the next sentence, marked by *enim* (1–2):

Non enim corona consessus vester cinctus est, ut solebat; non usitata frequentia stipati sumus; non illa praesidia quae pro templis omnibus cernitis, etsi contra vim conlocata sunt, non adferunt tamen oratori terroris aliquid, ut in foro et in iudicio, quamquam praesidiis salutaribus et necessariis saepti sumus, tamen ne non timere quidem sine aliquo timore possimus.

For the usual circle of listeners is missing; the habitual crowds are nowhere to be seen. Instead you can see military guards, stationed in front of all the temples. They are posted there, it is true, in order to protect us from violence, but all the same they cannot fail to inflict some fear on an orator. This ring of guards is, I repeat, both protective and necessary, and yet the very freedom from fear that they are there to guarantee has something frightening about it.

Here the basic antithesis is *vis/oratio*, 'force' or 'violence' versus 'discourse' – a key theme for the speech, because human discourse is meant to mark the progress we have made from that primitive stage where we clubbed one another like cavemen – a stage to which Milo and Clodius had temporarily returned.[19] The law-court is the house and shrine of IVS, that is, 'law, justice, jurisprudence', the triumph of reason and civilization. *Ius* is what guarantees, in legal/rhetorical situations, the efficacy of *oratio* as a means of settling human differences. But the presence of the soldiers stationed about the forum threatens the toppling of *ius* by its opposite – and anagram – VIS, and this is the focus of Cicero's fear: for he is easily by this time of his life the incarnation of oratory in Rome; he embodies in his own person the civilizing power of rhetoric. This antithesis of *vis* versus *oratio* is echoed in the third sentence, which is completely structured as a contrary-to-fact condition – a powerful antithetical structure in itself (2):

> Quae si opposita Miloni putarem, cederem tempori, iudices, nec enim inter tantam vim armorum existimarem esse orationi locum.

> If I believed these precautions to be aimed against Milo, gentlemen, I should bow to necessity and conclude that amid all this weapon-power there was no place for an advocate at all.

Schematically one might frame it thus (in the inferential pattern known as *modus tollens*): If X were true, then Y; but not Y; therefore not X. The implied part of this syllogism, set out in the contrary-to-fact condition, is picked up by *sed me recreat* in the next sentence (2):

> Sed me recreat et reficit Cn. Pompei, sapientissimi et iustissimi viri, consilium, qui profecto nec iustitiae suae putaret esse, quem reum sententiis iudicium tradidisset, eundem telis militum dedere, nec sapientiae temeritatem concitatae multitudinis auctoritate publica armare.

> But on this point the wisdom of the sage and fair-minded Gnaeus Pompeius has relieved and reassured me. For once he has committed a man to a court to be tried, he would certainly not regard it as compatible with his sense of justice to place that same man at the mercy of troops bristling with arms. And it would also, surely, be inconsistent with his sound judgement to add official incitement to the violence of a wild and excited mob.

Here Cicero begins to weave together into one strong cord the antithetical strands he has already been spinning out:

21

- fear versus confidence
- legal process (*ius*) versus force of arms (*vis*)
- the gripping fear of social disintegration versus the calming and civilizing presence of *Pompey*, who hovers (if we may believe Cicero in this speech) like a guardian angel over Milo in his plight.

This leads, by *quam ob rem*, to a series of *non/sed* (*not X but Y*) structural antitheses in §3, where Cicero is embroidering, or 'amplifying', a *paradox*: all these soldiers should not frighten me but relieve me; they assure me of (3):

- physical safety,
- emotional strength,
- silence (a very practical consideration in the forum, especially on this occasion):

> Quam ob rem illa arma, centuriones, cohortes non periculum nobis, sed praesidium denuntiant, neque solum ut quieto, sed etiam ut magno animo simus hortantur, nex auxilium modo defensioni meae verum etiam silentium pollicentur.

Consequently, what all these weapons and centurions and cohorts surely promise is not danger but a safeguard. They are meant to encourage us to be not only calm but determined as well; as I speak in defence of Milo they assure me physical security, but they also guarantee an uninterrupted hearing.

In the next sentence, *reliqua vero multitudo* institutes a new antithesis: the *soldiers* versus the *civilians*. The latter category is broken down by a sort of *diairesis*, or division, into two groups: those who are favourably disposed toward Milo and who tremble on his behalf (*nec eorum quisquam*) versus those rabble who had been roused by Clodius' madness (3):

> Reliqua vero multitudo, quae quidem est civium, tota nostra est, nec eorum quisquam quos undique intuentis, unde aliqua fori pars aspici potest, et huius exitum iudici exspectantis videtis, non cum virtuti Milonis favet, tum de se, de liberis suis, de patria, de fortunis hodierno die decertari putat.

All the other Roman citizens in this audience are sympathetic. From any and every point overlooking the forum you can see crowds gazing this way, and there is not a single soul among them who does not applaud the sterling qualities of Milo. And every one of these persons feels the same conviction: that not only Milo's future but his own, and the future of his children and his entire country, everything he possesses in the whole world, is at stake in this court today.

The principle underlying *antithesis* is, as I have said, *disjunction*: not 'both X and Y' (what I call *conjunctive* parallelism) but (in some form) 'not X but Y'. The parallel construction that is conjunctive, that is, not what I would call antithetical, is used all along in this *exordium* and indeed everywhere in Cicero, for example:

- turpe sit . . . minimeque deceat
- novi iudici: nova forma
- veterem consuetudinem fori et pristinum morem iudiciorum
- non cinctus est . . . non stipati sumus . . . non . . . non adferunt
- nec iustitiae . . . nec sapientiae

On the conceptual level this conjunctive principle works too, and is very deeply (if subliminally) ingrained in the whole rhetorical set-up:

- I am *pro Milone* (and fearless); hence you should be too
- Pompey is *pro Milone*; hence you should be too
- Every citizen worth his salt is *pro Milone*; hence you should be too

For all the sophistication of Cicero's rhetorical approach, this principle is very primitive. It is something like sympathetic magic, on a par with the *hieros gamos* or 'sacral wedding' that was intended to ensure a plentiful harvest: the act performed is supposed to bring about, by analogy, a resonance in the intended area of focus.

Milo himself also provides a conjunctive parallel for the *iudices* ('jurors', 3):

> Quorum clamor si qui forte fuerit, admonere vos debebit ut eum civem retineatis qui semper genus illud hominum clamor- esque maximos prae vestra salute neglexit.

> And if their racket reaches your ears, it should, I hope, warn you of the necessity of cherishing as a fellow-citizen the man who has always spurned individuals of that type, however loud they shout, because his one preoccupation is with the safety of you all.

What is implied is that just as Milo ignored the political agitation of the *Clodiani* in favour of the needs of the good citizens, so now you, *iudices*, must return the favour to him.

What we have then is another antithesis being implied: *bad people* versus you, the *iudices* (bad people being defined as anyone inimical to Milo). That is, two of these three points – [1] Milo, [2] you the *iudices*, [3] the *Clodiani* – are paired off with reference to the third, in two different ways:

- (conjunctive) Milo ignored the *Clodiani*; hence you should do so as well
- (disjunctive) The *Clodiani* [bad] were opposed to Milo; hence you [good] should favour Milo

In section 4 we come to a typical turn in Cicero's train of thought – a pattern evinced repeatedly in his oratory:

> Quam ob rem adeste animis, iudices, et timorem, si quem habetis, deponite. Nam si umquam de bonis et fortibus viris, si umquam de bene meritis civibus potestas vobis iudicandi fuit, si denique umquam locus amplissimorum ordinum delectis viris datus est, ut sua studia erga fortis et bonos civis, quae voltu et verbis saepe significassent, re et sententiis declararent, hoc profecto tempore eam potestatem omnem vos habetis ut statuatis utrum nos qui semper vestrae auctoritati dediti fuimus semper miseri lugeamus an diu vexati a perditissimis civibus aliquando per vos ac per vestram fidem virtutem sapientiamque recreemur.

So give me your attention, gentlemen. If you feel any nervousness, dismiss it from your minds. For here is the greatest opportunity you have ever had to declare your attitude towards a fine and gallant gentleman, a citizen of proven loyalty. You who are members of our country's most distinguished Orders have often expressed your appreciation of goodness and bravery by looks and words, but this is your unequalled chance to clothe those sentiments in actual votes and deeds. For here and now a vital decision is yours and yours alone to give. We, for our part, have never failed in devotion to your authority, and now it is for you to decide whether we must continue to mourn in miserable hardship or whether instead, by your staunch, courageous and wise support, our prolonged persecution by these ruffians can at long last come to an end, so that we may be revived.

This pattern functions as follows. [a] He makes a number of points, which he sums up in a 'therefore' of some type (here *quam ob rem*); [b] on the basis of these, he exhorts the *iudices* in a series of imperatives (or the equivalent, such as jussive noun clauses):

• quam ob rem adeste . . . deponate. . . ut statuatis

These two sentences comprising section 4 exhibit a remarkable shift. Until *utrum . . . an* toward the end there is no interplay of disjunction and conjunction. The pattern is entirely conjunctive, and almost every word is involved in some sort of conjunctive parallelism:

• si quem habetis . . . / adeste . . . deponite
• si umquam / si umquam / si denique umquam / hoc profecto tempore
• de bonis et fortibus viris / de bene meritis civibus
• potestas vobis iudicandi fuit / locus . . . delectis viris datus est
• voltu et verbis saepe significassent / re et sententiis declararent

There is also extensive *echoing* of significant words and forms. This is another kind of conjunctive thematic parallelism, or perhaps of a type somewhere between the thematic and the structural:

• timorem, si quem *habetis*/eam potestatem omnem vos *habetis*
• de *bonis et fortibus* viris/erga *fortis et bonos* civis
• bene meritis *civibus*/fortis et bonos *civis*
• *potestas* vobis iudicandi fuit/eam *potestatem* omnem

After such close interplay of conjunction and disjunction, this patch of language, purely conjunctive in both form and content, gives a sense of release, of gathering momentum and smooth force – comparable to the Latin hexameter, where the pattern of long syllables tends to conflict with the ictus of the words in the first half of the line, but to coincide in the second half, for example, *Aeneid* 1.1–2:

> Árma virúmque cáno, Tróiae quí prímus ab óris
> Itáliam fáto prófugus Lavíniaque vénit

We come next to another antithesis constructed around an indirect question with *utrum . . . an*: *ut statuatis utrum nos . . . lugeamus an . . . recreemur* (4). This antithesis is something of an *aria da capo*: not only does it have a resumptive force, bringing us back to disjunctive parallelism after the smooth sailing of the purely conjunctive passage; it synthesizes several disjunctive and conjunctive themes already touched upon in the *exordium*:

- fear (or, here, sorrow, *lugeamus*) versus confidence
- *Clodiani* versus *boni* (*a perditissimis civibus . . . per vos*)
- assimilation of *iudices* to Cicero (*dediti fuimus; per vos ac per vestram fidem virtutem sapientiamque*)
- assimilation of the *iudices* to Pompey (especially in the word *recreemur*, which echoes *sed me recreat et reficit* in section 2)

Once again we have structural disjunction:

- utrum . . . lugeamus/an . . . recreemur
- semper dediti fuimus/semper . . . lugeamus
- diu vexati a perditissimis civibus/per vos . . . recreemur (the participle *vexati* has a concessive force and might well have been answered by a *tamen*)

but it is laced with a conjunctive parallel, another *amplificatio*:

- per vos/ac per vestram fidem virtutem sapientiamque

It is no coincidence that we have such a synthesis of themes along with a reintegration of disjunction and conjunction at this strategic moment, which is focused directly on Cicero's relationship with his audience. This question about the jury's decision is highly charged emotionally, and framed in the following terms: not 'Are you going to acquit my client?', which would be far more neutral, but 'Are you going to disappoint me?'

Section 5 is markedly disjunctive:

> Quid enim nobis duobus, iudices, laboriosius, quid magis sollicitum, magis exercitum dici aut fingi potest, qui spe amplissimorum praemiorum ad rem publicam adducti metu crudelissimorum suppliciorum carere non possumus? Equidem ceteras tempestates et procellas in illis dumtaxat fluctibus contionum semper putavi Miloni esse subeundas, quia semper pro bonis contra improbos senserat; in iudicio vero et in eo consilio in quo ex coniunctis ordinibus amplissimi viri iudicarent numquam existimavi spem ullam esse habituros Milonis inimicos ad eius non modo salutem exstinguendam sed etiam gloriam per talis viros infringendam.

> For the situation in which my client and myself find ourselves is in the highest degree painful and anxious and distressing. When he and I originally took up politics, we nourished the hope that the amplest rewards might come our way. But what

has happened? Instead we suffer from incessant, tormenting fears of the cruellest penalties. I always realized Milo would be buffeted by storms and tempests of every other kind, that is to say of the kind encountered on the troubled waters of popular meetings. But in a trial, conducted in a court of law, where the most eminent members of all the Orders in the state pronounce their judgements, I never imagined for a moment that the enemies of Milo could entertain the smallest hope that such men might lend themselves to damaging his splendid reputation – much less that they would actually be willing to ruin him utterly.

Here Cicero contrasts *spe*, 'hope', with *metu*, 'fear', and *crudelissimorum suppliciorum*, 'the cruellest penalties'; then, the *fluctibus contionum* with the serenity and order of the legal system,[20] and *pro bonis* with *contra improbos*.

Section 6 consists basically of two complex sets of conditional clauses that together pose a major disjunction (I shall number them [i] and [ii] in the English):

Nisi oculis videritis insidias Miloni a Clodio esse factas, nec deprecaturi sumus ut crimen hoc nobis propter multa praeclara in rem publicam merita condonetis, nec postulaturi ut, quia mors P. Clodi salus vestra fuerit, idcirco eam virtuti Milonis potius quam populi Romani felicitati adsignetis. Sin illius insidiae clariores hac luce fuerint, tum denique obsecrabo obtestaborque vos, iudices, si cetera amisimus, hoc nobis saltem ut relinquatur, vitam ab inimicorum audacia telisque ut impune liceat defendere.

[i] Far be it from me, I repeat, to ask that you should condone anything he may now have done on the grounds of his many outstanding services to the state. On the contrary, what I propose to do instead is to make you see, with your own eyes, that it was Clodius who subjected Milo to a treacherous attack. And if, again, the death of Publius Clodius has in fact proved your salvation, it is not my purpose to demand that you ascribe this to Milo's valour rather than to the good fortune of the Roman people. [ii] However, if I can make it clear as day (as I shall) that it was Clodius who laid this plot, then, gentlemen, and then only, I shall have one favour to ask of you most earnestly: even if all else be taken from us, I beg and beseech

27

you, leave us this one thing at least: the right to defend our lives when they are threatened by the brutal weapons of our foes.

The disjunctive parallelism of these two blocks is marked by *nisi oculis videritis* and *sin ... clariores hac luce fuerint*. But here, too, in among the disjunction is woven a good deal of conjunctivity. There is some amplification, which as we have seen has a conjunctive effect:

- quid laboriosius/quid magis sollicitum/[quid] magis exercitum
- dici/fingi
- tempestates/procellas
- in iudicio/in eo consilio.

And the conjunctive formula *non modo ... sed etiam*[21] is used to join *salutem exstinguendam* and *gloriam infringendam*. The first of the two conditions in §6 has the conjunctive formula *nec ... nec*[22] in the apodosis.

Most striking of all, however, is the conjunctive presentation of Milo and Cicero as a pair of Roman statesmen (*nobis duobus*, 5) as having the same aspirations and subject to the same pressures. The pair is to be taken, for all intents and purposes, as a unit. This close identification of Milo with Cicero subtly imputes the latter's powerful ethos to the former.[23]

Paradox

Paradox (the word comes from the Greek *para doxan*, 'contrary to expectation') is useful rhetorically because its expression implies that the audience is privileged to learn something that, because of its counterintuitive nature, they might not otherwise discover. This concept pervades the entire *exordium* of the *Pro Milone*, beginning with the first sentence: It is untoward for one to speak fearfully on behalf of a fearless man, and yet I find myself very much afraid. The second sentence embodies another paradox: here the telltale words are *ut solebat* and *usitata*. Things are not as they should be here, he says, not as they normally are – they are *para doxan*. (Cicero is referring, of course, to the presence of the armed guards at the trial.) But in section 3 this is reversed yet again to form a new paradox: These men are actually here not to threaten me but to protect me, not to sabotage the rhetorical situation but to ensure its health. Thus paradox surrounds Cicero's involvement in the case, and (we find) it surrounds Milo and Clodius as well. Milo 'has always spurned individuals of that type, however loud they shout, because his one preoccupation is with the safety of you all' (3); Clodius' death has turned out, oddly enough, to be the salvation (or 'health') of the body politic (6).

Paradox extends even to the *iudices*. Cicero says, 'I never imagined for a moment that the enemies of Milo could entertain the smallest hope that such men might lend themselves to damaging his splendid reputation – much less that they would actually be willing to ruin him utterly' (5). The implication of course is that this threatens to obtain, even as Cicero intervenes rhetorically. So he uses this paradox to make explicit one of his rhetorical goals: he can now present his defence of Milo in terms of preventing a serious disequilibrium in the social order. Such an approach both justifies his defence and encourages the jury to align themselves with him.

There is in the *exordium* another curiosity that classifies not so much as a paradox presented by Cicero as a paradox in his own train of thought. He not only pleads self-defence for Milo, but espouses the right to self-defence in general, even theoretical terms: '. . . even if all else be taken from us, I beg and beseech you, leave us this one thing at least: the right to defend our lives when they are threatened by the brutal weapons of our foes' (6). He is appealing to our deeply ingrained sense of this right, and hoping that in the vigour of our assent we will lose sight of the fact that self-defence, especially against a gang of thugs like Clodius' henchmen, itself entails a hefty share of *audacia telaque* ('brutal weapons'). As it is, however, he achieves, with the greatest deftness, another *aria da capo*: at the end of the *exordium* he returns to the first theme he invoked, that of fear at the presence of *armed* guards. Those he had turned, by an agile use of paradox, from a liability into an asset. Now he conjunctively associates Milo's arms-bearing with those cohorts and centurions, by a conjunctive anaphoric use of the words *defensioni meae* (3) and *defendere*. The guards are Cicero's defence; it is right and good for them to be there; Milo owes his life to the exercise of his right to self-defence, and should certainly be acquitted on that account. This is a paradox in Cicero's own thinking because, in pressing the point and advocating (or even condoning) physical violence, he risks undermining his own earlier paradox between *vis* and *oratio*. In view of this delicate problem it may also be no coincidence that just at this point the *exordium* ends, and is followed not (as normally) by a *narratio* outlining the facts of the case, but by a *praemunitio*. Such a

29

procedure is adopted only in extraordinary circumstances, for instance when an unusual set of factors threatens to prejudice the jury against the defendant. Accordingly the advocate attempts to fortify (-*munitio*) his client's case in advance (*prae-*) of the defence proper.[24]

There is something that is shared by paradox and antithesis – something disjunctive about them both. Accordingly Cicero uses them both to the utmost in his *exordium*, thereby setting the tone for his whole speech. Nothing is ordinary about this rhetorical situation: the set-up of the jury, the time-limit allowed the *patroni*, the uproar over the whole situation. Everyone knew that Milo was responsible for the death of Clodius, and even Cicero had to admit it. So he has to resort to extraordinary means – to magic, as I have said – to bring about the acquittal of Milo. We happen to know that his defence did not in fact succeed in court: the original version was a failure, and Milo was sent into exile. But Cicero revised it before publication, sending the new version to Milo to read. Milo is said to have commented that it was a good thing Cicero hadn't given that version, because otherwise he would never have had the chance to sample the wonderful seafood in Marseille![25] Luckily for us, however, this second version was preserved – not only a paragon of oratorical perfection but a powerful testimony to my assertion that by virtue of his profound knowledge of the time-honoured patterns of eloquence, coupled with the magisterial capacity to bend or even break the rules when necessary, Cicero provides in the pages of his own oratory the surest demonstration of the heights to which Roman rhetoric was capable of reaching.[26]

NOTES

1 Except as noted, translations from Latin here are my own.
2 On this topic, see Cicero's citation of Aristotle in *Brut.* 46.
3 These have been expertly collected in the two volumes of Malcovati 1975.
4 Once thought to be by Cicero, this was formerly known as the *Rhetorica Secunda*. It is now commonly attributed to one Cornificius. Its close resonances with the *De Inventione* have been explained by a theory that its author and Cicero may have studied with the same teacher. A Loeb translation, with notes of unusually high quality, appears in Caplan 1954.
5 So speculates Kennedy 1972: 107.
6 See the discussion in Kennedy 1972: 102–4. Molon is mentioned explicitly in *Brut.* 312.
7 Cicero's use of the word *rhetor* here is a bit ambiguous. A Greek loan-word, in classical Greek it meant simply 'speaker', while in Latin it came

to have the sense of 'teacher of rhetoric' (the sense most apt here). But Isocrates was a *rhetor* in both senses; at any rate he worked, like Lysias, as a logographer, and his extant writings are presented in the form of orations.

8 See Kirby 1990b: 4 and n. 8.
9 See Kennedy 1972: 209 and n. 88 for discussion of this topic. On the lost dialogues of Aristotle, see, e.g., Chroust 1973, esp. vol. 2.
10 On this shift see especially Solmsen 1941: 35–50, 169–90.
11 Hence Cicero's contention, in the letter to Lentulus Spinther (*Fam*. 1.9), that the three books of the *De Oratore* 'stay away from the commonly taught precepts' (*abhorrent a communibus praeceptis*, 23).
12 See the extensive bibliography in Kennedy 1972: 215 n. 95.
13 Kennedy 1972: 215–17.
14 I omit, in view of the limitations of space, discussion of some minor treatises – the *Partitiones Oratoriae* (*c.* 54 BCE), the *De Optimo Genere Oratorum* (52 BCE) and the *Topica* (44 BCE).
15 See Douglas 1957: 18–26; *contra* O'Sullivan 1992: 114 n. 52.
16 For a profound recent study on the cognitive value of such categories, see Lakoff 1987.
17 Antithesis was listed as one of the Gorgianic figures, thus counting as a device of *style* (*lexis, elocutio*); by that system the word should be restricted to what I have termed disjunctive structural parallelism. But Quintilian (*Inst*. 5.10.2) and the author of the *Rhetorica ad Herennium* (4.25–6) show awareness of the use of *contrarium* as a principle of *enthymeme*, which is a matter not of *style* but of *invention* (*heuresis, inventio*). This I call *disjunctive thematic parallelism*.
18 Translations of passages from the *Pro Milone* are adapted from those by Grant 1969.
19 On the use of discourse in resolving conflict as the mark that distinguishes humans from the lower beasts, see Kirby 1992: 50–1. On the antithesis of *peithô/bia*, comparable in Greek thought to Cicero's *oratio/vis*, see Kirby 1990a: 213–28.
20 I would be very surprised if, in this context with *tempestates, procellas*, and *fluctibus contionum*, the word *subeundas* were not intended to suggest a pun on *undas* (waves).
21 The unwary may mistake this for disjunction. Note that the *non* negates, not the predication itself, but specifically *modo*.
22 Here, too, the negation involved in *nec ... nec* should not be misconstrued as disjunction. Both clauses are negated (*nec deprecaturi sumus ... nec postulaturi*) and are thus *joined*.
23 On the ethos of the *patronus* as distinguished from that of the client, see Kirby 1990b: 17–38.
24 The most famous other example of *praemunitio* in Cicero's speeches is probably that in the *Pro Caelio*.
25 Reported in Dio Cass. 40.54.3.
26 I am much indebted to my learned friends Scott Carson, Christopher Craig, and Neil O'Sullivan for their help in various ways. This essay is for Patricia and Kip.

3

Caecilius, the 'canons' of writers, and the origins of Atticism

Neil O'Sullivan

In an age when there is much talk of 'canons' in the sense of 'authoritative lists of approved (rather than "genuine") texts', it is curious that even the second edition of the *Oxford English Dictionary* (1989) does not recognize that meaning in English. But from classical scholarship that meaning has now spilled over into more general use.[1] The important point has been made, though, that the Greek word *canon* was never used by the Greeks or Romans in this sense. In fact, only in the Christian era does something approaching this meaning occur, and naturally it is used of what is perceived as the genuine body of Holy Scripture. It is never used to refer to any body of secular literature.[2]

We need to go further than this simple observation, for we are not just dealing with semantics. Not only did the ancients not use 'canon' in this sense, but in fact they had no word at all to express what 'canon' has meant since the late eighteenth century in classical scholarship: that is, an authoritative select list of authors.[3] That very fact is significant. For the early Church, it was most important that some commonly accepted body of texts was regarded as authoritative: a religion based on books could hardly have it otherwise. But there was no equivalent need to have an agreement about the important texts for the study of pagan literature. And in fact there was no such agreement – hence, no word for 'authoritative select list'. For there were no such lists in antiquity: when speaking of the various 'canons' of ancient authors we are using a metaphor from later religion, and one that suggests a rigidity quite out of step with the way ancient literature was studied by the ancients themselves.

What certainly did exist in the ancient world were lists of authors regarded by their compilers as representing the best in a particular genre. This of course is something quite different from a 'canon'; it

32

is merely a list and need carry no authority at all.[4] Viewed in this light, the absence in a given text of any reference to such a list need not imply that the list was unknown to the author of that text. Such lists, to repeat, were not 'canonical', and authors aware of them could pay as much or as little attention to them as they wished. Some discussion of the so-called 'canon of orators' illustrates the dangers of an unrealistic idea of the importance such necessarily arbitrary and in no sense 'official' lists had for ancient critics. The fact that Cicero nowhere refers to a list of ten orators has been taken as proof positive that he knew of no such list and that it therefore did not exist in his lifetime.[5] But why *should* he have referred to it? It would have been for him just one particular list of praiseworthy orators, not one to which he would have felt bound to respond, let alone follow. (The possibility that the list of ten orators was composed at exactly the time when Cicero was turning his mind to the history of oratory will be canvassed later.) After all, he had his own lists of orators (*Brut.* 27ff., 285; *De Or.* 3.28). The same argument must hold true for Dionysius of Halicarnassus, who gives six Attic orators, inter-changing Isaeus and Lycurgus.[6] Quintilian himself gives six (*Inst.* 10.1.76–80) and then later twelve (12.10.21–4).

Quintilian's dismissive attitude to the list of ten – if indeed he refers to it at all – places such lists in context. He seems to mention it once (*Inst.* 10.1.76), but does not seem to regard it as binding. He never tells us who was in that list, and both lists he does give us contain orators not admitted to the usual list of ten as it was known later. The list of ten as such clearly had no influence on his work, and the phrase containing it could easily be dropped from his *Institutio Oratoria*, the longest surviving treatment of oratory from antiquity, and we would be none the wiser about his acquaintance with the list. If the list rates the barest of mentions here, its omission from earlier and shorter works cannot imply that their authors did not know it.

The eighteenth oration of Dio of Prusa (whose reliance on earlier lists is stressed by Ludwig Radermacher,[7]) Quintilian's contemporary, bears this out. Clearly, if Quintilian knew a list of ten Attic orators, his Atticizing contemporary did as well. And yet he never mentions it in a speech listing the desirable reading for one being given a rhetorical education. In section 11 of that speech he mentions Demosthenes, Lysias, Hyperides, Aeschines and Lycurgus. The same five orators are mentioned in a different order by Tacitus (*Dial.* 25.3); again this is contemporary with, or slightly later than,

Quintilian's passing mention of the ten, and there is no mention of the list here.

The implication should be clear by now: Cicero's silence no more indicates the non-existence of the list of ten Attic orators when he wrote than does the similar silence of Dio and Tacitus. The same can be said about the absence of any reference to the ten in Dionysius of Halicarnassus; the added fact that Dionysius of Halicarnassus knew Caecilius of Calacte, to whom the *Suda*[8] attributes a work *On the Character of the Ten Orators*, cannot be regarded as making it any more likely that he would have felt obliged to mention the list if Caecilius had already produced this work when he was writing. Not only is the nature of the relationship virtually unknown – our only information is that Dionysius of Halicarnassus refers to Caecilius as 'very dear' at *Epistle to Pompeius* 3 while agreeing with his opinion that Demosthenes was influenced by Thucydides – but it is unreasonable to imagine that, given the provisional nature of such a list of ten, Caecilius would have taken offence at Dionysius' apparent failure to mention it.[9]

2

To understand the nature of the ancient so-called 'canons' is to be in a better position to appreciate what counts as evidence for their existence or otherwise at a particular time. But what in fact is the evidence for the emergence of these select lists in the first place? We find in three passages in Quintilian the explicit evidence for the existence of such select lists as drawn up by the Alexandrian critics: at *Institutio* 10.1.59 we learn that there were three iambic poets 'accepted' by Aristarchus (*ex tribus receptis*), at 10.1.54 that Apollonius of Rhodes did not feature in the *ordo* of epic poets established by Aristarchus and Aristophanes because they decided to exclude all contemporaries, and at 1.4.3 that the ancient grammarians were so severe that they not only marked verses and books as spurious, but there were some authors they admitted to their *ordo* and others they excluded. On the basis of this evidence – which relates to poets only – it is clear that not all writers known to the Alexandrian scholars were included in the lists they drew up. But does this mean that others were excluded on the grounds of quality? That is the usual interpretation.[10] But there is no positive evidence that this criterion was applied, and indeed the only criterion for exclusion mentioned by Quintilian is that of being of the librarians' own time (*sui temporis*): that is, the Alexandrian scholars were the original Dead Poets Society. Can we thus conclude that there was no other criterion for exclusion, and that the Alexandrian scholars included all the (genuine) poets from earlier ages they knew of in their lists? Such indeed was the view of Wilamowitz-Moellendorff.[11] It is true that some sort of ranking even of dead poets can be discerned before the Alexandrian critics: Heraclides of Pontus (fr. 179)[12] in the fourth century had already picked out three tragedians – doubtless the surviving ones – for special discussion, and it could be argued that such a selection is almost a prerequisite for the plot of Aristophanes' *Frogs* from the end of the previous century.[13] But, as a minimalist position, Wilamowitz-Moellendorff's view cannot be shown to be wrong. What this means is that we have to look beyond Alexandria for the first systematic drawing up of lists of approved authors, and that we cannot even be sure that the Alexandrians had select lists of poets, much less prose writers.[14]

The first strong evidence for the drawing up of these lists takes us to the early second half of the first century BCE in Rome. We are in fact now in a position where the purpose of such lists becomes clear: they are polemically motivated by the rhetorical theories that developed at this time. This is perhaps what we should expect anyway: the drawing up of the list of ten orators was linked by Brzoska in an influential study to the rhetorical practices in Pergamon in the second century BCE.[15] There are troubles enough with that view, but the belief that a particular group of orators should be selected as worthy of special attention by those who were themselves deeply involved in the practice of oratory seems, a priori, a reasonable one, and it is not surprising that Brzoska linked the canon with imitative Atticism. However, believing that Atticism arose in the middle of the second century, he was naturally inclined to fix the drawing up of the most common list of Attic orators to about this time.[16] As we will see, there is some argument for linking the canon with the beginning of Atticism, but later work has discredited Brzoska's views of the time and place of the latter.[17] And we should go further than he did and link not just the lists of orators, but of other writers as well, with rhetorical studies. For that is what the evidence unambiguously suggests.[18]

3

The fragments of Cicero's lost dialogue *Hortensius* (which can be dated to 45 BCE) have been held to contain some of the earliest evidence for select lists of authors. Most significant for our purposes is the following fragment (15[19]) dealing with historians:

> quid enim aut Herodoto dulcius aut Thucydide gravius, <aut Xenophonte copiosius> aut Philisto brevius, aut Theopompo acrius aut Ephoro mitius inveniri potest?

> For what can be found that is sweeter than Herodotus, or more solemn than Thucydides, < or richer than Xenophon > or more concise than Philistus, or sharper than Theopompus or milder than Ephorus?

Admittedly allowance must be made for the incomplete state of the text, but two points stand out here: we are being presented with (and, to judge from the other fragments, urged to read) these historians as especially excellent in their ways,[20] and Hellenistic historiography is completely excluded.[21] The list is thus quite different from that found in the earlier work (55 BCE) *De Oratore* 2.55ff. There Antonius is giving a list of Greek historians who, while not practising public oratory, still show the influence of rhetoric in their writing. He mentions Herodotus, Thucydides, Philistus, Theopompus, Ephorus, Xenophon, Callisthenes *and Timaeus*. The final addition seems all the more significant because, as Wilkins notes,[22] it is an afterthought. In a context not stressing excellence, we note the addition of a Hellenistic historian, and one who was a special target of early Atticist polemic.[23]

The exclusion of Timaeus from the list in *Hortensius* seems to coincide with its transformation into a collection (based on quality) of recommended reading. Is this just coincidence? Here I would refer to the point, forcefully made by Wilamowitz-Moellendorff,[24] that Cicero shows no awareness of Atticism and Asianism as stylistic terms in the *De Oratore*; we have to wait until *Brutus* and *Orator* (both 46 BCE) for that; in the former Timaeus is described as practising one form of Asianist style (325). The *Hortensius* of the following year contains perhaps the earliest list of recommended reading within a particular genre. Its exclusion of any Hellenistic prose is suggestive, and finds an interesting parallel in the list of orators in *Brutus*, which has suffered a similar constriction in relation to the *De Oratore*. Consider the list in the latter work at 2.93–5: beginning with Pericles, it continues as far as Menecles and his brother Hierocles, whom Antonius had actually heard speak. Douglas notes of this passage 'the whole account of Greek oratory there closely corresponds with that in *Brutus*',[25] so it is all the more interesting that the discussions in that work end with Demetrius of Phalerum (37–8) or his contemporaries Demochares and Charisius (286), admittedly at the beginning of the Hellenistic age, but described in such a way as either to mark their break from the orators who had gone before or at least to show them as the last breath of Attic oratory. At sections 286–7 the line is drawn before Hegesias, that monster of Asianism, and he is implicitly denied the title of 'Attic'.

In his attitude to the development of both history and oratory Cicero seems to have undergone the same sort of change between 55 and 46 BCE; the fact that this coincides with the first clear evidence for the existence of Atticism does not seem coincidental. We may find our suspicions confirmed by examining what is probably the next oldest list of recommended reading after the *Hortensius*, that found in the fragmentary *On Imitation* by the avowed Atticist Dionysius of Halicarnassus.

Although not complete, enough of this work survives for us to have much more confidence about it than about *Hortensius*. Dionysius of Halicarnassus arrived in Rome in 30 BCE (*Ant. Rom.*1.7) and began working on his early history of the city: it is usually assumed that his rhetorical writings were composed during the twenty-two years he was engaged in this task,[26] but clear evidence is lacking. The relative chronology of these minor works is also unclear, but Bonner has plausibly argued that *On Imitation* is the first of them.[27] The most important of the fragments (fr. 6 of Usener and Radermacher[28]) is actually an epitome of the second book, which set out a list of poets, philosophers, historians and orators to be imitated (*Epistle to Pompeius* 3); *Epistle to Pompeius* 3–6 reproduces the section on historians in its original fuller form. The fragments of this work thus contain the first examples of 'best authors' over a number of genres, and the purpose of these lists is clear: as Bonner observed, the essay is 'a purely practical handbook for use in the rhetorical schools',[29] and writers of poetry and prose are 'criticised for their rhetorical, not their inherent value'.[30] But to return to the relationship between this work and *Hortensius*: the historians picked out by Dionysius of Halicarnassus are Herodotus, Thucydides, Xenophon, Philistus and Theopompus. The list is not identical to that offered by Cicero, but it is similar in excluding Hellenistic historiography. This is less surprising in a polemical Atticist like Dionysius, but it does underline the Atticist flavour in these lists.

Nowhere is this Atticist flavour more clearly seen than in the lists offered by Quintilian in book 10. It is of considerable significance that both here and in the roughly contemporary Dio 18 we find recommended reading described, as in Dionysius, very much from the viewpoint of rhetorical education. The relationship between the lists in Quintilian and Dionysius has been the subject of speculation, but it seems clear that the similarities can only be explained by assuming either that Quintilian has used Dionysius as his source, or that they both draw on a common third source. If the latter option is more plausible, we must still acknowledge the strongly rhetorical interests of this source.[31] The historians Quintilian (*Inst.* 10.1.73–5) recommends are Thucydides, Herodotus, Theopompus, Philistus, Ephorus, Clitarchus and Timagenes; he mentions Xenophon in this context but feels he belongs more with the philosophers. This time the exclusion of Hellenistic prose is made more pointed by the inclusion of Timagenes (treated as the first historian for centuries), a first-century BCE figure whose conflict with the professed Asianist Craton[32] and friendship with Asinius Pollio[33] show him to have been an Atticist. Quintilian's source is aggressively Atticist, and Timagenes is included for this reason, not, *pace* Radermacher,[34] because of his interest in Alexander. The Atticist bias of the early list of recommended historians shows itself again, if not quite so spectacularly, with Dio 18.10 where the historians recommended are Herodotus, Thucydides, Theopompus and Ephorus.

In looking at the select lists of historians, we noticed that the general list in *De Oratore* 2.55ff., based on no particular qualities and including Hellenistic writing, gave way in Cicero's work to a list of particular excellences that excluded postclassical work once he had become aware of the Atticist movement. We can trace something similar with his attitude to philosophers. In *De Oratore* 3.56ff. he discusses the relationship between philosophy and rhetoric and runs briefly through the history of the former, going down as far as Carneades (214/3–129/8 BCE). This philosopher was influential on Cicero, and his style is spoken of with admiration here and elsewhere (68[35]). But by the time we get to *Brutus* 120 the situation is different. Cicero agrees with the judgement of the Atticist Brutus – a supporter of the 'old Academy' according to the manuscripts – who follows the philosophers who expound their ideas with *suavitas dicendi et copia* ('sweetness and richness of language'). The style of the Academics and Peripatetics is described as necessary (though not sufficient) to produce the perfect orator, while that of the Stoics is rejected as unsuitable (admittedly there are reservations already about them in *De Or.* 2.159 and 3.66). But as he goes on to mention particular philosophers, he restricts himself to three (*Brut.* 120–1):

> Quis enim uberior in dicendo Platone? . . . Quis Aristotele nervosior, Theophrasto dulcior?

> For who is richer in language than Plato? . . . Who is more vigorous than Aristotle, or sweeter than Theophrastus?

We immediately notice two points of detail. Like the fragment from the *Hortensius*, the writers are here presented as having particular, unsurpassed excellences.[36] And, like the fragment again, clearly Hellenistic work is excluded.

This later list has much in common with the list of philosophers in Dionysius of Halicarnassus. At *On Imitation* fr. 6.4,[37] if we accept with Usener and Radermacher that the recommendation of the (spurious) Pythagorean writings is not due to Dionysius, we have recommended for study Xenophon, Plato, Aristotle and the last-named's pupils: Theophrastus most readily springs to mind. Plato, Xenophon, Aristotle and Theophrastus are again commended by Quintilian, *Institutio* 10.1.81–4 (the Stoics are commended too, but for their content rather than their style). Of philosophers Dio 18.13 recommends only 'the Socratics'; of them only Xenophon is named. Note too that Velleius Paterculus, in a passage emphasizing that the period productive of literary genius was very short, refers to a list he has given of leading philosophers, which unfortunately has perished from the surviving text. But his reference to it makes it clear that it must have ended at or soon after Aristotle (1.16):

> Philosophorum quoque ingenia Socratico ore defluentia omnium, quos paulo ante enumeravimus, quanto post Platonis Aristotelisque mortem floruere spatio?

> And all the gifted philosophers, inspired by Socrates, whom I just listed – how long after the death of Plato and Aristotle did they last?

4

What then can we conclude about these select lists of prose writers? In the first place, we note that they are not fixed: variations occur even between the works of one author when they are given. This bears out the point made earlier about lists of orators: 'authoritative lists' of ancient writers did not exist. But the second conclusion to be drawn shows us that the lists are by no means arbitrary; for they are clearly of a strongly Atticizing bent. The lists of recommended orators, historians and philosophers, although not identical, all show the same spirit by excluding Hellenistic work. In this they present a marked contrast with earlier works of Cicero, where lists of authors are neither for the purpose of recommending reading nor anti-Hellenistic in bias. Furthermore, Cicero's works preserve vital evidence for the third conclusion we can draw from the survey. What seems to be the first extant list of recommended reading can be dated to 45 BCE and is to be distinguished from lists of orators, historians and philosophers found as late as 55 BCE in his work. Clearer are the prescriptions of Dionysius of Halicarnassus, probably datable to the 20s BCE. Finally, Dionysius gives us the first opportunity to see what is the general trend in the purpose of our lists: that is to say, they are drawn up to present models for rhetorical imitation. It is not the lack of reference to a particular 'canon' of orators until the first century BCE that means that such a list did not exist until then, but this conclusion is strongly suggested by the fact that this time coincides with the drawing up of lists of other writers for the purpose of rhetorical imitation.

The lists' Atticism, the date and place of their first appearance, and their apparent purpose all point to one source, which is the Atticist movement, a rhetorical school that began in Rome in the middle of the first century BCE. It has rightly been pointed out that it is extremely difficult to attribute the origins of this movement to any one individual, but at the same time the evidence that we have does point to Caecilius of Calacte as the most likely contender.

The data for determining the period of Caecilius' life are meagre and contradictory enough. Essentially, they consist of three notices in the *Suda*. S.v. Caecilius[38] we are told that he was a *rhetor* who taught in Rome under Augustus and until Hadrian (ἕως Ἀδριανοῦ) [sic!], s.v. Hermagoras[39] again that he taught under Augustus in Rome, and s.v. Timagenes[40] that the latter taught 'in Rome both under Pompey and after him, and under Augustus and afterwards at the same time as Caecilius (ἅμα Κεκιλίῳ)'. Almost the only inference we can safely draw from these notices is that he was active in Rome under Augustus. We could have concluded the same from the reference to him in Dionysius of Halicarnassus mentioned in section 1 above – and it is possible that the *Suda* or its source had only this information on which to draw. Hardly any more can be gleaned from these notices: in the first the phrase 'and until Hadrian' must be corrupt, and in the last it is unclear which period 'at the same time as Caecilius' refers to.

The further attempts to determine the period in which he was active, based on such data as the career of his supposed teacher Apollodorus (Quint. *Inst.* 9.1.12 does not establish the relationship) and the highly uncertain date of the treatise *On the Sublime*, are not very convincing.[41] We are faced, then, with the information that Caecilius worked under Augustus and possibly later. Could he have taught earlier? Some indeed have suggested that he was active in the age of Cicero.[42] He may have had a long teaching career – as long as that of Timagenes with whom the *Suda* links him. There is one piece of evidence that suggests that he may have already achieved some eminence early in the Augustan period. Dionysius of Halicarnassus' reference to him, as we have seen, has some claim to having been written close to 30 BCE, yet there seems to be a deferential tone to it already. Brzoska, who regarded Caecilius as a younger contemporary, felt that the tone implied that he could not have been much younger.[43] But with no strong arguments to make Caecilius younger at all, a more natural reading of the passage would be to see him as an already established, as a more authoritative and older figure. Before going on, it is worth pointing out that this reference to Caecilius – the only clearly contemporary one we have – is in the context of Dionysius of Halicarnassus' discussion of the historians he recommends for reading, a discussion that we have already seen as linked to Atticism.

Wilamowitz-Moellendorff[44] put forward a stronger argument for regarding Caecilius as older. Dionysius of Halicarnassus' preface to *On the Ancient Orators* is written from the viewpoint of victorious Atticism;[45] Caecilius, on the other hand, writes rather from the midst of the struggle. The works attributed to him in the *Suda* seem to have had a programmatic – even vitriolic – character: *How the Attic Style Differs from the Asianic*, the first Attic lexicon, and (unless this is just another name for the latter) two books *Against the Phrygians*, a clearly contemptuous way of referring to the practitioners of the Asianist style. Amongst his works too we find a title *On the Character of the Ten Orators*. His faults are those of the zealot: in his enthusiasm for Lysias and criticism of Plato (see below), he is the sort of one-sided Atticist against whom Cicero's *Brutus* inveighs.

On the other hand, it has been argued by George Kennedy[46] that his work *On the Character of the Ten Orators* must have been published after Dionysius of Halicarnassus wrote his preface to *On the Ancient Orators*, for the latter sets forth the questions he will address in his work (4): 'Who are the most important (ἀξιολογώτατοι) of the ancient orators and historians? What were their styles (προαιρέσεις) of life and writing? What of each (παρ' ἑκάστου) should we imitate or avoid?' Dionysius proceeds to say that he has not come across any work that deals with such issues; hence Kennedy's conclusion that Caecilius' work had not yet been published. But is the inference necessary? We actually know nothing about Caecilius' work apart from its title,[47] so it would seem rash to make any claims based on its apparent content. Perhaps we can go further than cautious scepticism. It is clear from this programmatic passage of Dionysius, and from what we have of the work *On the Ancient Orators* itself, that his focus was very much on individual orators and their differences. Did Caecilius have such an interest? He may, particularly early in his career, have been inclined to overlook the many differences between the Attic orators in an attempt to present them as a single body worthy of imitation. The singular *On the Character* (περὶ τοῦ χαρακτῆρος) *of the Ten Orators* need not mean that he wrote of just one style that they all shared (cf. the plural προαιρέσεις in Dionysius' project), but it is at least consistent with this hypothesis. So also is the title of another work from the *Suda*: *How the Attic Style* (ὁ Ἀττικὸς ζῆλος) *Differs from the Asianic* – once more the title suggests that there is just one sort of Atticism. Note too how his description of Antiphon's oratory (in Phot. *Bibl.* 485b) seems to shade off into a general description of the qualities of 'the ancient orators'. Finally, consider the criticism in Cicero, *Brutus* 285–7, one of the earliest documents witnessing to Atticism. Here the objection made is that the general term 'Attic' is too broad, and covers a wide range of styles. It is implied that the Atticists have not made the necessary stylistic distinctions. Perhaps this was true of the early stages of Caecilius' work: we know from the *Suda* article that at one point he wrote a whole book comparing Demosthenes with Aeschines, but of course we have no idea of the chronology involved. For all these reasons, then, we need not assume that *On the Character of the Ten Orators*, let alone any other work of Caecilius, was written after Dionysius' preface to *On the Ancient Orators*.

The appearance of the Atticist controversy late in Cicero's life, and the description he gives of it are, I believe, consistent with the hypothesis that Caecilius was, if not the father of Atticism, at least present at its birth. The old claim that he was the first to suggest the so-called 'canon' of ten Attic orators has recently been revived in the context of his Atticism,[48] and the two naturally go together. But we can say more than this, for not only is the existence of a select list of writings complementary to the concept of any form of classicism, but it is actually indispensable to it. That is to say, it must have a consciously formulated group of writers who form the standard to be imitated. Atticism cannot have arisen without the formation of some sort of list.[49] On the other hand, although it is at least conceivable that lists based on perceived quality could arise outside the context of an imitative classicism – such as the select lists of poets some believe the Alexandrian scholars drew up – the evidence above suggests that they grew up in just such an imitative context.[50]

<h1 style="text-align:center">5</h1>

The connection between Caecilius and a fundamental stage of Atticism seems fairly clear. So too the complementary connection between him and the selection of prose writers for study: the list of ten orators attributed to him suggests this for oratory, and other testimonia certainly indicate that he was also interested in sorting the wheat from the chaff in other genres. In the field of history his own works on the Sicilian slave wars (Ath. 272f.), and on the historical accuracy of orators (*Suda*), show some indication of an interest in the practice of historiography. The title *On History* (Ath. 466a) perhaps suggests a wider survey, but the one surviving fragment is anecdotal and does not support the notion. We know that he read Thucydides and concluded from the praise of Antiphon at 8.68 that the orator had been the historian's teacher ([Plut.] *Lives of the Ten Orators* 832e) – an assumption that tells us something about the relationship he saw between the two fields. Naturally he rated the Attic historian Thucydides highly, as we can deduce from his view that the greatest of Attic orators, Demosthenes, had learnt from him (see section 1 above on Dionysius' *Epistle to Pompeius* 3). But we have more detailed references to criticisms he made of two historians. It is not recorded where he made them, but the nature of the criticism is explicitly aesthetic. In other words, the historians are examined as prose writers above all. Two passages from the essay *On the Sublime*, a work professedly written against Caecilius' views on the subject (1), record his views on historians. Chapter 4 of the work is devoted mainly to criticism of 'frigidity' in Timaeus; only a few examples are given, because Caecilius 'had already collected most of them' (4.2) (there must have been many in the thirty-eight books of Timaeus' *History*). The first criticism is clearly just of a contrived thought, but the remaining two are based on feeble punning and are stylistic. If this is indicative of the criticism Caecilius made of Timaeus, the contrast with Polybius is instructive. The latter attacks Timaeus fiercely in book 12 of his *History*, but essentially on the grounds of his content, and above all on his lack of accuracy. 'Longinus', on the other hand, seems to regard his non-stylistic elements with more respect, and calls him 'learned' (πολυΐστωρ) and 'ingenious' (ἐπινοητικός); but it is as prose writer, not as historical thinker, that 'Longinus' and his apparent source consider him. Caecilius had obviously spent much time going through Timaeus looking for infelicities of language, and his evident rejection of the Hellenistic historian, no less than his regard for Thucydides, is consistent with what we have seen of his Atticist enthusiasms. Furthermore, it should be seen in the context of the absence of Timaeus from the lists of recommended historians mentioned above.

The other historian Caecilius criticized was Theopompus. The first point to make is that the evidence does not allow us to assume that Caecilius made the same sort of extensive examination and rejection of him as of Timaeus, for we only hear of one particular criticism. In the context of ἰδιωτισμοί ('everyday expressions'), 'Longinus' 31.1 mentions the word ἀναγκοφαγῆσαι, 'to eat under compulsion', which Theopompus[51] used metaphorically of Philip putting up with situations. 'Somehow or other', adds 'Longinus', 'Caecilius found fault with this.' Why? The suggestions that the word is a bold compound (thus Brzoska[52]) or a bold metaphor (thus Jacoby[53]) go clearly against the context in which 'Longinus' places the word; he regards it as a vulgar, everyday expression, and it is surely this which accounts for its absence from surviving texts before Theopompus. Its lack of literary pedigree, and its use in colloquial speech, seem to have been enough to condemn the word in the eyes of the Atticist Caecilius,[54] for Atticist polemic turned the charge of vulgarity against Asianist oratory.[55] As we will see further below, the condemnation of Hellenistic prose did not mean the automatic approval of all prose before the death of Alexander. Nor should we expect it to: already Theopompus' master Isocrates – no friend of vulgar words[56] – had remarked on his pupil's need for restraint in use of language (Cic. *De Or.* 3.36). Caecilius clearly did not regard all pre-Hellenistic Greek as equally worthy of imitation.

This emerges again in his notorious criticism of Plato. Once again, however, caution is needed in determining his exact attitude, for all we know about this criticism is the report of a very hostile witness who gives no details to speak of. In a context describing criticisms of Plato's metaphors, 'Longinus' 32.8 says that, on this basis, Caecilius said that Lysias was altogether superior to Plato. This is where the information about Caecilius' opinions ends. 'Longinus' then follows with two opinions of his own: that Caecilius loved Lysias more than himself, and that he hated Plato even more than he loved Lysias. But, as Russell observes, this is a mark of 'Longinus'' polemical methods and evidently unfair to Caecilius, who was no uncritical admirer of Lysias.[57] This is shown by Photius, *Bibliotheca* 489b, where it is recorded that Caecilius did not regard the orator's powers of arrangement as equal to his powers of invention. Ironically, this draws on a criticism of Lysias' work first made by Plato himself; in *Phaedrus* 236a the arrangement of the model speech attributed to Lysias is contrasted with its invention, and at 264b the former is claimed to be quite deficient. These facts put the claims of 'Longinus' in some sort of perspective. Brzoska reasonably suggests a parallel with Dionysius of Halicarnassus' criticisms of Plato;[58] these are in the context of preferring Demosthenes (cf. *Epistle to Pompeius* 1), and in attacking Plato's grand style the harshness of his metaphors is also mentioned (*Demosthenes* 5, repeated in *Epistle to Pompeius* 2). Yet the critique is clearly not one-sided, although a hostile reporter could have made it appear so. Dionysius of Halicarnassus, it will be recalled, explicitly included Plato in his recommended reading in *On Imitation*, and Caecilius' criticism would not seem to rule out the possibility that he may have had an influence in the formation of such lists, especially in the light of the very positive assessment of Plato's style – praising its accuracy, purity, simplicity and pleasing rhythms – which is attributed by the third *Life of Aeschines*[59] to Caecilius, Idomeneus and Hermippus.

6

The facts that no reference to either Atticism or the select list of orators can be certainly placed before Caecilius, when seen in the light of his own work, do not seem to be just coincidental. Further activity in drawing up lists of recommended prose authors may also be suspected, not only because such lists appear as Atticism is born, but also because he was clearly interested in the stylistic qualities of non-oratorical prose. Which is what we should expect, for Atticism was basically a stylistic revolution: Hellenistic rhetoric in general seems to have been far more interested in *inventio* than in *elocutio* (one thinks of the development of *stasis* theory above all).[60] A final thought about Caecilius' role in all this concerns the name by which the proponents of the classicizing new style described their opponents. Why the connection with Asia? There was nothing specifically Asian about the style; rather, it was a style that was presented as holding sway throughout the entire Greek world from the death of Alexander. One of its most notorious practitioners was the Sicilian Timaeus, active soon after Alexander and designated as Asianist in one of the earliest testimonies to the Atticist movement (Cic. *Brut.* 325). Obviously, the contrast was to be with Attica, but that Asia should have been chosen seems another reason for doubting that the new movement was begun by Apollodorus of Pergamum,[61] or by Dionysius of Halicarnassus. Caecilius' interest in his native island is shown by his historical researches, and he may have wished to spare it the ignominy of beginning the corruption of Greek literature.

The select lists of orators and other prose writers did not in themselves ensure the survival of those contained in them. The most crucial step in the survival of these particular orators may have already taken place before the drawing up of the list of ten, which may be only a reflection, through the mirror of a general desire for archaism, of this older and even more mysterious process.[62] There was not, as we have seen, uniformity in these genre lists, and we have seen several writers recommended for study who now survive only in fragmentary form. Even amongst the orators inclusion in what was later the usual list of ten did not guarantee survival: it is only by the chance discovery of papyrus that we have anything substantial of Hyperides.[63] But while differing in details, the lists we have seen are essentially the same in overall conception. This conception was that of Atticism as it arose in the mid-first century BCE, and it was this spirit, rather than any particular list, which was important not only for the survival of older literature, but for the subsequent nature of Greek itself. The exact contribution that Caecilius made to this conception cannot now be known; he may well have been behind particular lists of writers recommended for imitation, but such lists were subject to variation and were only the expressions of deeper ideas. Whatever the details, there are strong reasons for believing that Caecilius made an important – perhaps *the* important – contribution to these ideas and thus to the intellectual development of the ancient world.[64]

NOTES

1 Consider only Harold Bloom's *The Western Canon: The Books and Schools of the Ages* (1994).
2 Pfeiffer 1968: 207.
3 As is admitted by Pfeiffer 1968: 207.
4 See the disagreements in the lists assembled by Kröhnert 1897.
5 Douglas 1956: 30–40, esp. 31–4; Worthington 1994b: 244–63, esp. 250–1.
6 In his *On the Ancient Orators* (*pr.* 4) and elsewhere he lists Lysias, Isocrates, Isaeus, Demosthenes, Hyperides and Aeschines, while in *On Imitation* fr. 6.5 (Usener and Radermacher 1899–1929: 2.212) Lycurgus is substituted for Isaeus.
7 *RE* 10.1873, 1876.
8 Adler 1928–38: 3.83.
9 In any case, we do not possess everything that Dionysius wrote: see Roberts 1901: 7. Furthermore, we learn from [Plut.] *Lives of the Ten Orators* 838d and from Schol. Dem. *Olynthiac* 2.1a (Dilts 1983: 49) that the two could disagree.
10 Thus Pfeiffer 1968: 203–8.
11 Wilamowitz-Moellendorff 1900b: 63–71. He argues that the basis of acceptance was authenticity, not quality; cf. Kennedy 1963: 331.
12 Wehrli 1967–9.
13 Cf. Kröhnert 1897: 25; Wilamowitz-Moellendorff 1900b: 63.
14 *Pace* Smith 1995: 66–79.
15 Brzoska 1883. See the searching examination of the argument in Hartmann 1891: 14–21 and now in Smith 1995: 67–9.
16 Brzoska 1883: 6–7, 46 (the canon and imitative Atticism), 32 (the beginning of Atticism), 55 (the date of the 'canon': it was selected 'imitationis gratia *c.* 125' BCE).
17 See especially the great study of Wilamowitz-Moellendorff 1900a.
18 In what follows I have restricted myself to the lists of prose authors, for they give a clearer indication of their compilers' interests than do the poetic lists. But, as we have seen, it is by no means certain that formal selected lists of poets existed before this time either.
19 Grilli 1962.
20 For the significance of individual excellences, see Dion. Hal. *Is.* 19.
21 'Hellenistic' is a modern term, but the death of Alexander the Great is seen as *the* turning-point of stylistic history by the Atticists (Dionysius of Halicarnassus, preface [1] to *On the Ancient Orators*). Theopompus admittedly outlived Alexander but, like Theophrastus below, lived most of his life before 323 BCE.
22 Wilkins 1888–92: 2.31 *ad* 58.
23 See pp. 43–4.
24 Wilamowitz-Moellendorff 1900a: 1–2.
25 Douglas 1956: 32.
26 Thus Roberts 1901: 5–6; Bonner 1939: 2.
27 Bonner 1939: 36–7.
28 Usener and Radermacher 1899–1929.
29 Bonner 1939: 39.

30 Bonner 1939: 40.
31 Radermacher in *RE* 10.1875.
32 *FGrH* 2A 318 no. 88 T2.
33 *FGrH* 2A 318–19 no. 88 T3–4.
34 *RE* 10.1876.
35 See also Wilkins 1888–92: 3.37 *ad* 68. But the reference in *Acad*. 1.46 is inconclusive, and Cicero may not have spoken of Carneades' style with admiration as late as this.
36 Cf. the list in *Orat*. 62: again, just Theophrastus, Aristotle, Xenophon and Plato.
37 Usener and Radermacher 1899–1929: 2.210–11.
38 Adler 1928–38: 3.83.
39 Adler 1928–38: 2.411.
40 Adler 1928–38: 4.549.
41 Cf. Brzoska in *RE* 3.1175–6.
42 See Müller's opinion reported in *RE* 3.1176.
43 *RE* 3.1175.
44 Wilamowitz-Moellendorff 1900a: 5; cf. Wilamowitz-Moellendorff 1900b: 70.
45 *Pace* Worthington 1994b: 257, he can hardly have 'spearheaded' the movement, which Cicero shows was active at least sixteen years before he arrived in Rome.
46 Kennedy 1972: 364 n. 86.
47 I mention in passing the edition of the fragments of Caecilius (and much else besides) by Ofenloch 1907. The book contains over fifty 'fragments' of *On the Character of the Ten Orators*, not one of which is attributed by its source to this work.
48 By Worthington 1994b: 255–9.
49 *Pace* Brzoska 1883: 46; Dihle 1977: 176. The latter's view that Roman Atticism was not concerned with imitation is contradicted by, e.g., Cic. *Brut*. 67, 284–91.
50 Wilamowitz-Moellendorff 1900b: 66 denies that the list of ten orators was ever meant to supply models for imitation, but the contemporary parallel of Dionysius of Halicarnassus suggests otherwise. And see above on 'the' Attic style – the differences between earlier orators may not have been as apparent to those who had grown up on a strong diet of Hellenistic oratory.
51 *FGrH* 2B 592 no. 115 fr. 262.
52 *RE* 3.1179.
53 *FGrH* 2B (Commentary) 391 no. 115 fr. 262.
54 See Wilamowitz-Moellendorff 1900a: 40.
55 Dionysius of Halicarnassus, preface to *On the Ancient Orators* 1 and 2.
56 See Norden 1915: 114.
57 Russell 1964: 156 *ad* 32.8.
58 *RE* 3.1183.
59 Dilts 1992: 6.
60 Thus Wilamowitz-Moellendorff 1900a: 44.
61 Cf. Wilamowitz-Moellendorff 1900a: 46–9; Kennedy 1972: 338–9.

62 Hartmann 1891: 38–9, 43; Wilamowitz-Moellendorff 1900a: 42; 1900b: 66–70. Was the list essentially a catalogue of surviving work?

63 Conversely, there was still a demand for speeches of those off the list: the forged speech now under the name of Demades did not exist at the time the list of ten was coming into existence (Cic. *Brut.* 36), nor even much later (Quint. *Inst.* 2.17.13; 12.10.49), but its forger thought it enough to attribute it to an Athenian orator.

64 I am very grateful to John Kirby for commenting on a draft of this chapter and to my brother Patrick, whose help was invaluable in completing the final version.

4

The style is the man: Seneca, Tacitus and Quintilian's canon

William J. Dominik

There was much controversy and debate among writers of the first century on matters of style (*elocutio*), namely the selection of individual words (*dictio*) and the generation of syntactic patterns (*compositio verborum*). The writings of the period are replete with references to and discussions about the various forms, functions and styles of rhetoric and literature. The *Institutio Oratoria* of Quintilian (*c*. 35–*c*. 96 CE) and the *Dialogus de Oratoribus* of Tacitus (*c*. 55–after *c*. 117 CE) constitute some of the most important passages on rhetorical and literary criticism of the early imperial period. Stylistically the comments of Quintilian and Tacitus are often pointed and memorable, none more so than Quintilian's polemic against the younger Seneca (*c*. 4 BCE–65 CE) in *Institutio* 10.1 and Marcus Aper's defence of postclassical rhetoric in the *Dialogus*. The stylistic contrast between Quintilian and Seneca, standard-bearers of neo-Ciceronianism and postclassicism respectively, and the debate between Aper and his scholastic opponents exemplify the aesthetic controversies of the age. While Seneca promoted and Aper defended a style of expression that in their view reflected the changed attitudes and circumstances of the early principate, Quintilian attempted to modify the prevailing imperial style.

1

The first chapter of *Institutio* 10 is significant for its evaluation of Greek and Latin authors according to genres (47–131). Quintilian's comments on specific writers and the various styles are made primarily from the standpoint of their appropriateness in the training of aspiring orators and in shaping their styles (cf. 10.1.44–5), but they are also literary judgements. Since Quintilian's discussion of Seneca's perceived faults and talents (126–31) has heavily coloured subsequent judgements of Seneca and his style, the passage merits critical examination and consideration of its rhetorical and historical contexts. Just as there had been a reaction during the early empire against the style of Cicero, so there evolved a counter-movement led by Quintilian against the postclassical style.[1] Quintilian, in effect, fought a rear-guard action against the postclassical style that was so popular in the first century and which for him was epitomized in the style of Seneca and his imitators. This apparently had been the purpose of his earlier *De Causis Corruptae Eloquentiae*.[2] Quintilian was not only concerned about the influence of Seneca and his style on his students, but he also harboured some resentment against Seneca for his role in the anti-Ciceronian reaction. Quintilian argues that his criticism of Seneca was part of an attempt to bring style back into line with severer standards at a time when it was corrupted and weakened by every kind of error (*Inst.* 10.1.125); he maintains his aim was to prevent Seneca being preferred to those authors who were superior to him (126). As Quintilian asserts that the only model in the hands of the young at the time was Seneca (126), the 'corrupt style of speaking' (*corruptum dicendi genus*, 125) to which he refers applies to Seneca and his imitators; the severer standards are those of the neo-Ciceronian style advocated by Quintilian.

Quintilian structures his discussion of Seneca by framing his praise of Seneca (10.1.128–9) with general criticisms of Seneca's qualities (126–7, 130–1). It seems that Quintilian wishes to emphasize the faults of Seneca, since he begins and ends with them. Quintilian also mentions a number of Seneca's positive qualities. From his discussion it is apparent that he considered Seneca a writer of extraordinary talent who possessed a wide range of abilities. Most of the praise appears in the middle of the passage, although there is a specific criticism for virtually every compliment given. Seneca was intelligent, industrious and learned, but he was often misled by those who researched certain subjects for him (128). How was he misled? Quintilian does not tell us. Seneca was extremely versatile, dealing with almost every department of knowledge and writing widely across the generic spectrum (129). He was also admirable in his denunciations of vice but lacked critical power in philosophy (129).

Quintilian's discussion of Seneca is notable for its emphasis on the latter's popularity and the attractiveness of his style (10.1.126–7, 130). Seneca probably was no less influential in prose style during his own time than Cicero had been in his own age; he may even have been more influential, judging from Quintilian's comments on his popularity and on the Atticists' criticisms of Cicero (Tac. *Dial.* 18.4–5; Quint. *Inst.* 12.10.12–15; cf. 12.1.22). Although Quintilian's use of the past tense may suggest that the vogue of this style had already waned when he was writing, his remarks give the impression that many Roman audiences of the early principate still preferred the aesthetic of Seneca to the more restrained style advocated by Quintilian. Seneca does not include himself among those who sought to win the attention of the young with his style (*Ep.* 20.2), but they nevertheless admired and attempted to imitate him. Quintilian viewed the postclassical style represented by Seneca not only as a threat to the style he favoured but also as a challenge to his own established school of rhetoric. From his comments on Cicero it may appear that Quintilian was attempting to reassert the pre-eminence of the neo-Ciceronian tradition in opposition to the postclassical style among orators and writers; if this was the case, it shows that his *Institutio* was already out of step with prevailing trends when it appeared in 95. For despite the efforts of Quintilian and his suggestion that the stylistic influence of Seneca had waned (*Inst.* 10.1.125–6), it is difficult to see in the first century a sustained movement toward neo-Ciceronianism away from the postclassical style. That a generation after the death of Seneca Quintilian feels compelled to deal at length with Seneca bears witness to the endurance of Seneca's influence.

Seneca maligned the styles of Cicero and Ennius and the archaism of Vergil (Gell. *NA* 12.2; cf. Sen. *Ep.* 108.32–4); this is no doubt what Quintilian means when he contends that Seneca criticized authors superior to himself (*Inst.* 10.1.126). According to Quintilian, Seneca disparaged authors whose style was different from his own because he was afraid he would fail to please those who admired them (126). This assertion seems gratuitous, since Seneca's popularity and implied disclaimer of attempting to allure the ears of the young would appear to obviate the need for him to condemn other writers for this reason. In Quintilian's view, the young imitators of Seneca fell as far short of his level as Seneca did of the ancient writers (126); furthermore, it was his faults alone that pleased his young admirers, who vainly sought to imitate him (127). Even if it were true that Seneca's influence corrupted the young who attempted to imitate his style, Seneca cannot be held responsible for the poor attempts of his young admirers to imitate him. In fact, Seneca attempted to curb the excessive stylistic tendencies of Lucilius (e.g., *Ep.* 115, esp. 1, 18; cf.

100), the type of youthful imitator to whom Quintilian refers in his discussion of Seneca. But in the eyes of Quintilian, Seneca continued to remain the single most important exponent and chief source of the postclassical style.

Quintilian's criticism of Seneca's philosophical practice (*Inst.* 10.1.129) suggests the latter's method of argumentation was superficial and lacked precision. One of the root causes of Quintilian's ambivalent judgement of Seneca seems to be his apparent hostility toward the contemporary practice of philosophy (e.g., 1 *pr.* 15, 5.11.39, 11.1.33–5, 12.2.6–9, 12.3.11–12; cf. 10.1.123), a reflection of the breach between rhetoric and philosophy in antiquity.[3] Quintilian, who considered rhetoric to be the basis of all education, viewed contemporary philosophy as a challenge to its supremacy. While he acknowledges the orator should read philosophy, this is only because orators have abandoned to the philosophers much of what should form part of their own concern (10.1.35–6; cf. 1 *pr.* 11). Quintilian displays little understanding of philosophical theories, since he seems to equate philosophy mainly with frivolous disputations and with those who have withdrawn themselves from public affairs (cf. 11.1.35). In his antipathy toward the philosophers of his own time, there is even a hint of a grudge. Quintilian claims that the orator must borrow from the philosopher material that rightly belongs to oratory but has been lost to philosophy (1 *pr.* 13, 12.2.8–10; cf. 10.1.35, 12.2.5); he suggests philosophers have taken over from oratory the moral training of the future orator (1 *pr.* 11–19, 10.1.35, 12.2.9); and he scorns those who, wearied by the labour required to learn rhetoric, escape to the study of philosophy as a refuge for their indolence (12.3.11–12). The fact that philosophy is the last genre treated by Quintilian in his discussion of Greek and Latin authors is a strong indication not only of his view of its relative importance to the practice of oratory but also of his general aversion to the philosophers, including Seneca.

Quintilian also shows little awareness in the *Institutio* of the role of the changed political conditions in the development of philosophy in the early empire, but he was not likely in any case to be sympathetic to the philosophers, who were known during the Flavian period for their disinterest in public affairs and in a few cases for their active opposition to the emperors.[4] Nor was Seneca likely to be excluded from this group, given the ambiguous nature of his role in Nero's administration. Perhaps this explains why Quintilian's discussion of Seneca seems to have more of an air of a political pamphlet than it does of a rhetorical treatise. As the Atticists had shown when they attacked Cicero for his perceived Asianist tendencies (Quint. *Inst.* 12.1.22, 12.10.12; Tac. *Dial.* 18.4–5), Quintilian demonstrates that the critique of rhetorical style can be used as a stick with which to beat your opponents, and this may account for some of his tendentious but vague references to Seneca's style.

Quintilian's equivocal judgement has influenced modern critics tremendously in their assessment of Seneca, although explanations of his discussion vary enormously. Some critics believe Quintilian's comments constitute nothing but the meanest criticism,[5] while others perceive in them an attempt on the part of Quintilian at a fair and balanced assessment.[6] These are Quintilian's specific stylistic criticisms of Seneca (*Inst.* 10.1.129–30):[7]

> His style is for the most part corrupt (*corrupta*) and extremely dangerous because it abounds in attractive faults (*dulcibus vitiis*). . . . For if he had despised certain expressions (*aliqua*), if he had not coveted what was incorrect (*parum recta*),[8] if he had not been fond of all that was his own, and if he had not enfeebled the authority of his writing with trifling epigrams (*minutissimis sententiis*), he would have gained the universal approbation of the learned instead of the passionate approval of boys.

Despite disagreement among scholars, it is apparent that from the viewpoint of Quintilian the main problem – due to the defects he perceives in Seneca's style – is with the latter's stylistic influence on others and the attempts to imitate him by young orators learning their art. Stylistically the works of Seneca contain some striking epigrams (*sententiae*), according to Quintilian, and there is much worth reading for edification (129), but Seneca's excessive use of certain stylistic devices renders his style over-refined and ornate – in a word, *corrupta* (129). Quintilian reveals here the limits of his conception of style. In his view, Seneca's talent was admirable (130–1), but he should have allowed himself to be guided by the taste of others (130), these others presumably being an orator like Cicero or even himself. Seneca's 'attractive faults' (*dulcibus vitiis*, 129), particularly his 'trifling epigrams' (*minutissimis sententiis*, 130), are what Quintilian disapproves of most of all. He also criticizes Seneca for 'certain expressions' (*aliqua*, 130), perhaps a reference to his use of word-play and word-contrast. Elsewhere in the *Institutio*

Quintilian defines what he considers to be the stylistic faults of the 'corrupt style' (12.10.73):

> [It] exults in the licence of words or runs riot with childish epigrams (*puerilibus sententiolis lascivit*) or swells with unrestrained pomposity or rages with empty commonplaces or glitters with ornamentation that will fall to ground if lightly shaken, or regards extravagance as sublimity or raves under the pretext of free speech.

Quintilian probably had Seneca in mind when asserting that the corrupt style 'runs riot with childish epigrams' (*puerilibus sententiolis lascivit*; cf. 8.5.13), since it recalls his specific criticism of Seneca's epigrammatic brevity and his popularity among the youth of his time (10.1.130).

2

Why does Quintilian leave his treatment of Seneca until last? Quintilian maintains there is a general, though false, impression that he condemns and even detests him (*Inst*.10.1.125). Presumably now that Quintilian has virtually finished with his survey, he can turn to Seneca and clarify his feelings about this writer and his style. Quintilian's criticisms of Seneca are all mentioned in the past tense, which reminds the reader that whatever disagreement Quintilian had with Seneca was in the past, since Seneca had died about a generation earlier. However, that Quintilian commences his treatment of Seneca in a defensive manner shows that the memory of his criticisms could be expected to be still fresh in his reader's mind. The denial of animus against Seneca at the beginning of his discussion (125) may seem initially sincere, but any sincerity is soon undermined by the weight of his subsequent criticisms. These criticisms, and their positioning at the endmost part of his survey, may afford the impression that Quintilian separates Seneca from the rest of his survey so as to stigmatize him as a stylistic contagion to be avoided by all but the most mature students of rhetoric. Indeed, this is the case in so far as Seneca should be read, according to Quintilian (131), only by those who have honed their skills by reading less dangerous writers and who wish to exercise their critical faculties in assessing his merits and faults. From his ambivalent treatment of Seneca, it is apparent that Quintilian finds him a most difficult writer to treat, yet because of this and his prominence, Seneca emerges as one of the most important writers discussed in his survey.

This difficulty in assessing Seneca might be reason enough for Quintilian to defer the discussion of him until the end of his survey, but Quintilian appears to have more practical reasons for treating Seneca separately. Quintilian classifies all existing literature within traditional genres and there is generally little attempt, with the exception of his discussion of Greek tragedy (10.1.66–8), to consider these genres as part of a larger process of the natural evolution and development of literature. Such lack of sophistication is perhaps not surprising, given his main purpose of providing a reading list suitable for the training of an orator. Since Seneca was versatile and attempted a number of genres (cf. 125), he slots easily into a number of generic categories. Given his important role in the development of Roman tragedy, for instance, he should have been mentioned in the discussion of this genre (cf. 97–8). But Seneca is discussed separately only under the rubric of Roman philosophy (123ff.), the final category in Quintilian's survey of Latin authors. Ovid, by contrast, is mentioned under Roman epic (88), elegy (93) and tragedy (98). Admittedly Cicero is discussed mainly as an orator (105–16), which is to be expected, but he also rates a mention under the category of philosophy (123). Perhaps one of the reasons Seneca is treated separately is that he does not really conform to Quintilian's generic expectations of a writer. Certainly his style does not fit into any of the three traditional stylistic classifications of plain, grand and intermediate mentioned by Quintilian as a prelude to his survey (10.1.44; cf. 12.10.58ff.).

Quintilian could have excluded Seneca altogether from his survey, as he does other authors mentioned as worth reading but not discussed (10.1.45), but Seneca is such a major figure and identified so closely with the postclassical style that Quintilian can hardly fail to discuss him. The discussion of Seneca is the second longest devoted to a single author in Quintilian's survey, a strong indication of Seneca's importance in his reading programme. Only the discussion of Cicero is longer. Although Quintilian considers Seneca's style to be affected, corrupt and inelegant, he must be included in the select group of authors that should be read as a means of acquiring command of the language. Just before commencing his survey Quintilian indicates he is going to discuss only a few of the most eminent authors (44; cf. 37). He concludes his survey by acknowledging again the talent of Seneca but asserting that it deserved to be devoted to better aims (131). Just after this he refers to those authors he has discussed as worthy of study (10.2.1), which emphasizes the unique, if equivocal, role that Seneca has to play in the education and training of an orator. Elsewhere Quintilian lists him among a half dozen orators whose distinguishing qualities point to the high standard of contemporary oratory (12.10.11). What Seneca lacked, in Quintilian's view, was not talent (*ingenium*) but judgement (*iudicium*).[9] Since Seneca is the last writer treated in Quintilian's survey, the reader is likely to leave behind this section of the *Institutio* with the memory of Quintilian's ambivalent assessment of Seneca uppermost in mind.

3

What canon was Quintilian advancing in his judgement of Seneca?[10] If Quintilian was attempting merely to restore the classical prose style of one hundred years earlier to favour, he would have been open to the charge of imposing upon his students a stylistic standard more suited to a past age than his own. Unquestionably the *Institutio* betrays the legacy of Cicero, which Quintilian exerts in an attempt to subordinate his students' styles to his own stylistic model. To Quintilian Cicero was the supreme exemplar of rhetorical excellence, embodying all the stylistic qualities of the best orators of the past (12.10.12; cf. 10.1.105–12, 10.2.25, 12.1.20). But Quintilian's style is not really Ciceronian: his vocabulary is typical of his age, and his phraseology is less ample and symmetrical than Cicero's. In some ways, he even seems to have been influenced by Seneca, for instance in his frequent use of poetic or rare words, in his piling up of substantive adjectives, and particularly in his epigrammatic turns of phrase. These stylistic qualities and his praise of some features of contemporary oratory (10.1.19) suggest Quintilian did not so much seek a strict revival of Ciceronianism as a modified form more in keeping with the spirit of the contemporary age, or possibly a Ciceronian invigoration of the more restrained imperial style he favoured. What is clear is that the main disagreement between Quintilian and Seneca is stylistic. While Seneca represented the style of a contemporary age that sought expression for its ideas in new and varied forms, Quintilian sought to represent the standard of the best oratory of the past in a modern form.

But was Quintilian judging Seneca by the standards of an age different from his own? To Seneca and other writers of the time the postclassical style was a natural form of expression, entirely suitable for the contemporary age. Seneca describes the stylistic qualities he admires in a letter from his friend Lucilius (*Ep.* 59.5):

> You have your words under control. Speech does not carry you away nor pull you beyond the limit of what you have resolved upon. Many are enticed by the grace of some appealing words to write on something they had not intended to take up, which has not happened in your case. All your words are concise and appropriate to your purpose. You say as much as you want and you mean more than you say. This bears testimony to the importance of your subject. It is clear that your mind also contains nothing superfluous and bombastic.

The emphasis in this description is on the careful manipulation and control of language, compression, brevity, effective allusion, and the exclusion of bombastic expression and overblown images. A modern scholar could be forgiven for thinking that its author was Quintilian. But there was nothing unnatural about the postclassical style, provided that it was not given to the sort of excess that Seneca cautions against. In *Epistle* 114 Seneca explains how a corrupt style emerges and gains popularity during a particular age. Seneca's explanation revolves basically around the idea that style reflects the character of the individual (*talis hominibus fuit oratio qualis vita*, 'man's speech is just like his life', 1). Style is determined by personality and the age. As tastes change and history takes its course, inevitable development and change occur. Was Seneca referring to his own age in this description?[11] Not likely, judging by the examples he gives of a corrupt style: they are all from writers before his time. Maecenas, patron of Augustan literature, is adduced as an example of a corrupt style reflecting the depraved character of an individual (4–8; cf. 21–2), while the archaisms, brachylogy, abruptness and obscurity of the historian Sallust are furnished as examples of stylistic faults made fashionable by an individual and imitated excessively by other writers (17–19). Significantly there is no suggestion on the part of Seneca that the stylistic practices of his own period are corrupt.

Quintilian's criticism of Seneca would lead the reader to think that Seneca and other practitioners of the postclassical style wrote with more rhetorical extravagance and redundance than Cicero, but it was in fact Cicero who was accused of being pleonastic, repetitive, overexuberant and undisciplined by his Atticist critics (Tac. *Dial.* 18.4–5; Quint. *Inst.* 12.10.12–15; cf. 12.1.22); he in turn criticized his detractors for their narrow conception of Atticism and argued that he was actually more Attic than they were (cf. Cic. *Orat.* 24–32, 76–90; *Brut.* 284–91).[12] Quintilian may have considered the style of Seneca and his imitators to be more Asianic than any other style, but in its preference for epigrammatic expression, it most nearly resembled Atticism. Compared with the flowing amplitude and artistic symmetry of the Ciceronian period, the Senecan sentence appears terse, clipped and disjointed. Periodic abundance and stateliness had gradually given place to an abrupt, antithetical style. An imperial audience would have expected an orator to employ such stylistic devices as epigram (*sententia*), hyperbole, antithesis, paradox, commutatio, asyndeton, epitrochasmus, anaphora, polyptoton, homoioteleuton, paronomasia, alliteration and assonance. These devices helped to produce the defining characteristics of the postclassical style: epigrammatic brevity, vivid dramatic narrative, rapid shifts of focus, incongruity and discontinuity, expansion of ideas, elaborate description, and marked rhetorical and emotional effects. In the *De Optimo Genere Oratorum* Cicero gives the three functions of oratory as *docere* ('to instruct'), *delectare* ('to delight') and *movere* ('to move', 3).[13] Although didactic discourse was still composed during the empire, postclassicism contributed to and reflected the shift in interest from *docere*, the didactic function, to *delectare* and *movere*, the aesthetic and emotional functions of an oral or written text. The emphasis was upon the immediacy of the subject's experience – the spontaneous thought or emotion as it was being imagined or felt, rather than on the final, ordered expression of a fixed idea or feeling.

4

Quintilian's *Institutio* and Seneca's *Epistles* bear testimony to the vigorous debate among writers of the early principate on matters of style. A similar discussion occurs in Tacitus' *Dialogus de Oratoribus* where Vipstanus Messalla and Marcus Aper debate the merits of past and present oratory. Probably composed during the reign of Nerva (96–98),[14] the *Dialogus* had a dramatic date of about 75 CE. Aper's defence of modern oratory helps to situate Quintilian's criticism of Seneca and the postclassical style in its historical context (*Dial.* 16–23). The transition from republic to empire exerted a deep and lasting influence on the political consciousness of Romans. It also affected the direction of public and political oratory. Such activity was constrained within the limits imposed by the new political order. The languishing of deliberative oratory in the empire was partly due to the loss of the senate as a venue for serious political debate under emperors who became progressively authoritarian in their rule. Despite its diminished importance in the political arena, oratory continued to assume a considerable role in the courts, in the schools, and even an increased role on the public stage. Given the political situation and requirements of the period, it is scarcely surprising that new trends emerged, for both orator and writer were compelled to adapt to the changing circumstances and demands of their age in order to achieve success.

The need for the artist to change with the times is a key theme in the vigorous apology that Aper conducts of postclassical rhetoric in the *Dialogus*. Aper's defence forms a striking contrast to the canon advanced by Quintilian. The issue of style in the *Dialogus* arises in the course of a discussion on an alleged decline of eloquence in the contemporary age. Romans themselves argued for a decline in eloquence.[15] But there was much debate and disagreement about whether there was such a decline. How seriously should we take Roman self-evaluations attesting to a decline in eloquence?[16] We should at least view them with circumspection, since these statements are made with considerable articulateness. Aper makes precisely this point in respect of oratory: he insists that Messalla's predilection for past standards blinds him to his own eloquence and that of his contemporaries (*Dial.* 15.1):

> You do not desist from admiring only what is old and anti-
> quated, while moreover you ridicule and despise the learning
> of our time. I have often listened to you speak when, forgetting
> how eloquent you and your brother are, you maintained there
> was no orator of the present age who could match those of
> the past.

Even Quintilian did not believe there had been a decline in the standard of oratory:[17] he speaks highly of the orators of his own day for their powers of expression and description (*Inst.* 10.1.122). As can be seen from his comments on Seneca and his imitators, not all orators spoke according to the taste of Quintilian. Undoubtedly there were bad orators, just as there were during the time of Cicero. But Aper argues in the *Dialogus* that there is no real difference between the orators of his day and those of Cicero's; the main difference is in the preference of modern audiences for point and elegance (17–20).

Modern critics frequently claim that either Messalla or Maternus represents the real feelings of Tacitus.[18] While there is some evidence for both of these positions, it is unlikely that either figure really represents Tacitus' views. When Messalla criticizes the rhetorical teaching of his day (*Dial.* 29–35), there is no compelling reason to exclude the school of rhetoric upheld by Quintilian from this indictment.[19] According to Messalla, proper rhetorical training was not based on the fantasies of the declamation school but on real issues.[20] The world of declamation was often violent and spectacular; this atmosphere both reflected and was reinforced by the outbursts of political violence that occurred during the reigns of the Julio-Claudian and Flavian emperors. Declamatory exercises, which required the ability to engage in clever argument, were excellent preparation for the declamation hall. The diminished role of political oratory in the imperial period encouraged the growth of rhetoric as a social pastime where orators practised their skills for intellectual fame and enjoyment. Some orators turned to the public theatre in order to display their talents and the exercises they declaimed became an end in themselves distinct from practical oratory. Messalla criticizes the schools that gave rise to public declamations, but Quintilian holds a high opinion of the role of rhetorical training (*Inst.* 12.1.25) and of the utility of declamation (2.10.2). While Messalla might be a spokesman for Tacitus' view of contemporary education, the perspective of Messalla, who praises the ancient orators, especially Cicero, more nearly resembles the view of Quintilian than it does of Tacitus.

As for Maternus, he displays an awareness of the social and political context that has given rise to the present state of oratory, which is notably lacking in Quintilian. Maternus' analysis shows that the causal relationship is not just between time and style but between politics and genre. The entire discussion is notable for its treatment of the influence of the political circumstances of the age upon oratory and the responses of individual orators to the altered social and political conditions. Tacitus, shortly after the publication of Quintilian's *Institutio*, abandoned oratory and undertook writing history as a means of expressing himself, just as Maternus had abandoned legal oratory to write tragedies. But Maternus' praise of the emperor as 'one man wise before all others' (*sapientissimus et unus, Dial.* 41.4) seems tainted with irony, given that he appears to have offended the emperor Vespasian by reciting a potentially subversive play praising Cato (cf. 2.1, 3.2), an archetypal republican hero, and plans to write a political drama on Thyestes (cf. 3.3), a mythical tyrant.[21] The Maternus of the *Dialogus* may have been either Curiatius Maternus, who was executed for delivering a practice speech against tyrants (cf. Dio Cass. 67.12.5) under Domitian,[22] or possibly the Maternus who suffered death as a result of offending Vespasian (cf. *Dial.* 13.6),[23] in which case his death would have served to enhance the irony inherent in his praise of the imperial system.

While Tacitus' employment of a neo-Ciceronian style to record a conversation taking place a generation earlier has the effect of suggesting a different period of time, the style, structure and vocabulary of the *Dialogus* appears to have been determined partly by the generic requirements for a dialogue on an oratorical or literary theme.[24] But the style of the *Dialogus* probably owes more to aesthetic and political considerations than to temporal and generic factors. Although the *Dialogus* has some points in common with the *Institutio*,[25] its style represents an ironic challenge to that employed by Quintilian only a few years earlier in the *Institutio*. In fact, an attitude of hostility to Quintilian can be detected in the *Dialogus*. This hostility seems not to be limited to Quintilian's attitude toward oratory and rhetorical training but may have a political basis rooted in Quintilian's view of the Flavian dispensation. While Tacitus portrays Domitian as a ruthless tyrant for the duration of his reign (*Agr.* 3.2), Quintilian appears to have supported, even if superficially, the Domitianic regime (cf. *Inst.* 4 *pr.* 2; 10.1.91), and he benefited greatly from the Flavian dynasty (cf. Suet. *Vesp.* 18; Quint. *Inst.* 4 *pr.* 2; Juv. 7.186–9; Auson. *Grat. Act.* 7.31). In marked contrast to the *Institutio*, the *Dialogus* reveals an awareness of the evolutionary nature of society and the changed political conditions under the principate. This is no doubt partly due to the fact that Tacitus brings the insight of a senator, magistrate, orator and historian to his writing of the *Dialogus*.

5

Marcus Aper, Messalla's opponent in the second set of paired speeches in the *Dialogus* (14–26), has a larger share of the debate and is delineated more clearly than any of the other interlocutors. Tacitus mentions in the introduction that one of the characters in the debate, which turns out to be Aper, will take a point of view opposite to the others (4.1), while Messalla (15.2; cf. 28.1) and Maternus (16.3, 24.2) remark that Aper, in advocating the postclassical style, has merely taken on the role of an opponent; however, Aper gives no such indication himself that the views he advances are anything but his own. It is significant that his arguments, which constitute a powerful defence of the style of his contemporaries, are never actually refuted by the other speakers. Aper maintains that styles and trends change according to the conditions and prevailing tastes of the age (18–19). He is able to view the situation from a historical perspective and sees the necessity of adapting oratory to the requirements of a new age. Aper argues against an absolute relativity of standards in style and the idea of a decline in oratorical standards. While it is possible, even likely, that Tacitus has offered some of his own opinions in the speeches of Messalla and Maternus, he may have identified himself most with the views of Aper. Given the terse, pointed stylistic qualities of his later prose works, he probably sympathized with Aper's arguments on the necessity of a change in style from Ciceronian extravagance, diffuseness and redundancy (cf. 18–20, 22–3, esp. 18.2–3, 19.2, 19.5, 20.1, 23.3).[26] Tacitus, who shows signs of the influence of Senecan prose style in his historical writings, seems further to have identified himself with Aper through his judgement of Seneca as 'a man whose pleasant talent admirably suited a contemporary audience' (*viro ingenium amoenum et temporis eius auribus accommodatum, Ann.* 13.3).[27] As Tacitus perceived, Seneca was expressive of the Zeitgeist. People were impatient of the elaborate long-windedness favoured by earlier generations (cf. *Dial.* 19.2). By his own standards and those of Cicero, to whom the real test of oratory is its ability to win the approval of the multitude (*Brut.* 183–9), Seneca has met the requirements of a good style. Even Quintilian, who maintains that the degree of eloquence is determined by the extent of a speech's effectiveness upon its audience (*Inst.* 12.10.44), admits that Seneca's genius succeeded at achieving what it set out to achieve (10.1.131).

Seneca remarks in *Epistle* 114.13: 'Style has no fixed laws; it is changed by the usage of the people, never the same for any length of time' (*oratio certam regulam non habet: consuetudo illam civitatis, quae numquam in eodem diu stetit, versat*). Aper too demonstrates an awareness that style changes with altered social conditions and is part of a natural process of aesthetic change in popular taste (*Dial.* 18.2, 19.2). In the view of Aper, the audience now was more sophisticated and knowledgeable, with some training in the rudiments of rhetoric (*Dial.* 19.5), and therefore demanded a vivid, ornate, epigrammatic style instead of the homoiological, unadorned style of a figure like Cicero (20.1–5). The preference for the post-classical style among orators represented an improvement in aesthetic standards, not a decline (19.1). Aper praises the elegance of the modern type of oratory (19.5, 20.2–6, 21.3, 23.6) and criticizes specific flaws in earlier styles (21.4; cf. 22.3). The new style was more graceful, elegant and attractive, as preferable over the old style as a house of marble and gold is over one made of stone and bricks (20.6–7). Aper touches upon some important points here, since the postclassical style, with its use of short, sharp sentences and avoidance of amplification, represents an attempt to overcome what he identifies as some of the shortcomings of the classical Ciceronian style: pleonasm, repetition, rhetorical extravagance and indiscipline. The postclassical style, with its use of paradox, shock and novelty, was more emotionally direct, spontaneous, variable, forceful and immediate than classical Latin. It transcended the old stylistic bounds of the somewhat logical and predictable manner of Ciceronian expression and restored to the Latin language some of the vigour and strength of archaic Latin, thereby helping to fulfil the stylistic potential of the language. Seneca believed the periodic style of Cicero, with its predictable phrasal structure, well-rounded periods, modulated pace and gradual expansion, hampered the natural expression of speech. Seneca found much of Cicero's prose *gradarius* ('too slow', *Ep.* 40.11; cf. 100.7) and its composition lacking in variety (114.16), while he probably missed in him the pointed expressions so dear to his own generation. Seneca's fondness of short phrases, balanced clauses, word-play, allusiveness, loose syntactic structure, and antithetical and paradoxical expression was generally in accord with the sensibilities of his contemporary audiences, which Aper observes would have possessed at least a reasonable measure of academic learning, literary astuteness and aesthetic sensibility (*Dial.* 19).

The arguments of Aper in the *Dialogus* serve as a strong defence of postclassical tendencies in oratory and in the process challenge the notion of a decline in eloquence. Tacitus, like Aper, realized language must change not only to prosper but to survive, as his own works bear witness. The pointed style of his *Histories* and *Annals* is probably as much a response to the expansiveness of the neo-Ciceronian style employed in his *Dialogus* as it is an exemplification of the style required for a historical work. Our own assessment of

Tacitean style would be radically different if we possessed only the *Dialogus*. The popularity of the Tacitean style is evident in that it immediately established itself alongside Sallust as a model of historical writing in place of Livy and Caesar, who were known for their period-building. The same stylistic phenomenon is exemplified in the figure of Pliny, whose *Panegyricus* represents a similar evolution in style from his earlier *Epistles*; as with the works of Tacitus, the stylistic differences cannot be explained by generic factors alone. Not only was there a diversity and range of styles during the late republican period and early principate, but individual writers employed different styles according to their stage of development and sometimes according to their particular subjects.

Unlike the second-century archaists Fronto (*Ad M. Ant. de Orat.* 2)[28] and Aulus Gellius (*NA* 12.2), who loathed Seneca, Quintilian was no blind traditionalist. But while Quintilian is likely to have approved of the neo-Ciceronian style of Tacitus' *Dialogus*, it is unlikely that he would have thought much of the terse, pointed style of Tacitus in the *Histories* and the *Annals*. Quintilian's conception of style is not static, since he maintains that an eloquent style is one that is well suited to a contemporary audience (cf. *Inst.* 12.10.43–6), but he still has in mind a new orthodoxy of neo-Ciceronianism and is less willing than Seneca to allow for styles that differ significantly from his own canon; he therefore overlooks to some extent the fact that style is essentially a reflection of society, which is generally far more complex, dynamic and heterogeneous than he seems to apprehend. On the other hand, Seneca realizes different ages call for different styles. Whereas Ciceronian *decorum* ('appropriateness') had been the order of the day, Seneca approved of Lucilius for choosing words that express what he wishes to say instead of what he should say (*Ep.* 59.4–5; cf. 52.4, 115.2). For Seneca stylistic matters should be subordinated to the ideas of the speaker. An excessive concern for words and their arrangement is what constitutes the 'corrupt style' for Seneca. Marcus Aper attempts to consider oratory in its social, political and historical contexts. This method of criticism for the most part goes unattested in ancient literary criticism. What Aper attempts to explain is the notion of evolution in oratory and the various processes through which it passes. To Aper oratory was, as indeed it was to the Romans, an expression of national life, constantly changing in form, not bound by rigid rules, but responsive to social and political influences, so that it was only in the light of its environment that literature could be fully understood. When there is such a close connection between life and speech, there can be no fixed standards and rules.

The postclassical style was both function and product of its age. The differences between the postclassical aesthetic and those of the classical norm cannot be described in absolute terms. While the stylistic qualities of postclassical rhetoric reflect a general change in aesthetic sensibilities, the factors responsible for this change defy ready definition and explanation on account of their sociological complexity. However, this shift in aesthetic appears to have been not only a natural extension of the classical norm and an anxious reaction to the influences of the Augustan classical achievement, but also a response to the oppressive political environment and a reflection of changed social conditions, manners and literary taste. An amalgam of aforementioned factors resulted in a turning away from classical propriety and rigid generic categories and aided in the development of a complex, ornate and paratactic style whose appeal depended on the finely tuned rhetorical sensibilities of a contemporary audience, which looked for and expected precisely this kind of discourse. In place of Ciceronian correctness, harmony, proportion, fullness and rhythm, contemporary audiences developed a predilection for incongruity, discordance, disproportion and point. The postclassical style of expression was an index of the new attitudes produced by the changed social and political circumstances of the early empire. To Seneca, Aper and other writers and orators this new style was a better way of reflecting upon contemporary society than the classical style.[29]

NOTES

1 My references to '*the* postclassical style' in this chapter may appear to obfuscate the complexity of the stylistic phenomenon discussed. I wish to stress from the outset that I do not suggest that this style is monolithic in nature; nor do I mean to equate 'postclassical' merely with 'Seneca' or the term 'classical' just with 'Cicero'. There are any number of different styles used in the first centuries BCE and CE that could be described as 'postclassical' (or 'imperial') and 'classical' (or 'neo-Ciceronian'). For instance, Tacitus' style can be distinguished from Seneca's, but they have enough features in common to be identified as 'postclassical'. The style of Cicero is radically different from that of Caesar, his exact contemporary, but it is unmistakably of the 'classical' variety. For a more nuanced discussion of the ranges of style involved, see Leeman 1963.

2 See, e.g., Brugnoli 1959; Gelzer 1970; Heldmann 1980: 12–19; Brink 1989.
3 For a recent discussion see Halliwell 1994.
4 The philosophers were banished twice by Domitian, once in 89 and a second time in 93 (or 95).
5 E.g., Alexander 1934–5; Seel 1977: 94–5.
6 E.g., Kennedy 1969: 112–13; Trillitzsch 1971: 67–8; Laureys 1991.
7 All translations in this chapter are mine. Except where indicated, the edition used of the *Institutio Oratoria* is by Winterbottom 1970; all other Latin texts cited are from the Teubner series.
8 Peterson 1892 adds *recta* to Halm's 1868–9 (the first modern edition of the *Institutio*) reading of *parum*, which Winterbottom 1970 follows.
9 Cf. Heldmann 1980: 15–16.
10 I use the word 'canon' in the ancient rhetorical sense to refer to a stylistic model advocated by an individual writer, in this case, Quintilian; cf. Pfeiffer 1968: 207.
11 As argued by Williams 1978: 14.
12 The bibliography on these terms and the Atticist–Asianist controversy is vast; see, *inter alia*, Wilamowitz-Moellendorff 1900a; Norden 1915: 131–52, 251–72; Hendrickson 1926; D'Alton 1931: 208–65; Austin 1948: 161–4; Leeman 1963: 91–111, 136–67; Bonner 1968: 444–9; Russell 1981: 48–51; Dihle 1994: 49–53.
13 For variants of this triad, see Cic. *De Or.* 2.310; *Orat.* 69.
14 On this dating see Murgia 1980; Barnes 1986.
15 For contemporary Roman discussions on the decline of oratory, see Petron. *Sat.* 1–4, 88, 118; Tac. *Dial.* 1, 24–41 *passim*; Sen. *Controv.* 1 *pr.* 6–7; Pliny *HN* 14.2–6; Pers. 1.15–18, 32–6, 121; Juv. 1.1–4, 12–14; Vell. Pat. 1.17; cf. [Longin.] *Subl.* 44. For modern treatments of the Roman discussions, see Kennedy 1972: 446ff.; Heldmann 1982: 213–99.
16 Limitations of space preclude even a brief treatment of this topic. It seems to me, however, that the various Roman discussions of decline occur in contexts where this *topos*, deeply etched in the Roman mindset, is brought to bear upon series of essentially unconnected social, moral and political issues; but that is a subject for another essay.
17 *Pace* Kühnert 1964; Fantham 1978: 102ff., esp. 112.
18 E.g., Kennedy 1972: 517ff. (Messalla); Luce 1982: 1014 (Maternus).
19 Cf. Alberte 1993.
20 During the early empire the final stage of a Roman's formal education consisted of declamatory exercises (*declamationes*) known as *suasoriae* ('deliberations') and *controversiae* ('disputations'). On declamation see Parks 1945: 62–101; Bonner 1949; Clarke 1953: 85–99; Leeman 1963: 219–37; Kennedy 1972: 312–37; Winterbottom 1980; Russell 1983.
21 Cf. Köhnken 1973: 32ff., esp. 46; Heldmann 1982: 283. It is not my purpose here to discuss the contradictory views of the political situation offered by Maternus in his first (11–13) and second speeches (36–42); on this see Heldmann 1982: 257ff., 271ff.; Luce 1993: 11ff., esp. 22; Bartsch 1994: 106ff.
22 See, e.g., Matthiessen 1970.
23 See, e.g., Luce 1993: 19 and n. 44.

24 This is suggested by Leo 1898: 169ff., esp. 172ff. The style recalls Cicero's *De Oratore*, which reports a conversation of Cicero over thirty years earlier (cf. *De Or.* 1.5; *Att.* 4.13.2).

25 Recent studies of the relationship between the *Dialogus* and *Institutio* include those of Güngerich 1951; Barwick 1954; Michel 1962: 195–6; Leeman 1963: 320–3.

26 Compare Cicero's comments on the exuberance of his early style (*Orat.* 107–8).

27 I do not interpret this comment disparagingly, as most modern commentators do. This is not to suggest that Aper (or Tacitus) approved of *delatores* ('informers') such as Eprius Marcellus and Vibius Crispus. It is apparent that Aper does not admire them (cf. *Dial.* 8.1), but they are none the less exemplars of oratorical talent and success.

28 Haines 1920: 2.101–2.

29 I thank Edward George, John Hilton, John Kirby, Bernhard Kytzler and Peter Toohey for their written comments and suggestions on an earlier version of this chapter.

Part II

RHETORIC AND SOCIETY

5

Field and forum: culture and agriculture in Roman rhetoric

Catherine Connors

The techniques of oratory systematically described and practised by the Greeks were viewed by Romans with the mixture of enthusiasm and suspicion that marked Hellenization in general.[1] This essay examines representations of rusticity and agriculture in Roman rhetorical texts in the context of these cultural negotiations. Rhetoricians oppose rusticity to the good orator's urbane sophistication, *urbanitas*.[2] Excluded from the rhetorical training available to the urban élite, rustics make poor orators; therefore, incompetent or unpolished orators are metaphorically called rustic. At the same time, in addition to contrasting rusticity with oratorical competence, rhetoricians use the cultivation of land as a metaphor for the proper cultivation of oratory. Both of these metaphorical strategies were already available in the Greek tradition, and Plato's Socrates playfully points to the apparent potential for contradiction between them: considering whether good can result when an ignorant orator persuades an ignorant state, Socrates asks, 'What sort of harvest do you think rhetoric is likely to reap thereafter from what it sowed?' 'Not at all good', says Phaedrus. 'Well,' says Socrates, 'do you think we have reproached rhetoric in a more rustic way (*agroikoteron*) than we ought?' (*Phdr.* 260 c–d).[3] Transplanted to Rome, these rustic metaphors flourished. Yet in Rome, the idealized rustic is a powerful icon of upright living and immunity to the corrupting influences that increase as Rome controls more land and imports more culture: being rustic increasingly means not being at all Greekish. Accordingly, representations of rusticity in Roman rhetorical texts are utterances in a discourse that can acknowledge or conceal the potentially suspect foreignness of imported rhetoric.

Ancient accounts of metaphor emphasize its ornamental and persuasive functions (Arist. *Rhet.* 3.1405a; *Rhet. Her.* 4.34.45; Cic.

71

De Or. 3.155–68, *Orat.* 92; Quint. *Inst.* 8.6.4–18). On this view, the effects of figurative language are greatest when the figures strike the reader emphatically; metaphor is at its least effective (that is to say metaphorically dead) when its transfer of meaning from one thing to another is so familiar as to be unnoticed. The comparisons of language to crop to be examined in the second section of this essay must have had an ornamental and persuasive function.[4] But the metaphorical impact of words such as *agrestis* ('rustic'), *fructus* ('fruit', 'harvest'), and *cultus* ('cultivation') in rhetorical discourse seems negligible: should they be included in analyses of rhetorical representations of rusticity? Probably, for persuasive arguments can be made that metaphor is not simply a decorative and detachable element of discourse but is something essential and ineradicable in human language, and that uses of metaphor, even of very familiar metaphors, structure our experiences of the world.[5] According to this view, for example, a significant sense of definite and perceptible boundaries emerges in English from calling academic specializations 'fields' rather than, say, mountains or caves, even though the topographical metaphor in 'field' is quite dead.

RHETORIC AND RUSTICITY

Rhetorical texts associate rusticity with a lack of oratorical sophistication in several ways. In the *De Oratore* Crassus discusses relations among *natura* ('natural capacity'), *ars* ('skill') and *exercitatio* ('practice') in the development of the orator. He asserts that the natural rusticity of some people cannot be overcome by training: 'There are some men who stammer so in their speech, or are so discordant in tone, or so uncultivated and rustic in their appearance or gesture (*aut ita vultu motuque corporis vasti atque agrestis*) that even if their talents and skill are sufficient, still they are not able to join the ranks of orators' (Cic. *De Or.* 1.115; cf. *Brut.* 286, *Orat.* 172; Quint. *Inst.* 1.11.16, 6.3.17, 107). The language of country people is viewed as a measure of simplicity and plainness. Thus if even rustics use metaphors such as 'bejewelled vines' or 'joyful fields', then metaphor in moderation is appropriate to the plain style (Cic. *Orat.* 81; cf. Quint. *Inst.* 8.6.6, 1 *pr.* 16, 2.21.16, 6.3.13, 11.3.117). An opposition between rusticity and rhetorical sophistication is given dramatic form in a *controversia* discussed by Quintilian (*Inst.* 7.1.41–63). Two brothers, one 'eloquent' (*disertus*) and one 'rustic' (*rusticus*) go to court over the estate of their father who died intestate. The eloquent one unsuccessfully defended their father on a charge of treason and accompanied him into exile (the rustic brother did not appear in court, but being rustic, would not have been any help). When the rustic brother won a reward for heroism, he requested the restoration of his father and brother. The dispute turns on whether the law stipulating that a son who does not defend his father is disinherited prevents the rustic son from obtaining his share of the estate. In this fictional case, declaimers could focus on contrasting eloquent arguments with rustic ones, and the ventriloquized discourse of the uneducated rustic brother would become a vehicle for educated rhetorical competition.

Obviously, such rhetorical representations of rusticity as a lack of oratorical sophistication reinforce the formal and informal institutions that imported and reproduced Greek rhetoric for the Roman élite. A corresponding excess of sophistication and training is regularly associated with theatricality. Some training in gesture and voice at the hands of theatre professionals is judged appropriate (Quint. *Inst.* 1.11.4–14, 11.3.4–7), but rhetoricians disapprove of excessive development and exploitation of theatrical techniques (*Rhet. Her.* 3.14.24, 15.26; Cic. *De Or.* 1.251, 3.220, *Orat.* 86).[6]

Cicero is generally content simply to recommend that theatricality be used appropriately (*De Or.* 1.156; *Orat.* 56–7), but the *De Oratore* closes with an account of delivery that explores the issues in more depth. Crassus says that the effective use of voice and gesture is essential for oratorical success and cites Demosthenes as his first example. As his second example of the power of delivery, Crassus cites Gaius Gracchus' famous speech just before he was murdered, saying that his performance brought even his enemies to tears. The quotation itself has a theatrical cast, for Gaius' dilemma, *quo me miser conferam? quo vertam?* ('Wretched as I am, where shall I betake myself? Where shall I turn?', *De Or.* 3.214) recalls the dilemma of Ennius' *Medea*, quoted by Crassus soon thereafter: *quo nunc me vertam?* ('Where shall I turn now?', 3.217). After discussing the use of gesture and the glance to communicate emotion, Crassus returns to Gaius as an exemplar: he used to have a slave stand behind him and play notes on an ivory flute to guide his manipulation of vocal pitch. Thus, Gaius spoke with a kind of latent theatricality, being 'accompanied', as actors were, by a piper, but one whose notes would be unheard, presumably, by the audience. Crassus evidently approves of modulating one's pitch, saying even that to begin by shouting would be 'something rustic' (*agreste quiddam*) but recommends that his interlocutors leave the flute-player at home and instead bring only the habits of modulation to the forum (*De Or.* 3.225–7; cf. Val. Max. 8.10.1; Quint. *Inst.* 1.10.27–8; Dio 25.85.2.). Crassus makes an aesthetic point about Gaius' effective vocal technique. Yet Gaius' meaning as an exemplar inevitably extends beyond aesthetics: his oratory set forces in motion that ended in his death, and even though in the final crisis his delivery made his enemies weep, they still killed him. Thus Gaius is an exemplar not only of the power that theatrical techniques can impart to oratory but also of the dangerous consequences such power can have. This representation of his passions only just held in check seems a fitting end to the *De Oratore*, whose third book begins with Cicero looking ahead to the death of Crassus and the turbulent events of the Social War soon to follow the end of the dialogue (3.8). Seneca (*Controv.* 1 *pr.* 8) and Quintilian (*Inst.* 1.8.3, 1.11.1–3, 11.3.19, 22–4, 57–60, 88–91, 103, 181–4) more vehemently and explicitly condemn the effects of theatrical influences upon rhetorical practice, and Tacitus' Messalla finds contemptible those who blur boundaries between acting and oratory and boast that their speeches can be sung and danced to, saying that from such orators arose the saying that at Rome 'our orators speak sensuously (*tenere*) and our actors dance articulately (*diserte*)' (*Dial.* 26.3).

In effect, such rhetorical representations of rusticity and acting have complementary functions. Disparaging references to rusticity make oratorical training essential, while warnings against excessive theatricality hold imported rhetorical techniques in check. Setting oratory against both rusticity and theatricality replicates the physical and temporal separation of the business of the city from the business of the country and the business of the theatre: rusticity takes place outside and prior to contemporary Rome, while theatre takes place in the city but only on holidays. Of course, a whole set of oppositions comes into play when rusticity and theatricality are opposed: rusticity is traditional, native and hardworking; theatricality is newer, at least partly a Greek import, and often construed as decadent and effeminate.[7] The contrasts emerge clearly in Varro's disapproval of his fellow Romans: in early Rome men came into the city only for market day, and male bodies made healthy by farming needed no exercise in Greek gymnasia. In his own time though, grain and wine are imported since traditional agriculture has yielded to a culture of spectacle: 'Virtually all the heads of households have crept within the city walls, abandoning sickle and plough, and they prefer to move

their hands in the theatre or the circus than among the crops or vines'
(*Rust. 2 pr.* 1–3).

Such fairly standard oppositions between ancient rusticity and
effeminate, foreign theatricality are occasionally complicated in
interesting ways. In the *De Oratore*'s discussion of diction, Crassus
recommends a balanced diction: orators should avoid being either
excessively effeminate or excessively rustic. He singles out Lucius
Aurelius Cotta[8] for affecting a rustic accent, asserting that Cotta
'thinks that what he says will seem venerable (*priscum*) if it is
thoroughly rustic' (3.42). Cotta thus uses rusticity to distance himself
temporally from contemporary Rome: he aims to sound as Romans
sounded before they became so cosmopolitan, before Greek influences were felt so pervasively. Crassus says critically (3.46; cf. *Brut.*
137) that Cotta's broad accent (elsewhere termed 'as far as possible
from similarity to Greek enunciation', *Brut.* 259) imitates not the
oratores of antiquity but *messores* ('reapers'). Moreover, contrasting
Cotta's artificial rusticity with the accent of his wife's mother Laelia,
Crassus observes that since women converse with fewer people than
men do, their pronunciation remains more stable; listening to his
mother-in-law makes him think he is listening to Plautus or Naevius.
From the sound of Laelia's voice he can therefore infer what her
father and ancestors sounded like (*De Or.* 3.45). In Crassus' view,
Cotta's affected rusticity is to be disparaged; the fact that Laelia's
discourse is genuinely female rather than affectedly effeminate gives
it an admirable purity. The conventional boundaries between male
and female, oratorical and theatrical, urbane and rustic, authentic and
artificial seem not to be operating conventionally here: this female
preserves the voice of her male ancestors; this theatrical language is
not a decadent contemporary artifice but the relic of a simpler past.
Yet Crassus' play with the conventions that construe oratory as
language that is neither female nor theatrical nor rustic is designed
not to subvert those conventions but to deprecate Cotta's affected
antiquity. Laelia is an archive for storing and transmitting male
discourse – to Crassus: with access to this archive Crassus, not Cotta,
knows the authentic sound of the venerable past.[9]

In the discussion of Cotta's accent the opposition between rusticity and Greekness is clear. Remarkably, rusticity can be such a
powerful signal of not being at all Greekish that it can make even
someone declaiming in Greek sound less than Greek. According to
Seneca, Agroitas of Massilia (his name is derived from the Greek
agroikos, 'rustic'), whom Seneca quotes in Greek, 'spoke with such

uncultivated technique (*arte inculta*) that you would know he had not frequented the Greeks, and with such forceful *sententiae* ("expressions") that you would know he had frequented the Romans' (*Controv.* 2.6.12).

The issues at stake in the separation of rusticity and theatricality from appropriate oratory are also dramatized in anecdotes about Hortensius, an exponent of the luxuriant style of oratory and life. Hortensius was said to have been admired by the renowned actor Roscius (Val. Max. 8.10.2). He defends his Greek theatrical sophistication in the face of an insult from the 'rather rustic' Torquatus, who calls him not just an actor, as others had, but 'Dionysia', the name of a well-known dancing girl: 'Indeed I would rather be a Dionysia, Torquatus, than be what you are, a stranger to the Muses, to Aphrodite, to Dionysus' (Gell. *NA* 1.5.3). Macrobius records a story that Hortensius watered his plane trees with wine and in a court case once asked Cicero to change places with him in the order of speaking so that he could do this for a plane tree he had planted in Tusculum (*Sat.* 3.13.3). And at the close of Varro's handbook on prudent farming Hortensius stands as a paradigm of imprudence. He dotes on his pet fish in extravagant fishponds at his villa in Baiae and instead of serving them to his guests, he feeds them himself and buys fish from Puteoli for dinner (*Rust.* 3.17.5–7).[10]

NATURE, CULTURE AND ORATORY

Cicero seems to have been the first to apply the noun *cultura* to intellectual pursuits when he termed philosophy 'the cultivation of the mind' (*cultura animi*, *Tusc.* 2.13).[11] Cicero's development of this particular figure undoubtedly draws upon, and should be viewed in the larger context of, the overlapping spheres of the verb *colo* and its derivatives. Depending upon the context, *colo* can be variously translated as 'cultivate', 'inhabit', 'take care of' or 'worship'; underlying these uses is the notion that labour or care of some kind is expended upon fields, the gods, or the human body or mind. As we shall see, rhetoricians associate good rhetorical language with a good harvest, good rhetorical training with the care of vines, language that is too elaborate or abundant with the luxuriant natural growth of uncultivated weeds or grasses, and language that is not artful enough with land that is uncultivated, dry or thorny. Something of the familiar quality of comparisons between mind and land emerges from Quintilian's discussion of similes: 'So if you should say that the mind must be cultivated, you would use a comparison to land, which when it is not cultivated, yields thorns and thickets, and when cultivated produces fruit' (*ut, si animum dicas excolendum, similitudine utaris terrae, quae neglecta sentes ac dumos, culta fructus creat, Inst.* 5.11.24).

How contradictory is it to compare oratory to crops while opposing rusticity to good rhetoric? The social and cultural boundaries that exclude rustics from oratory are reinforced when a lack of rhetorical sophistication is troped as rusticity, but they are blurred when the cultivation of language is figured as the cultivation of land: the fiction that oratory is like farming makes the orator's productions seem in some subliminal way less foreign and more like the hard rural work that Varro and others recall so nostalgically. Such fictions have ideological as well as decorative or persuasive functions.[12] The fact that rhetorical expertise was imported to Rome from Greece is implicitly played down when the work of rhetoric is figured as the native work of farming. When the work of elaborating language is assimilated to labour on the land, the image serves to 'naturalize' the artificial acculturation of the élite through imported rhetorical education.

This 'naturalization' of rhetoric is carried out overtly in discussions of the contributions of nature (at a universal or an individual level) to the development of rhetoric. A related strategy argues that persuasive language, rather than being a relatively recent Greek import, actually arose in ancient times. Thus Cicero's *De Inventione* asserts that people came together in society when a persuasive man convinced them to do so; rhetoric (*oratio*) is prior to all practices based on logical reasoning (*ratio*) and even set in motion the practice of agriculture (1.2; cf. *De Or.* 1.33).[13] While criticizing imitators of Thucydides in the *Orator ad M. Brutum*, Cicero turns the argument around, focusing on cultural innovations rather than natural developments. Playfully comparing the development of rhetoric after Thucydides at Athens with the invention of agriculture at Athens by Triptolemus, he says: 'What great perversity is there in men that they would eat acorns once grain has been discovered? Or could food be cultivated (*excoli*) with the aid of the Athenians, but not oratory?' (31).

Fruitful Fields

The *De Oratore*'s discussions of whether oratorical training should emphasize technique or mastering a broad body of knowledge yield agricultural figures which maintain that an individual's nature partially determines his capacity for success in oratory. Crassus thus says that some natural talents are necessary and cannot be grafted on (*inseri*) or bestowed by art (1.114). Antonius too emphasizes the importance of natural talent, saying of Sulpicius that his oratory was formerly too elaborate, but this was not a fault in a young man: as in vines it is easier to prune than to cultivate new growth, so with young orators (2.88; quoted at Quint. *Inst.* 2.4.9). In assessing Sulpicius' subsequent oratorical development Antonius says that Nature herself was leading him into the noble and splendid style of Crassus, but that Sulpicius' assiduous practice and imitation of Crassus was essential too (*De Or.* 2.89). Still, though Sulpicius has advanced in his training, he should practise writing more to achieve a condensed style because his style, while acceptably exuberant in his youth, now needs cutting back: 'as rustics are wont to say about grass, that in exceptional fertility there is a certain luxuriousness that has to be grazed off (*depascenda*) by the pen (*stilo*)' (2.96).[14] Antonius also naturalizes rhetorical expertise when he proposes that a well-educated orator will know how to choose commonplaces effectively without needing a collection of ready-made defences suitable for particular charges, 'which masters usually teach their students' (2.130). 'I need a cultivated talent (*subacto mihi ingenio opus est*) like soil ploughed not once but left fallow and ploughed again, so as to be able to produce a better and more abundant harvest. And the cultivation (*subactio*) is practice, listening, reading, and writing' (2.131; cf. Varro *Rust.* 1.29.1).[15]

By comparing the development of rhetorical expertise with the processes of growth, rhetoricians make oratory seem part of nature as it exists in the rhythm of the seasons. In the *De Oratore*, arguments in favour of a broad definition of oratorical training and expertise use metaphors from nature as it exists in space, as a topography divided up by natural or legal boundaries.[16] Crassus, arguing for a wide-ranging education, says that orators, like poets, roam wherever they choose, anywhere in the world (1.70). Good rhetoric, according to Cicero, 'has no specific territory (*regionem*) in whose boundaries it is held enclosed (*saepta*)' (2.5). For Crassus, eloquence is one and the same whatever subject it is expended upon, that is, 'whatever shores of discourse or regions it travels to' (3.22). Oratory and philosophy flow from a common source of wisdom, as the rivers of Italy flow east and west down from the Apennines (3.69); the implication is that an eloquent Roman is master of both. In light of

Rome's developing sense of global empire, formulations of oratory's boundless range seem to measure oratory not just against nature's realm but empire's – and Cicero had initially framed the *De Oratore*'s history of eloquence in imperial terms, saying that it arose after Rome attained its global empire and peace fostered rhetorical training (1.14).[17] In the *Brutus*, however, rhetoric is not symbolically boundless. Here Cicero's history of oratory emphasizes the variety in the tradition, and oratory, as we shall see below, is divided up and mapped onto the contrasting lands of Attica and Asia (51, 285, 325–6). And, in the dialogue's closing moments, Eloquentia is figured as the orphaned daughter of Hortensius, a virgin under the guardianship of Cicero and Brutus who must be kept sheltered (*saeptam*) at home away from importunate suitors (330).

The subtle manoeuvrings involved in Quintilian's representation of the role of nature in fostering rhetoric have recently been analysed by Fantham.[18] Agricultural similes are frequently used to drive the point home. At the end of the preface to his first book, Quintilian remarks that rules and principles avail nothing without the assistance of nature (*natura*) and explains that students lacking natural talent (*ingenium*) derive no more benefit from technical training than barren land derives from technical treatises on agriculture (*Inst.* 1 *pr.* 26). The mind as field metaphor underlies the view that young minds should not be 'vacant' (*vacare*, 1.1.16). Precocious minds rarely produce sound fruit (*frugem*) (1.3.3) and their growth is shallow, like that of seeds cast upon the soil (1.3.5). The varied tasks of oratorical training and practice are compared to the varied labours of the agricultural year (1.12.7). Quintilian develops the vine image to 'naturalize' the role of imitation in the development of the orator; thus boys enjoy imitating their fellow students, just as vines, before they attain their full height, are supported by the lowest branches of nearby trees (1.2.26). A comparison between education and vines is also implicit in Quintilian's quotation of Vergil, *Georgics* 2.272 in a discussion of the formation of character (*Inst.* 1.3.13). Like seeds, eloquence needs an environment that will foster growth (2.9.3). Like plants, students do not thrive in a dry environment: 'Therefore we must avoid above all, especially in the case of boys, a dry (*aridus*) master, just as for plants that are still young we avoid dry (*siccum*) ground without any moisture' (2.4.8). Later, in discussing the importance of nature and training (*doctrina*) for adult orators, Quintilian again turns to an agricultural comparison. Nature is more important to average orators, training to perfect orators; in the same way, completely unproductive land does not benefit from even excellent cultivation and good land can have some yield without any cultivation, but really good land will produce more under cultivation than it would if left alone (2.19.2). Still, even though natural talent is important, a second analogy re-emphasizes the contributions of training. If Praxiteles carved a statue out of a millstone, even an uncarved block of Parian marble would be superior, but if he carved Parian marble, its value would derive more from his skill than from the value of the stone: 'Perfect art is better than the best material' (2.19.3). Quintilian implicitly uses naturalness as a criterion for measuring the appropriateness of rhetorical ornament. Ornament must be manly, strong and pure (*virilis et fortis et sanctus*) and must avoid effeminate smoothness and cosmetic colouring, which are unnatural effects. Analogies argue that true beauty in ornamented or cultivated language derives from utility and not from frivolous decoration, for example: 'Shall I judge a farm in which someone points out to me lilies and violets and anemones growing of their own accord to be better cultivated than one where there is a full harvest or vines weighed down with fruit?' So too the most beautiful way to cultivate olive or fruit trees is the most useful, and the best-looking horse or athlete is the fastest and strongest (8.3.6–11).[19]

Tacitus acknowledges far more openly than Quintilian that oratory under emperors differs from oratory in the republic.[20] Tacitus too makes figurative connections between oratory, the natural world, and empire in the *Dialogus* but, as we might expect, these are much bleaker than those we see in Cicero and Quintilian. At the beginning Tacitus recalls that Iustus Fabius has often asked why, though earlier ages bloomed (*floruerint*) with oratorical genius, the current age is barren, an *aetas deserta* (*Dial.* 1. 1). Aper argues that Maternus should not give up oratory for poetry, saying (9.4) that Saleius Bassus' pursuit of poetry yields only short-lived praise, 'like a plant cut down in its first growth or in bud', and does not get to the point of producing an actual harvest (*frugem*). In addition, a poet needs to work in solitude, abandoning civilized life and retreating into the woods and groves (9. 6); thus the poet's work is imagined to take place in areas untouched by agriculture. Maternus too figures the cultivation of oratory as the cultivation of land, representing himself as a draught animal when he says that he has decided to 'unyoke' himself from legal practice (*me deiungere a forensi labore*, 11. 3). Instead, he will seek out the wilder places, untouched by cultivation. And Maternus says that he considers the peace and quiet of withdrawal from civic life among the principal benefits (*fructus*) of poetry (12. 1). Maternus' praise of poetry grows out of a nostalgic vision of a golden age before land was cultivated and before oratory was practised: 'But that was a fortunate and, as poets call it, golden age, empty of criminals and orators and overflowing with bards and poets who sang of deeds nobly done rather than defended what had been committed ignobly' (12. 3). Thus while for Cicero oratory creates culture, for Maternus it arrives with crime. Repudiating oratory, Maternus revises Cicero's narrative of progress, which connects oratory with agriculture and all the other arts of culture, into a narrative in which oratory (like agriculture and the labour it entails) is a symptom of a post-golden age decay.

Grass

The labour required to produce effective rhetoric from native talent can be compared to the removal of weeds or grasses that flourish in an uncultivated field; such *herbae* are generally eaten by animals and consumed by humans for medicinal or magical purposes (see the cook's joke at Plaut. *Ps.* 822–5). According to Cicero, the ideal orator will choose from among his stock of commonplaces (*loci*) intelligently (*Orat.* 48; cf. Quint. *Inst.* 8 *pr.* 23): 'Nothing is more bountiful (*feracius*) than human intelligence, particularly that which has been cultivated (*exculta*) by training. But just as productive and fertile fields yield not only crops but also weeds (*herbas*) that are very harmful to them, so sometimes from these commonplaces are produced trivial, irrelevant or useless arguments.' Although it would be better to avoid declamation altogether, Quintilian says, he recognizes that students like it, and he compares declamatory excess to green grass, which is appealing to cattle but not good for them. A declaimer can indulge, but he should realize that, like cattle that must be bled after gorging on green grass, he too must carefully rid himself of the after-effects of rhetorical excess (2.10.6).

In the *Dialogus*, the familiar agricultural metaphor is again given a new emphasis. Aper, the defender of oratory in the modern style, compares the pleasures of extemporaneous oratory to uncultivated plants: 'For, in relation to talent, as on land, though some things are sown and tended for a long time, still what springs up of its own accord is more pleasing' (6.6). Maternus, who abandons oratory for tragedies with a political message, also compares oratory and uncultivated plants when he explains the history of oratory and its relation to the nature of particular communities. Oratory is not an index of the health of a polity but of the absence of a controlling force within the community and its consequent vulnerability to disturbance, he says; that is, oratory 'does not grow (*oritur*) in well-constituted communities' (40.2). Thus Athens is famous for its orators, not Sparta, Crete or Persia. Likewise in Rome, eloquence was more powerful while civic order was vulnerable to disturbance, 'just as an uncultivated field has some more flourishing plants (*herbas*)' (40.4). Once again Maternus' metaphors suggest that the practice of rhetoric is more problematic and dangerous than it appears in either Cicero or Quintilian. Maternus participates in the tradition of comparing rhetorical production to natural growth. But by envisioning oratory not as the crop (*fructus*) that labour wins from cultivated land but as the plants produced without labour (*herbae*) from uncultivated land, Maternus positions his account of oratory against Cicero's. This rupture of connections between civilization, agriculture and oratory undercuts Maternus' praises of the imperial silence that has replaced the eloquent forum.

Thickets

An excessively plain style is described as 'dry' (*aridus*, corresponding to the Greek *xeros*; *Rhet. Her.* 4.11.16; cf. Demetr. *Eloc.* 236–9). Roman rhetoricians also associate the dry style with thorny and uncultivated land. Antonius comments on Mnesarchus' Stoic views of rhetoric: 'This was a thorny (*spinosa*) and meagre (*exilis*) discourse and was very alien to our way of thinking' (*De Or.* 1.83; cf. 2.159; *Orat.* 113–14).[21] Elsewhere Cicero remarks (*Brut.* 117) that the Stoic Quintius Aelius Tubero was in life as he was in oratory: 'hard' (*durus*), 'uncultivated' (*incultus*) and 'rough' (*horridus*). Quintilian recommends that young boys not read much of the archaic Cato and Gracchus, otherwise, they will become wild and barren (*horridi* and *ieiuni*); they should also be sheltered from the opposite extreme, the appealing 'little blossoms' (*flosculi*) of modern decadence (*Inst.* 2.5.21–2).

Associations between unadorned discourse and uncultivated, dry, or otherwise unproductive land can be gracefully turned to self-deprecating effect. Quintilian fears lest his exposition of technical matters be too 'dry' (*arida*) and 'barren' (*ieiuna*) for students (3.1.3). In a more elaborate figure, Cicero compares his composition of the *Brutus* to the cultivation of a neglected field (*Brut.* 16):

From the new harvest I have nothing with which to pay back, as farmers do, what I have received – all growth has been so checked and its blossom has been so burned up and parched with thirst for its earlier abundance. Nor can I repay you from things put by, for these lie in gloomy storerooms and my every approach (I had practically the only key) to them has been frustrated. Consequently, I shall plant a crop, as it were, in uncultivated and abandoned land, which I shall tend so carefully that I shall be able to pay back the generosity of your gift with interest provided my mind can do what a field can, which, when it has lain undisturbed for many years, usually yields a more abundant crop.

Agricultural self-deprecation is taken to another amusing extreme in the *De Oratore* when Iulius Caesar Strabo characterizes his discourse on wit as unproductive, and indeed unhealthy, land: he says it is a stopover in the Pomptine marshes (*De Or.* 2.290; cf. 234). The conceit is also humorously exploited in an anecdote reported by Seneca as a demonstration of Latro's love for *sententiae*. Once while Seneca and Latro were studying with Marullus, Marullus self-deprecatingly justified his extremely unadorned style with the explanation that the topic was thorny (Sen. *Controv.* 1 *pr.* 22):

> We were students together under Marullus the rhetor, a man who was rather dry (*aridum*) and who said very few things beautifully, but spoke in an unusual way. He blamed the meagreness (*exilitatem*) of his discourse on the theme of the *controversia* and said: 'Since I am making my way through a thorny patch, I have to place my feet carefully (*necesse me est per spinosum locum ambulantem suspensos pedes ponere*).' Latro said: 'By god, your feet aren't treading on thorns: they've got thorns in them (*non mehercules tui pedes spinas calcant, sed habent*).' And immediately, while Marullus was still in the middle of declaiming, Latro started to mention epigrammatic remarks (*sententiae*) that could be introduced into the arguments.

As Seneca tells it, Marullus uses a conventional self-deprecatory figure when he says that his dry material is thorny. Latro opportunistically shifts the referent of *pedes* from human feet to the metrical feet that are the elements of prose rhythm (on metrical prose see *De Or.* 3.182–6). Delighting in *sententiae*, Latro mocks the self-deprecatory convention and obliquely suggests a pun between *sentientia* and *sentes*, 'thorn-bush'.[22] Seizing upon the adjective meaning 'thorny' (*spinosum*), Latro sees the 'thickets' (*sentes*) implicit in the untamed landscape. And Seneca shows that by his witty, compact and symmetrical phrasing, Latro composes a well-turned *sententia* of his own in mocking Marullus.

Flowers

A flower metaphor can be used to describe a pleasing style: the Latin *floridus* is the counterpart of the Greek *antheros* (Quint. *Inst.* 12.10.58). Discourse that lacks figures and ornament lacks *flores*, 'flowers' (Cic. *Brut.* 233, 298; *Parad. pr.* 2; Sen. *Controv.* 9 *pr.* 1; Quint. *Inst.* 12.10.13.). Contemporary styles are called 'too flowery' by the younger Seneca (*Ep.* 114.16), while Quintilian (*Inst.* 2.5.22; 10.5.23; 12.10.73) characterizes such styles with the scornful diminutive 'little blossoms' (*flosculi*). In the *Brutus*, where in general Cicero argues that good oratory need not strictly adhere to a narrowly defined Attic standard of simplicity, the entertaining Demetrius of Phaleron is described as 'more flowery' than Lysias and Hyperides, but Cicero also says that 'the scent of Athens itself seems to waft out of his orations' (*Brut.* 285; cf. 37–8). This distinctive scent of Athens is surely that of Hymettan thyme, perhaps best known to Romans from the honey made from it (Cic. *Hort.* fr. 89[23] [Nonius 240M];[24] Pliny *HN* 11.32; Quint. *Inst.* 12.10.25). By evoking the scent of thyme Cicero polemically sharpens the metaphor in *floridior* ('more flowery') to take a position in current debates over the definition and merits of a distinctively Attic style.

Attica and Asia

Ostensibly natural connections between landscape and language underlie Roman narratives of the influence of Greek techniques and teachers on Roman oratory, which contrast Attic simplicity and directness with Asiatic luxuriance and theatricality. In a general way, Greekness is often associated with luxury and unreliability;[25] in discussions of style, however, Attica is singled out for the simplicity and straightforwardness of its oratory. Cicero remarks in *Brutus* 51:

> For once eloquence sailed out of Piraeus, it visited every island and travelled all around Asia, with the result that it sullied itself

with foreign customs and lost as it were all the soundness and health of Attic style, and almost forgot how to speak well. From here arose Asiatic orators, not to be disparaged in swiftness or fluency but lacking in compression and too overflowing; Rhodian orators are healthier and more similar to Attic ones.

The use of the term 'Attic' to describe a sparer, less elaborate style seems to have arisen in Rome as a response to the perceived Asiatic tendencies of Cicero and others (see Cic. *Brut.* 284–91; *Orat.* 23–32, 75–90.).[26] Asiatic style is characterized as overly showy, theatrical and effeminate. Cicero describes two kinds of Asiatic style, one marked by striking turns of phrase (*sententiae*), the other very rushing and abundant, and says that Hortensius used them both (*Brut.* 325–6). In discussing the decline of oratory in Greece, Tacitus' Messalla disparages the crowd-pleasing oratory of Ephesus and Mytilene (*Dial.* 15.3). Cicero describes the Asiatic style as full of excessive modulations and sing-song technique (*Orat.* 27) and remarks (57; cf. Quint. *Inst.* 11.3.58) that Phrygian and Carian rhetoricians make the *epilogus* (a concluding appeal to the emotions) sound like a *canticum* (a song such as an actor would perform in a comedy).[27] Thus the inappropriate mixing of acting and oratory is linked geographically to Asia.

In their ancient cultural context such stylistic distinctions made sense, up to a point at least, both in historical and geographical terms. Orators whose work could be characterized this way did come from Asia.[28] Calling an orator Asiatic can refer mainly to his country of origin, but even then it would be misleading to say that the term can be 'purely' geographical. For the ancients, geography was not laid out on the grid of latitude and longitude or indeed visible from space; in ancient ways of thinking, landscape always tells the story of a nation's character.[29] The performance of any Asiatic orator would be measured against preconceptions about the nature of Asia. And indeed, the perceived differences between Attic and Asiatic rhetorical styles correspond exactly to perceived differences between the landscapes of Attica and Asia and the resulting physiognomic and psychological contrasts attributed to their inhabitants. Attic oratory is implicitly associated with the hard-bodied work of farming in Attica, while Asiatic oratory is associated with the soft sluggish body that the easy climate of Asia was thought to produce. The Hippocratic treatise *Airs, Waters, Places* sets out this conception of Asia

(12): 'Asia differs very much from Europe in the nature of everything that grows there, vegetable or human. Everything grows much bigger and finer in Asia and the nature of the land is tamer, while the character of the inhabitants is milder and less passionate.'[30] The physical world of Asia influences the character of its inhabitants (16):

> The small variations of climate to which the Asiatics are subject, extremes both of heat and cold being avoided, account for their mental flabbiness and cowardice as well. They are less warlike than Europeans and tamer of spirit, for they are not subject to those physical changes and the mental stimulation that sharpen tempers and induce recklessness and hot-headedness. Instead they live under unvarying conditions. Where there are always changes, men's minds are roused so they cannot stagnate. Such things appear to me to be the cause of the feebleness of the Asiatic race, but a contributory cause lies in their customs, for the greater part is under monarchal rule.

The influence of this kind of geographical thinking was pervasive and long-lasting.[31] Cicero's view of the climate of Athens and the character of the Athenians derives from it (*Fat.* 7):

> We understand how great the difference is between the characters (*naturas*) of different places: some are healthy, others unhealthy (*pestilentes*); in some the inhabitants are phlegmatic (*pituitosos*) as though overflowing with moisture (*redundantes*); in other places they are parched (*exsiccatos*) and dried up (*aridos*). And there are many other things that are very different between one place and another. At Athens the climate is thin (*tenue*) and from this the Athenians are thought to be more intelligent (*acutiores*); at Thebes it is heavy (*crassum*) and so the Thebans are fat and sturdy.

In setting up an opposition between Attic and Asiatic oratory, while rhetoricians acknowledge the historical facts of the development of oratory in Attica and Asia Minor, they also derive the oratorical styles from their conceptions of the contrasting landscapes of Attica and Asia. Attica is small; Asia is big. The less luxuriant landscape and people of Athens 'naturally' produced a more rugged oratory, according to this way of thinking, while the luxuriance of Asia's lands and people produced correspondingly lush language and style. Quintilian thus derives the differences in Asiatic and Attic styles from the *naturae* of speakers and audiences (*Inst.* 12.10.17). To be sure, analysing Greek oratory in these categories is not really satisfactory, for Demosthenes, undeniably Athenian, does not fit the stylistically spare criterion that the Atticists seem to uphold, as Cicero argues (*Orat.* 23–7). Quintilian expostulates (*Inst.* 12.10.25, citing Men. *Georg.* 35–9):

> Why then do these critics think that oratory that flows in a gentle trickle over a pebbly stream-bed has a true Attic flavour and declare that the true scent of thyme is to be found there? I think that if they should discover in Attica an unusually fertile piece of land or an unusually bountiful crop, they would deny that it was Attic, since it was yielding more than it had received in seed, for Menander joked about the 'fidelity' of this land in paying back its deposits.

By distinguishing Attic and Asiatic styles, Roman ambivalence about the cultural influence of Greece is mapped onto the contrasting landscapes of Attica and Asia Minor; Greek influence at large can be separated into an austere Attic strain and a luxurious Asiatic strain. And when Attic oratory, or an exponent of it, is called *aridus* (Quint. *Inst.* 12.10.14), the austere landscape of Attica is in some sense serving as a figure for the spare style of oratory. In a way, the development of a distinctive Rhodian oratorical style proves the theory. When Aeschines brought Attic rhetorical studies to Rhodes, they became corrupted by foreign (i.e., Asiatic) influences, just as 'certain plants degenerate in a different land and climate' (*Inst.* 12.10.19).

Even without such explicit analogies as these, distinctions between Attic and Asiatic style are part of the overall pattern of supposedly natural connections made by rhetorical texts between rhetorical and agricultural work. To locate Attic style in Attica was to associate it with the hard work of farming there, while to locate Asiatic style in Asia was to evoke that region's richer yields and softer bodies.

By now, I confess, the temptation to indulge in rustic analogy has become irresistible. Perhaps it will be helpful to consider the material discussed here as a cultivated field. Walking between the rows, we can appreciate the rustic figures comparing rhetorical language to crops, grass, thickets and flowers individually: they are vigorous creations yielding pleasing effects in their immediate contexts. Stepping back to take in the whole farm with our gaze, we see these individual figures as part of a large and orderly pattern: rustic metaphors that compare the cultivation of land to the cultivation of language work alongside a range of other strategies to emphasize the role of nature in oratorical success. Like pointing out that nature gave language to humans, emphasizing the importance of natural talent for orators, arguing that certain kinds of figures (such as saying that productive fields are joyful) are natural because even rustics use them, or suggesting that imitation is a part of a process of natural development, comparing the cultivation of language with the cultivation of land makes the social practice of rhetoric seem more like a development of nature and less like an invention of culture. But there are other ways to look at a field besides taking in the view. One might consider what the crop has cost to cultivate, who does the work, and who benefits from the labour. So too, the representations of rusticity discussed here are created within a network of larger cultural negotiations, for talking about nature is inevitably a way of talking about culture. These figures make it look natural that élite men receive privileged access to persuasive speech. They should also lead us to question that process of naturalization.[32]

NOTES

1 Beard and Crawford 1985: 12–24 is a useful introduction to Hellenization; Gruen 1990: 158–92 describes an increasing self-confidence in Roman reactions to Greek intellectual imports.
2 On *urbanitas* and oratory see Ramage 1973: 52–76, 100–6, 125–32.
3 Translations are my own unless noted otherwise.
4 On the thematic and structural functions of figurative language in the *De Oratore*, see Fantham 1972: 137–75.
5 For a concise overview of metaphor, see Hawkes 1972; on the ways in which metaphor can structure experience, see Lakoff and Johnson 1980.
6 See also Gleason 1995: 103–21.
7 On Roman views of the actors and theatre, see Edwards 1993: 98–136.
8 See *RE* 2.2.2485 (Aurelius 100).
9 Elsewhere Cicero takes care to point out that he and Brutus have had access to this archive through Laelia, her daughters and her granddaughters; see *Brut.* 211 with Douglas 1966: 153 *ad* 211, who provides a helpful family tree.
10 For other anecdotes about Hortensius' extravagant tastes, see Varro *Rust.* 3.6.6, 3.13.2–3.
11 See further Novara 1986.
12 For a reading of ideological functions of metaphor in Cicero's descriptions of adapting Greek culture to Roman uses, see Habinek 1994.
13 For a comparable Greek view of *logos* as a civilizing force, see Isoc. *Antidosis* 253–4, 293–4.

14 For the use of grazing to prevent damagingly luxuriant growth, see Verg. *G.* 1.111–13; Pliny *HN* 18.161. For *stilus* used of an agricultural tool, see Columella *Rust.* 11.3.53.

15 Cf. also Leeman, Pinkster *et al.* 1981–89: 3.70.

16 See Fantham 1972: 162–3.

17 For representations of Rome as a global empire, see *Rhet. Her.* 4.9.13 (*imperium orbis terrae*) and the discussion of Nicolet 1991: 31–2.

18 Fantham 1995.

19 For a survey of Quintilian's metaphorical language, see Carter 1910; on p. 62 she reports that the five largest categories of metaphor are of nature (68, including 22 agricultural), athletics (19), art (18), navigation (14) and medicine (13).

20 See Michel 1962.

21 Cf. also the passages cited in Leeman *et al.* 1981–9: 1.177; for analysis of Stoic rhetorical theories, see Atherton 1988.

22 Plautus had constructed a similar though more obvious pun on the verb *sentio* (perceive) and *senticetum* (a thicket): 'Well you aren't in a thicket, so you don't get the point' (*non enim es in senticeto, eo non sentis, Capt.* 860).

23 From the edition of Müller 1890.

24 From the edition of Lindsay 1903.

25 On Cicero's manipulation of Greek stereotypes in his speeches, see Vasaly 1993: 192–205.

26 For an overview of these terms, see Dihle 1994: 49–59. Norden 1915: 131–52, 251–72 traces the evidence for Asiatic and Attic styles in Greek and Latin, respectively; his conclusions are critiqued by Wilamowitz-Moellendorff 1900a. Cf. Wooten 1975; Fairweather 1981: 243–303.

27 For similar comparisons between oratory and *cantica*, see Sen. *Ep.* 114.1; Quint. *Inst.* 11.3.13; Pliny *Ep.* 2.14.13.

28 At *Brut.* 325, for example, Cicero lists Hierocles of Alabanda, his brother Menecles, Aeschylus of Cnidus, and Aeschines of Miletus.

29 See Vasaly 1993: 131–55.

30 Translations of Hippocrates are those of J. Chadwick and W. N. Mann in Lloyd 1978: 159–60.

31 For the influence of these traditions in Rome, see Thomas 1982; Ross 1987: 54–74; Vasaly 1993: 141–5.

32 I am grateful to Alain Gowing, Sandra Joshel, Stephen Hinds, Alison Keith, Jennifer Kosak and John Webster for their generous assistance.

6

Gender and rhetoric: producing manhood in the schools

Amy Richlin

'An orator is, son Marcus, a good man skilled at speaking.' This famous line contains worlds of gendered cultural experience in each word. The orator is male, not female; father teaches son; the orator conforms to moral norms; he is trained; he speaks – in public, in a certain way. Yet the orator's gender was a crux of Roman culture and still demands study.

STATE OF THE QUESTION

The question of the relation of gender to rhetoric could not well have been considered before the Roman gender system itself came to be examined, and indeed seems not to have arisen.[1] Recent years have seen a surge of relevant research.[2] Most of this work, as well as my own, shows the influence of the Berkeley New Historicists, treating the rhetorical schools and performance halls as a locus of gender construction, a place where manhood is contested, defended, defined, and indeed produced.[3] Related approaches deal with Rome in the context of cultural studies, wherein ideological apparatus, of which rhetoric is surely one, are analysed as parts of an organic culture.[4]

This work, however, depends on a critical tradition allied to, but often divergent from, feminist theory.[5] Manhood and male sexuality have tended to take centre stage here, as, for example, in Stephen Greenblatt's influential work, or in the way John Winkler looked toward Michael Herzfeld's *Poetics of Manhood*.[6] The overwhelmingly male nature of ancient rhetoric naturally has promoted a similarly male focus in current work on gender and rhetoric, with a few exceptions.[7] It has at least been possible to study ways in which the female persona was used within the rhetorical schools, as if women were good 'to think with' – much like the 'elegiac women' described by Maria Wyke, textual figures doing generic work.[8] In the case of the *scholae*, the female can be seen to serve important social functions as well.[9] But real women are few and far between in rhetoric, so this chapter is regrettably lopsided.

A full study of the issue would have to consider the nature of the forum as gendered space; the socialization of Roman citizen boys into manhood through the study of rhetoric; the rhetorical handbooks as guides to gender construction; the subject matter of the extant rhetorical exercises; the analogy between gender and geography in the Atticist–Asianist debate; the relation between Greeks, Romans, and others in the rhetorical schools; the contrast between Greek ideas of the meaning of rhetoric and Roman ideas; and the ways in which womanhood is constructed in Roman culture through exclusion from rhetoric. This essay will focus mainly on gender construction in the rhetorical schools, spotlighting the elder Seneca.

THEORETICAL BASIS

Gender and public space.   Feminist theorists in architecture and geography have emphasized this axiom: 'Throughout history and across cultures, architectural and geographic spatial arrangements have reinforced status differences between women and men.'[10] These theorists have not dealt with pre-industrial Europe, but the ancient Mediterranean constitutes a prime example; the spaces of the forum and the *scholae* themselves separated male from female.

Gender construction.   Judith Butler analyses gender as 'performative – that is, constituting the identity it is purported to be'.[11] Current analysts of the masculine postulate that masculinity is particularly problematic, 'a precarious or artificial state that boys must win against powerful odds', and have often turned to the Mediterranean for examples.[12] This approach seems eminently applicable to the world of the forum, where the concern of the oratorical theorists with the precariousness of virility verges on the obsessive.[13]

Similarly, Wayne Koestenbaum traces connections between the singer's throat and the homosexual's body in opera. He notes: 'As long as there have been trained voices, there have been effeminate voices – tainted by affectation or "false" production. The ancients concurred in condemning such emissions.'[14] The conflict between female voice and male body problematizes the gender of orators as well as singers.

Orientalism. Finally, the Atticist–Asianist controversy forms part of the Roman attitude toward the East, so essential to Roman ideas of self/Other. Edward Said's definition of Orientalism as discourse helps to locate this debate over proper oratorical style in the context of Rome's relation to its empire and to other cultures.[15]

THE GENDERED FORUM AND THE *TIROCINIUM FORI*

During the late republic and early empire, the Roman forum was a major site for the establishment of the cultural meaning of gender. The forum was ringed by buildings in which the (male) business of running the Roman state was carried on; voting, political speeches, the censors' assessment of senators and knights, and jury trials were held in the middle.[16] Women's important business was carried on elsewhere, their girlhood togas dedicated at the temple of Fortuna Virgo in the *forum Boarium*, next to the temple of Mater Matuta; important women's cults were located outside of the *forum Romanum*, with the unsurprising exception of the temple of Vesta.[17] But freeborn Roman boys, each year on the day of the Liberalia (March 17), were brought by their fathers to the forum, clad for the first time in the *toga virilis*, in a *rite de passage* that may have included a physical inspection of the boy's genitalia; the day, then, links the male body with place, dress and male bonding.[18]

Indeed, apprenticeship to a great orator was an important factor in this Roman *rite de passage*. It was known as the *tirocinium fori* ('recruitment to the forum'); it paralleled the *tirocinium militiae* of a young officer (Tac. *Dial.* 34).[19] Cicero's remarks on the adolescence of Caelius (*Cael.* 6–15) demonstrate how the boy's sexual attractiveness to older men structured this transition to the forum. Apprenticeship included chaperonage (9):

> As soon as [his father] gave him his *toga virilis* . . . he was immediately handed over by his father to me; no one saw this Marcus Caelius in that flower of his youth unless with his father or me or when he was being instructed in the most honourable arts in the most chaste (*castissima*) home of Marcus Crassus.

The adolescent Caelius is passed from man to man in a way reminiscent of the 'traffic in women': from his father to Cicero to his teacher Crassus.

Whatever the process was really like, we have some attestations that it was charged with emotions and sentiments similar to those we attach to boarding school or summer camp, and that it involved a strong hierarchical bonding between seniors and juniors. Both Cicero (*Amic.* 1–2; cf. *Brut.* 304–12) and Tacitus (*Dial.* 2) write fondly of the days when they were sitting at the feet of their beloved mentors. This was a time of pride for young men; the younger Seneca writes to his friend (*Ep.* 4.2): 'Of course you cherish in your memory the joy you felt when you put aside your *praetexta* and took up the *toga virilis* and were led to the forum.'

Nothing resembling this process happened to a young woman, and our scanty evidence suggests that a woman orator was an anomaly.[20] Despite Cicero's praise of distinguished ladies who trained their sons to speak well (*Brut.* 210–11, cf. Quint. *Inst.* 1.1.6), the only list of women speakers is three names long and is presented less than enthusiastically: 'We ought not to keep silent even about those women whom the condition of their nature and the robe of decorum were not able to constrain into silence in the forum and the courts' (Val. Max. 5.3 *pr.*). Amaesia Sentia (5.3.1) is presented favourably, but Valerius says she won the nickname 'Androgyne' for her efforts; the speech of Gaia Afrania (5.3.2) is described as 'barking'; only Hortensia, daughter of the great Hortensius, wins undiluted praise (5.3.3). Justinian's *Digest* says flatly (3.1.1.5): 'It is prohibited to women to plead on behalf of others. And indeed there is reason for the prohibition: lest women mix themselves up in other people's cases, going against the chastity that befits their gender, and lest women perform the duties proper to men.' So speech is proper to manhood, but chastity seems to call for silence – a dilemma, in fact, for men.

STYLE AND GENDER IN PUBLIC PERFORMANCE

Considering how the forum served as the locus of the boy's transition to manhood, it is not surprising that the content of Roman oratory includes a consistent strain of invective in which rival orators impugn each other's masculinity.[21] But these gender terms were also applied by Roman theorists to literary style itself. The logical link

93

seems to be the principle *talis oratio qualis vita* (Sen. *Ep.* 114.1): a man's style indicates his morals, and his morals will affect the way he speaks.

Seneca's 114th epistle instances several kinds of undesirable personal/literary style, but harps on effeminacy.[22] Sometimes style is too inflated, sometimes *infracta et in morem cantici ducta* ('broken and drawn out in the fashion of singing', 114.1). On the connotations of *infracta* ('broken'), we may compare Seneca's association elsewhere (*De Vita Beata* 13.4): *enervis, fractus, degenerans viro, perventurus in turpia* ('emasculated, broken, degenerating from what a man is, on the way to disgusting things'). The terms *fractus* ('broken') and *enervis* ('emasculated'; literally, 'sinewless') recur in this kind of critique and normally connote a lapse in masculinity.[23] Seneca even rejects what he calls an 'immodest' (*inverecunde*) use of metaphor (114.1), exemplifying the Roman perception of even prose rhythm and rhetorical *figurae* as subject to the rules governing sexual behaviour (cf. 114.16 on unchaste *sententiae*). The *actio* ('movement') of each person is similar to his speech (114.2); thus the *lascivia* ('sexiness') of public oratory is proof of *luxuria* ('a degenerate lifestyle'). Seneca uses Maecenas as his case in point, reproaching him for a style in line with his effeminate affect (cf. *Ep.* 19.9, where Seneca describes Maecenas as 'castrated'). His speech is *soluta* ('loose'), as he himself is *discinctus* ('unbelted').[24] The epistle closes with an elaborate portrait of the affect of the effeminate man – his haircut, the way he shaves, the colours he wears, his see-through toga, the way he is willing to do anything to be conspicuous – and concludes, 'Such is the *oratio* of Maecenas and all others who err not by accident but knowingly and willingly' (114.21).

Seneca's own father's collection of remembered speeches and anecdotes, a memoir as well as a handbook, shows how gender and style served as signs in the rhetorical *scholae* of the early empire. This book was written by the elder Seneca for his sons and expressly dedicated to them, again marking the importance of the training of sons by fathers. Seneca invokes at the outset Cato's definition of an orator; like Seneca, his model addressed his definition of an orator to his son and wrote a book on rhetoric dedicated to that son.[25] Cicero wrote the *Partitiones Oratoriae* for his son Marcus, and the book is actually framed as a sort of dialogue, or catechism, the characters being 'Cicero' (that is, Cicero's son Marcus) and 'Father' (that is, Cicero). Seneca's three sons appear occasionally as the intended audience throughout his book; for example, at the end of

Suasoriae 2.23, Seneca remarks that the style of Arellius Fuscus 'will offend you when you get to my age; meanwhile I don't doubt that the very *vitia* that will offend you now delight you'. This goes along with an idea voiced by Cicero that the Asianist style is both more appropriate to young men than to mature men and more admired by young men than by old men (*Brut.* 325–7).

The elder Seneca depicts declamations in the *scholae* staged as verbal duels among the participants, exchanges of witty criticisms, establishing and contesting a hierarchy – often gendered, as in one story about Iunius Gallio (*Suas.* 3.6–7):[26]

> I remember [Iunius Gallio and I] came together from hearing Nicetes to Messalla's house. Nicetes had pleased the Greeks mightily by his rush [of language]. Messalla asked Gallio how he'd liked Nicetes. Gallio said: 'She's full of the god.' [Seneca says this is a Vergilian tag.] Whenever he had heard one of those declaimers whom the men of the *scholae* call 'the hot ones', he used to say at once, 'She's full of the god.' Messalla himself, whenever he met [Gallio] fresh from hearing a new speaker, always used to greet him with the words, 'Well, was she full of the god?' And so this became such a habit with Gallio that it used to fall from his lips involuntarily. Once in the presence of the emperor, when mention had been made of the talents of Haterius, falling into his usual form, he said, 'She's another man who's full of the god.' When the emperor wanted to know what this was supposed to mean, he explained the line of Vergil and how this once had escaped him in front of Messalla and always seemed to pop out after that. Tiberius himself, being of the school of Theodorus, used to dislike the style of Nicetes; and so he was delighted by Gallio's story.

The story points to several features of the game as played in the *scholae*. First, a speaker's style is rejected by labelling him as a woman. The style of the original target, Nicetes, is associated with Greek declaimers in particular and said to be characterized by *impetus*, a flood or rush of words. So the bad style is feminine, foreign, and overly effusive. Second, the people involved range from Ovid's friends and patron to Augustus; this august circle is following, like sports fans, questions of style among declaimers ranging from the Greek Nicetes to the consular Haterius. Moreover, these fans are also players: Tiberius' team affiliation is noted here; Messalla appears repeatedly in Seneca, sometimes as a noted declaimer himself

(*Controv. 3 pr.* 14), occasionally insulting another declaimer.

Another story shows how such insults were wielded during the actual declaiming of speeches in the *scholae* (Sen. *Suas.* 7.12):

> This *suasoria* [Should Cicero burn his writings to get Antony to spare his life?] was declaimed in the *schola* of the rhetor Cestius Pius by Surdinus. He was a young man of talent, by whom Greek plays were elegantly translated into Latin. He used to make sweet (*dulces*) *sententiae*, but often they were too sweet (*praedulces*) and broken (*infractas*). In this *suasoria*, when he had closed out his previous pretty thoughts with an oath [a common ornament of declamations], he added the words, 'So may I read you' (*ita te legam*). Cestius, the most witty of men, pretended he hadn't heard him so that he could insult this elegant young man as if he were unchaste (*impudens*), and said, 'What did you say? What? "So may I ream you?" (*ita te fruar*, literally "so may I enjoy you").'

For us, it is easier to see the mechanics of the situation than to understand Cestius' joke. The young man speaks, the master-declaimer interrupts, and gives his interruption a form that enables him to (verbally) penetrate the young man. It is harder to see what exactly it was that set him off. According to Seneca, Surdinus' style of speech was to make *infractas sententias*. I would assume it was not *ita te legam* that bothered Cestius but the unspecified list of *belli sensus* ('pretty thoughts') that preceded it.

The style wars came to play an important role in the history of Latin literature. One of the chief offenders, according to Seneca, was Arellius Fuscus, Ovid's teacher. Here Seneca deplores how Arellius trained the young philosopher Fabianus (*Controv. 2 pr.* 1):

> Arellius Fuscus' *explicatio* was splendid, indeed, but laborious and convoluted; his ornament (*cultus*) was too far-fetched; the arrangement of his words more effeminate (*mollior*) than could be tolerated (*pati*) by a mind preparing itself according to such sacred and staunch precepts; the overall effect of his oratory was its unevenness, since it was at one point slender (*exilis*), at another wandering and overflowing with excessive licence (*licentia*): his premises, his arguments, his narratives were spoken drily (*aride*), but in his descriptions, all the words were given their freedom (*libertas*), breaking the rules, as long as they sounded brilliant; there was nothing keen, nothing solid,

nothing shaggy; his oratory was splendid, and more sexy (*lasciva*) than happy.

The problem seems to consist largely in the relation between Arellius' style and poetry, a relation both literary and social (cf. *Suas.* 3.5); and poetry is connected with what is *mollior* ('more effeminate'), what is out of control, and what is *lasciva* ('sexy').

Yet, as Seneca makes clear, Arellius was highly thought of: 'No one was thought to have been a more elegant (*cultius*) speaker' (*Suas.* 4.5); his speeches are met with cheering (*Suas.* 4.4). Indeed, Seneca himself had a high opinion of Arellius and not only quotes him extensively but puts him among his top four orators (*Controv.* 10 *pr.* 13); Arellius' 'too cultivated and broken word-order' (*nimius cultus et fracta compositio*, *Suas.* 2.23) is evidently not just for young men. Seneca claims to have included *Suasoria* 2 just so his sons can know 'how brilliantly (*nitide*) Fuscus spoke – or how licentiously (*licenter*)' (2.10), leaving it to them to judge. And then, giving an extraordinary and charming insight into the world of the forum, he says, 'I remember that, when I was a young man, nothing was so familiar as these *explicationes* of Fuscus; we all used to sing (*cantabat*) them, each with a different lilt of the voice, each to his own tune.' 'Singing' speeches was a highly charged practice and Seneca hardly advocates it; still, there he and his friends were, warbling away at Fuscus' well-known words, which they all knew by heart.

The danger to young men of experimenting with extreme style is the theme of Seneca's account of the boy orator Alfius Flavus, who peaked too young, declaiming while still wearing the *toga praetexta*. This poor boy's 'natural force' was 'emasculated (*enervata*) by poetry' (*Controv.* 1.1.22). How did poetry spoil Alfius Flavus, we wonder, and what poetry was it? We find out in the *controversia* about the father who gave his son poison because he had gone mad and was chewing on his own body (*Controv.* 3.7):

> Alfius Flavus made this epigram: 'He was his own nourishment and his own ruin.' Cestius attacked him for speaking corruptly (*corrupte*): 'It is clear', he said, 'that you have read the poets carefully; for this is an idea of that man who filled this age not just with arts but with *sententiae* that are amorous. For Ovid . . . .'

And he goes on to quote Ovid's lines on Erysichthon. Seneca has plenty to say elsewhere about Ovid's style and its faults; here Ovid is responsible for leading young Alfius astray. His very way of turning a phrase is said to be erotic (*amatoria*), just like his subject matter. The adjective *corruptus* is often used in Seneca to deplore style (e.g., *Suas.* 1.12, 1.13) or to label anything he finds in bad taste. The story of Alfius Flavus points to a feeling that oratory is contaminated by influence from a certain kind of poetry – a kind of poetry that itself represents a falling-off from a manly style.

A correlative critique from within the world of poetry is presented in the first satire of Persius.[27] The relationship between the audience and the speaker's words is depicted by Persius as a sexual one (1.19–21):

> Then you may see, neither with right morals nor calm voice,
> the big Tituses tremble, when poetry enters
> their groins, and they are scratched where it's inmost by a
>   quavering verse.

The poet likewise is effeminate, as evinced not only by his clothing but by his manner of speech and by the content and style of what he says (1.32–35):

> Here some man, wearing a lavender cloak about his shoulders,
> speaking some rancid drop from his stammering nose –
> Phyllises, Hypsipyles, and something weepy from the bards –
> he squeezes it out and trips his words under his tender palate.

And Persius implicitly compares the manly style he claims for himself with the unmanly style he deplores. He puts this in physical terms (1.103–5):

> Would these things happen if any vein of our paternal balls
> lived on in us? Groinless (*delumbe*), on the tip of saliva,
>   this swims on their lips, and 'Maenad' and 'Attis' are all wet.

Content (Greek, orgiastic, female, transsexual), style (Greek vocabulary, line structure, *enargeia*, artistic syntax), and the feminized physical body of both speaker and audience unite to form what the manly satirist rejects. Ironically, the critic himself provides a flamboyant example of what he is criticizing; it would be hard to find a more artificial poet than Persius.

It is likewise ironic that the younger Seneca produced such a lengthy sermon on the corrupt style, since he himself was reproached as an outstanding case of it by Quintilian (*Inst.* 10.1.125–31).

Quintilian says that, much as he admires Seneca's style, he had occasion to criticize it (10.1.125–6, 127)

> when I was trying to recall [my students] from a corrupt style of speech, broken by all vices (*corruptum et omnibus vitiis fractum dicendi genus*), to a more severe standard. Then, however, [Seneca] was practically the only [author] in the hands of young men. . . . But he pleased [them] precisely for his vices. . . .

If only Seneca had had more self-control, Quintilian concludes, he might have enjoyed the 'approval of the learned rather than the love of boys (*puerorum amore*)' (10.1.130).

This modelling, as has been seen, is not peculiar to Seneca and his fans: style is seen above all as something that is passed on from older men to younger men. Seneca's sons like Arellius Fuscus; Alfius Flavus likes Ovid; teachers train students or ridicule them; young men have fun imitating noted speakers. Young men are said to have a weakness for the ornate style sometimes castigated as effeminate. Oratory, then, not only manifests gender attributes in itself but is a medium whereby older men seduce younger men – though in the word, not in the flesh.

To sum up: The forum was a place for activities that defined Roman male citizens; young men came there to begin their lives as adults and were there trained by older men. This was a time when their sexual identity was felt to be in jeopardy and, perhaps for this reason, to them is attributed a predilection for a style felt to be effeminate. The 'effeminate' style was so called by Roman rhetoricians for multiple reasons: they related it to the putatively effeminate body of the speaker; they found it even in phrasing, syntax and use of rhetorical figures. Orators used imputations of effeminacy to attack each other's style in a world in which men's reputations were on the line while they vied with each other in public performance. That the performative aspect of their world was a source of concern to them is amply attested by the next group of sources.

ACTING AND *ACTIO*

If one major source of anxiety about style was the danger of effeminacy, another – and related – source was the danger of resembling an actor. The sexuality of actors was itself suspect and actors (partly on that account) suffered a diminished civil status as *infames* – much like men marked as *molles*.[28] William Fitzgerald has suggested that poetry, as a public performance, might have been seen as itself akin to acting, hence tending to cast a shadow on the sexual integrity of poets.[29] Certainly this was the case for oratory; the handbooks are full of insistent disclaimers explaining how orators, though as talented as actors, though very like actors, are really not like actors at all.

The problem was not only that orators, like actors, performed in public. The problem was that orators used their bodies in performance in ways that resembled what actors did on stage. They used their voices for effect, and sometimes this reached the point that critics described as 'singing' or 'chanting'. They used their voices to impersonate different kinds of people, including women. And they moved their bodies. The effects to be achieved by various hand and arm gestures, arrangements of the toga, eye movements, and so on constitute the branch of oratory called *pronuntiatio* ('delivery'), or *actio* ('movement'); Quintilian devotes a whole section of the *Institutio Oratoria* to it (11.3), which he begins by stating *actio* to be preeminently the most important branch of oratory, appealing to authorities including Demosthenes and Cicero. Students who read the Catilinarians today rarely even hear of *actio*, and it is startling to realize that a Roman orator must have looked more like a hula dancer than like a television anchorman. And that is just what bothered the Roman critics – that oratory should be assimilated to dancing. So it is the orator as singer and dancer who runs the risk of looking like an actor, since actors sang and danced; moreover, this dancing was regarded as morally suspect *per se* (e.g., Macrob. *Sat.* 3.14.4–8, where Scipio watches the dancing school).[30] Acting and dancing were both closely associated in Roman thought with effeminacy and sexual penetrability; hence the oratorical style that employed flowing *actio* was associated with the 'effeminate' verbal style discussed above.

The conflation of ideas about oratory, sexuality, acting and dancing is easy to find in sources from the period. The earliest extant Roman rhetorical handbook, the *Rhetorica ad Herennium* (early first century BCE), discusses *pronuntiatio* with special attention to voice (3.19–28).[31] Considering the sexual overtones of *mollitudo*, it is striking that the *auctor* gives this name to one aspect of voice control; at the same time, the name is a good indicator of the hazards that await an orator who misuses his voice.

Such pitfalls for the oratorical vocalist and performer suggest this warning (*Rhet. Her.* 3.22): 'Sharp exclamation wounds the voice; it also wounds the listener, for it has something about it that is ungentlemanly (*inliberale*) and more suited to womanish clamours (*muliebrem ... vociferationem*) than to manly dignity (*virilem dignitatem*) in speaking.' Several sections (3.23–5) are devoted to *mollitudo*; the *auctor* observes that the speaker should use the 'full throat' (*plenis faucibus*), yet 'in such a way that we should not cross from oratorical practice to that of tragedy' (3.24). Finally, in the two sections he devotes to body movement, he argues that the purpose of gestures and facial expression is to make the argument 'more probable'; therefore (3.26): 'It is fitting that chastity (*pudorem*) and briskness (*acrimoniam*) should be on your face, and that in your gesture should be neither conspicuous charm (*venustatem*) nor anything disgusting (*turpitudinem*), lest we seem to be either actors (*histriones*) or construction workers (*operarii*).'

Comments on the theatre by other writers explain what underlies these caveats. Columella, who wrote on the quintessentially Roman and manly art of agriculture in the mid-first century CE, begins his book with a classic *locus de saeculo* that includes the following comment on the theatre (1 *pr.* 15): 'Astonished, we marvel at the gestures of effeminates (*effeminatorum*), that, by womanish movement, they counterfeit a sex denied to men by nature, and deceive the eyes of the spectators.' But both dancing and the theatre were extremely popular in Roman culture, and even that hero of Roman conservatism, Scipio Aemilianus, 'moved that triumphal and military body of his to a rhythmical beat' (Sen. *Tranq.* 17.4).

If Scipio was a manly dancer, this oxymoronic state seems to have been the precarious goal of the Roman orator. Quintilian's treatment of *actio* ('movement') is full of cautions about lapses in masculinity. Effeminate *actio* repels him (*Inst.* 4.2.39): 'They bend their voices and incline their necks and flail their arms against their sides and act sexy (*lasciviunt*) in their whole style of subject matter, words and composition; finally, what is like a monstrosity (*monstro*), the *actio* pleases, while the case is not intelligible.' In an extended passage (2.5.10–12), he complains that 'corrupt and vice-filled ways of speaking' (*corruptas et vitiosas orationes*) find popular favour out of the moral degradation of their audience; they are full of what is 'improper, obscure, swollen, vulgar, dirty, sexy, effeminate' (*impropria, obscura, tumida, humilis, sordida, lasciva, effeminata*). And they are praised precisely because they are 'perverse' (*prava*). Instead of speech that is 'straight' (*rectus*) and 'natural' (*secundum naturam*), people like what is 'bent' (*deflexa*). He concludes with a lengthy analogy between the taste for such speech and the admiration for bodies that are 'twisted' (*distortis*) and 'monstrous' (*prodigiosis*) – even those that have been 'depilated and smoothed', adorned with curled hair and cosmetics, rather than deriving their beauty from 'uncorrupted nature' (*incorrupta natura*). 'The result is that it seems that beauty of the body comes from bad morals.' The bad body, in Quintilian's book, is that elsewhere associated with the *cinaedus*;[32] bad speech is *effeminata*, good speech is 'straight' and natural, tallying with the common assertion that the actions of the *cinaedus* are 'against nature'. The effeminate body stands both by metonymy and synecdoche for the kind of speech that Quintilian rejects; bad speech is both like such bodies and produced by such bodies.

This critique is applied specifically to the voice.[33] 'The transition from boyhood to adolescence' is precisely the time at which the voice is in most danger, for physiological reasons: 'not because of [the body's] heat, but rather because of its *humor*, with which that time of life is swollen' (*Inst.* 11.3.28). That is, the voice is vulnerable to bad oratorical practice at just the age when the young man is most susceptible to penetration. A healthy voice is neither too rough nor too feeble (11.3.32); the extremes are expressed by strings of adjectives, constituting a spectrum of masculinity, although the voice itself is feminine, posing a problematical androgyny. It won't do to be too rough – we might think of the Stoic/pathics targeted by satire;[34] nor yet too smooth, explicitly effeminate. But the voice has to be both firm and sweet, great and pure.

Other aspects of *actio* also come in for regulation. It is important to be careful about your eye movements; your eyes should not be 'sexy (*lascivi*) and mobile, swimming and suffused with a certain kind of pleasure, or giving sidelong glances (*limi*) and, if I might say, venereal (*venerei*), or asking or promising anything' (*Inst.* 11.3.76; cf. Cic. *Orat.* 60). In a discussion of *vitia* in hand gestures, Quintilian quotes Cicero, who rules out 'cleverness of the fingers' but approves of a 'manly bending of the sides' (*Inst.* 11.3.122, cf. Cic. *Orat.* 59). The speaker even has to be careful about where he walks: approaching the opponents' bench is 'not quite chaste' (*parum verecundum*, *Inst.* 11.3.133). The arrangement of the toga is an art in itself (11.3.137): it should be 'shining and manly' (*splendidus et virilis*); the toga should come just below the knees in front and to the mid-knee in back 'because a longer length belongs to women and a shorter to centurions' (11.3.138). Among other possible flaws, throwing the fold from the bottom over the right shoulder would be 'loose and prissy' (*solutum ac delicatum*, 11.3.146).

Moreover, *actio* should not smack of acting or dancing. Quintilian insists that the orator's vocal training is not the same as that of singing-teachers (*phonasci*), though they have much in common; orators need (11.3.19): 'firmness of the body, lest our voice be attenuated to the thinness of eunuchs and women and sick people; this is achieved by walking, applying body lotion (*unctio*), abstinence from sex, and the easy digestion of food – that is, frugality.' For Quintilian, the orator's training should be rough and tough, as opposed to the coddling a singer might give his voice (11.3.23–4): 'For we do not need so much a soft (*molli*) and tender (*tenera*) voice as we do a strong and durable one.' We have to speak 'roughly' (*aspere*); so 'let us not soften (*molliamus*) our voice by pampering (*deliciis*) . . . but let it be made firm by practice'. Likewise, our movements should not look like dancing (11.3.128): 'Most of all should be avoided *mollis actio*, such as Cicero says was exhibited by a man named Titius, so that even a certain kind of dance was called "the Titius".'

The need to divide the orator from the actor shows up repeatedly in the oratorical handbooks. Cicero, in the *Orator*, calls for *actio* that is 'not tragic (*tragica*) nor of the stage (*scaenae*), but by a moderate movement of the body and face still expresses much' (86). The elder Seneca says of Cassius Severus (*Controv.* 3 *pr.* 3) that his 'pronunciation is that which an actor might produce, but still not that which could seem to belong to an actor'. A fine distinction. Yet Seneca puts into Cassius' own mouth a speech on oratory in which he draws on his own *morbus* – his theatre craze – to use the actors Pylades and Bathyllus as instances to illustrate a point (*Controv.* 3 *pr.* 10).

Quintilian emphasizes that too close an imitation of the comic actors will corrupt the youthful student (*Inst.* 1.11.2–3):

> Indeed, not every gesture (*gestus*) and movement is to be sought from the comedians. For although the orator ought to use both of these up to a certain point, still he will be very different from an actor; nor will he be excessive in his facial expression or his hand [gestures] or his body movements.

And again, arguing that orators need not study all the nuances of *gestus* (11.3.181–4), he suggests that *actio* 'should be moderated, lest, while we strive for the elegance of an actor, we lose the *auctoritas* of

103

a good and serious man' – a telling opposition (for further remarks on acting and oratory, see 1.12.14; 11.3.103, 123, 125).

One of the causes of the problem was the fact that orators had to impersonate various characters in the course of making speeches. Quintilian lists 'children, women, foreigners (*populorum*), and even inanimate things' as posing challenges to the orator's skill (11.1.42). The failure to observe the correct tone is especially a problem in the *scholae* because 'many emotions are acted out (*finguntur*) in the *schola*, which we undergo not as advocates, but as victims' (*non ut advocati sed ut passi subimus*, 11.1.55) – might we here posit that the lawyer stood to the client as active sexuality stood to passive? That what 'unmanned' the orator was too close an identification with the experience of the contesting parties? But here Quintilian is advocating a scrupulous adherence to the tone necessitated by the plot of the *controversia*: weep, be emotional, and do it consistently. Yet, paradoxically, what he rejects here is precisely the kind of style associated with acting and effeminacy elsewhere (11.1.56): *cantare, quod vitium pervasit, aut lascivire* ('singing/ chanting, a vice that has become pervasive, or sexy style').

A singing or chanting intonation is mentioned repeatedly as a vice plaguing the practice of oratory. It shows up as early as Cicero's *Orator ad M. Brutum* in a passage in which he discusses earlier Greek practices (57):[35]

> There is, however, even in speaking a certain rather muffled (*obscurior*) singing tone (*cantus*), not that peroration of the rhetors out of Phrygia and Caria that is almost an aria, but that which Demosthenes and Aeschines mean when one charges the other with modulations of the voice (*vocis flexiones*). . . .

As we have seen, the elder Seneca talks of himself and his friends, in his younger days, singing the purple passages from Arellius Fuscus. Seneca likewise calls Vibius Gallus crazy for his habit of singing out cues that he is about to begin a descriptive passage (*Controv.* 2.1.26): 'When he was about to describe love, he would say, almost like someone singing, "I want to describe love", just as if he were saying, "I want to have an orgy (*bacchari*)".' Quintilian suggests that singing may be taken up as the refuge of a weak voice; such a speaker may ease his 'weary throat and side by an ugly aria (*deformi cantico*)' (*Inst.* 11.3.13). He introduces an extended discussion of the vice of chanting by a list of other faults that includes spitting on bystanders and hawking up phlegm, continuing (11.3.57–60):

But any one of these vices would I prefer to the one that now is so belaboured in all court cases and in the *scholae* – that of chanting; I don't know whether it is more useless or more disgusting (*foedius*). For what is less fitting for an orator than a stagy modulation, not infrequently approaching the licence of drunks or carousers? (57) What indeed is more contrary to moving the feelings than . . . to loosen the very holiness of the forum by the licence of the Lycians and Carians? . . . (58) But if it is to be generally accepted, there is no reason why we shouldn't help out that vocal modulation with lyres and flutes – no, by God, with cymbals, which are closer to this ugliness. . . . (59) And there are some who are led by this pleasure of hearing everywhere what might soothe their ears, in accord with the other vices of their lives (60).

Here Quintilian brings together many elements of the critique of gender in style. Singing is repellent, ugly, in the sense that it is morally repugnant and like the improper body; it is associated with the stage or with drunks, recalling the younger Seneca's description of Maecenas' verbal style; it is associated with *licentia*, the opposite of the desired control of the body; it threatens to dissolve, to loosen, the forum, which is called 'holy', and opposed to the licence here attributed to Asia Minor (Quintilian seems to have the passage from Cicero's *Orator* in mind); it is associated first with the musical accompaniment of the stage and, climactically, with the cymbals of the eunuch priests of Cybele – an association both with Asia and with effeminacy. Finally, Quintilian hints that those who like this style have problems with vice in their own lives.

To sum up: the orator's training involved a surprising amount of physical work. The formalized list of appropriate gestures in *Institutio* 11.3 must have involved substantial practice for novices. The orator's vocal range was close enough to a singer's to necessitate training with a voice coach. But always, in these endeavours, the orator risked running to various extremes, among which effeminacy always looms large. The problem above all was how to avoid looking like a dancer and sounding like a singer, dubious statuses that themselves carried the stigma of effeminacy. But the beleaguered orator had even more to worry about; in Quintilian's tirade on singing, we see the traces of a further aspect of gender trouble in oratorical style: the threat to the virile forum from the effeminate East.[36]

THE ATTICIST–ASIANIST CONTROVERSY

The debate over oratorical style known as the split between Atticists and Asianists is well known and is discussed in detail by modern analysts.[37] But the Roman ambivalence over an art so markedly Eastern in origin was often expressed in terms of gender. The Orient, in Roman thought, was associated with luxury and a concomitant deviant sexuality – effeminacy, even self-castration.[38] Thus it was logical for a style of speech that came from the East to be labelled as effeminate. The problem was, if you wanted to be an orator, you had to submit to an Eastern regimen – Greek, if not absolutely Asiatic. A solution was to divide the East into less-East and more-East and to identify oneself with the lesser of the two evils. Hence the 'Atticists', who spoke of their style as more manly, claimed that it derived from the writers of Athens; the term 'Asianist' was applied to writing associated with the rhetorical schools of Asia Minor. 'Asianist' was generally a term of abuse, and it is hard to find an instance of someone claiming to be one, though it is not hard to find denunciations of the Atticists.

Quintilian discusses the difference between Atticists and Asianists at some length (*Inst.* 12.10.12–26) and gives an account of the origins of the two schools (12.10.16–17). In antiquity, he says, the Attic was good, the Asianist bad. The Attic speakers were *pressi* ('concise') and *integri* ('whole'), while the Asianists were *inflati* ('inflated') and *inanes* ('empty'); the former had nothing extra, the latter were lacking in both judgement and moderation. Some say, he continues, that this happened because Greek spread from Greece to Asia Minor and the Asianists tried their strength at eloquence when they were not yet skilled in speaking Greek; so they expressed ideas by circum-locutions because they did not know the right words; and then they kept up the habit. Quintilian, however, thinks that the difference is an ethnic one and stems both from the orators and their audience (12.10.17): 'The Attici, refined and discriminating, tolerated nothing empty or gushing (*redundans*); but the Asiatic race (*gens*), somehow more swollen (*tumidior*) and boastful (*iactantior*), was inflated with a more vainglory of speaking.' The Asiatics are thus branded both as upstarts on the rhetorical scene and as inherently, even physically, less capable of excellence.

These ethnic adjectives show up associated with gender adjectives in descriptions of the battle between Cicero and his Atticist op-ponents. Tacitus, in the *Dialogus*, preserves an interchange between Cicero, Calvus, and Brutus (18.4–5):

106

It is established that not even Cicero was without his de-tractors, to whom he seemed inflated and swollen (*inflatus et tumens*), not concise (*pressus*) enough, but jumping over the limits (*supra modum exultans*), overflowing (*superfluens*) and not Attic enough. In particular you have read the letters sent by Calvus and Brutus to Cicero, from which it is easy to gather that Calvus seemed to Cicero bloodless and worn (*attritum*) while Brutus seemed idle (*otiosus*) and disjointed. In return, Cicero indeed got bad reviews from Calvus as loose (*solutum*) and sinewless (*enervem*) and from Brutus, if I may use his own words, as 'broken and loinless' (*fractum atque elumbem*).

Compare Quintilian's report of the attack on Cicero (*Inst.* 12.10.12):

But even people of his own times dared to attack him as too swollen (*tumidiorem*), Asianist, gushing (*redundantem*), too repetitive, sometimes frigid in his humour, and in his composi-tion broken (*fractum*), jumping-over (*exsultantem*), and almost – which could not be farther from the truth – softer than a man (*viro molliorem*).

The list of adjectives associated with effeminacy is a familiar one, but thought-provoking in its connection with the East. We move from the familiar *mollis* ('soft') to the explicit and physiological *elumbis* ('loinless') and *enervis* ('sinewless'/'emasculated'), to a group of adjectives evoking space and substance: *inflatus* ('inflated'), *tumens*, *tumidus* ('swollen'), *exultans* ('jumping-over'), *redundans* ('gush-ing'), *superfluens* ('overflowing'), *solutus* ('loose'), *fractus* ('broken'). These adjectives, also familiar from Seneca *Epistulae* 114 (and cf. *Rhet. Her.* 4.16), are located in the body of the orator as well as in his speech, and in addition suggest a quality he may be passing on to the world around him; compare what Quintilian said about 'loosen-ing the holiness of the forum' by importing style from Lycia and Caria (*Inst.* 11.3.58). This fear of flowing, loosening, leaping the boundaries, breaking up, pervades Roman imagery of the city, state and empire.[39] In contrast, the Attici are *pressi* ('concise') and *integri* ('whole').

Yet the heroes of Roman oratory are not Brutus and Calvus but Cicero and Hortensius. Despite the problematic aspects of the Asianist style, the experts agree that it is more beautiful, more noble, and more effective than the arid wastes of the Atticists.

AMY RICHLIN

CONCLUSIONS

Although the feminine plays a major part in the world of the forum, real women themselves are almost entirely absent. The players in these all-male games seem to need the feminine both for their own enjoyment and in order to insult each other, but an actual female body does not belong in the forum. Indeed, the charming minutes of the elder Seneca's men's club convey no sense of lack; women are elsewhere, maybe in the women's club, but who cares?[40]

NOTES

1 No mention of the subject appears in the lengthy bibliography compiled by Sussman 1984.
2 For recent work on gender and Roman rhetoric, see Corbeill 1990; Santoro L'hoir 1992; Richlin 1992d; Gleason 1995; Richlin 1995: 204–5; Corbeill 1996; Gunderson 1996; Richlin 1996; Gunderson (forthcoming); Richlin (forthcoming a).
3 For a brief early discussion of sexuality and rhetorical style, see Richlin 1992a: 92–3. On the New Historicists see Veeser 1989. On cultural studies see Grossberg et al. 1992.
4 Bloomer 1995; Bloomer (forthcoming).
5 On the relations and divergences between the New Historicism and feminist theory on the body, see Richlin (1997).
6 Greenblatt 1980; Herzfeld 1985; Winkler 1990.
7 For consideration of women's participation in Roman oratory, see Hallett 1989: 62, 66; Richlin 1992d.
8 Wyke 1987; Wyke 1995.
9 For ventriloquism of the female in rhetoric, see Santoro L'hoir 1992: 29–46; Bloomer 1995; Richlin 1996.
10 Spain 1992: 3. For feminist theory on space, see also Women and Geography Study Group 1984; Ardener 1993; Rose 1993.
11 Butler 1990: 25.
12 Gilmore 1990: 11; cf. Brandes 1981; Herzfeld 1985; Winkler 1990; Gleason 1995.
13 For performative gender, compare work by Latinists on masculinity in Roman literary texts: Fitzgerald 1988; Fitzgerald 1992; Skinner 1993; Fitzgerald 1995: 34–58; Oliensis (forthcoming).
14 See Koestenbaum 1991; the cited passage is found on p. 218.
15 Said 1979; pp. 55–8 deal with Greek and Roman orientalizing.
16 On activities in the forum, see Stambaugh 1988: 112–19; Zanker 1990: 79–82; Moore 1991. On the gender significance of the shape of the forum of Augustus, see Kellum (forthcoming).
17 On Roman women's religion see Richlin (forthcoming b); on the androgyny of the Vestals, see Beard 1980.
18 On the Liberalia see Richlin 1993: 545–8. On Roman (unlike Greek)

108

rhetorical education as 'responsible for a whole cadre of young men', see Gleason 1995: 121.

19 See Bonner 1977: 84–5 with bibliography.
20 Richlin 1992d; cf. Bonner 1977: 135–6 on coeducation in secondary schools; Hallett 1989. On voice training for women as a health measure, see Gleason 1995: 94–8.
21 For overview and discussion see Richlin 1992a: 83–104, 278–84. For a parallel discussion of rhetoric and gender slippage, see Gleason 1995: 71–3, 75, 98–102.
22 For previous discussions of this letter, see Richlin 1992a: 4–5; Gleason 1995: 113.
23 On the sexual connotations of *fractus* and its compounds in the context of rhetoric, see Gleason 1995: 112; for other stereotypical adjectives used to connote effeminacy, see Richlin 1992a: 258 n. 3; Edwards 1993: 63–97, esp. 68–9; Gleason 1995: 67–70. On the vocabulary of Roman male gender variance, see ch. 4 of Williams (forthcoming).
24 For the connection of *discinctus* with effeminacy, see Richlin 1992a: 92, 280; Edwards 1993: 90; Corbeill 1996: 160 n. 81.
25 Bonner 1977: 10–14.
26 On the agonistic structure of Greek declamation in the second century CE, see Gleason 1995: 72–3, 122–6.
27 Richlin 1992a: 186–7 with further bibliography.
28 On these terms and the ideas behind them, see Bonner 1949: 20–2; Dupont 1985: 95–110; Edwards 1993: 98–136; Richlin 1993: 554–61; Edwards (forthcoming).
29 Fitzgerald 1992: 420–1.
30 Richlin 1992a: 92, 98, 101, 284; Gleason 1995: 106, 113–21; see also Edwards (forthcoming).
31 Also discussed in Gleason 1995: 104–5.
32 On this word see Richlin 1993.
33 On the voice and voice training see Edwards 1993: 86; Gleason 1995: 82–102, esp. 82–3.
34 See Richlin 1992a: 138–9.
35 On singing see Bonner 1949: 21–2, 59; Gleason 1995: 93–4, 108, 112, 117–18.
36 For a later version of this critique by a Greek writer (without the ethnic angle), see Lucian *Nigr.* 11 (actors who speak *gunaikôdes*, 'effeminately'); *Demon.* 12 (Demonax mocks Favorinus' prose rhythm as *agennês*, 'low-born', and *gunaikeion*, 'womanish'); and the extended description of an effeminate, chanting orator at *Rhêtorôn Didaskalos* 11–12, 15, 19. These and related texts are discussed in detail by Gleason 1995: 126–30, 132–8.
37 On Asianists and Atticists see Leeman 1963: 136–67. Gleason 1995: 107–8 de-emphasizes the issue.
38 On gender and the East see Griffin 1976; Balsdon 1979: 60–3, 225–30; Edwards 1993: 92–7; Skinner 1993; and for modern Orientalizing, Said 1979: 190.
39 On the use of the image of fluid body boundaries to express anxiety over the body politic, see Joshel 1992.

40 Sections of this chapter were delivered at a session on 'Configurations of Gender in Roman Literature' held on 29 December 1992 at the 123rd Meeting of the American Philological Association in New Orleans, USA. I thank the panel organizer, Micaela Janan, and my fellow panellists – William Fitzgerald, Holt Parker, Ellen Oliensis and Marilyn Skinner – for helpful discussion.

7

The contexts and occasions of Roman public rhetoric

Elaine Fantham

Both the vast scale of modern political societies and the overwhelming increase in communication by images or through the intimacy of electronic media explain why the concept of oratory has become alien and archaic, needing a social commentary to explain it to the modern reader. But the difference between Greek civic democracies and Rome also meant that interpretation was needed for a Roman to understand how an *orator* differed from an Athenian *rhetor*. Indeed, his course of study with Greek teachers of rhetoric would hardly prepare him for the divergence between oratory as practised at Rome and its past or current uses in Hellenistic Greece. My concern is with practice, not etymology, but it is still useful to take as guidance the earliest recorded uses of *orator* (from *orare*, 'to pray', 'request', 'plead'): these men are envoys in public life or intermediaries in the private world of comedy between erring lovers or sons and their mistresses and fathers.[1]

In classical Athens the *rhetor* was above all the politician, not as elected magistrate but as one with power to persuade the popular assembly. When the herald announced, 'Who wishes to address the people?' (Ar. *Ach.* 45),[2] the democratic principle entitled any citizen to speak, but reality ensured that officials would be recognized first and foremost. Although the first hearing in Aristophanes' mock assembly is given to ambassadors newly returned from Persia, this would normally go to established political figures. Yet we know that young men tried to become established in politics through speaking. In Xenophon's *Memorabilia* Socrates interrogates a young kinsman of Plato, Glaucon, who has embarrassed his friends by leaping up to speak in the assembly and persisting even when people try to drag him down from the speaker's platform (3.6). Glaucon wants to be a public speaker (*dêmêgorein*) so as to become a leader, but has no idea of public finances or military needs.[3]

At Athens and often elsewhere both policy and actual proposals were shaped by informal discussion in the smaller consultative council (*boulê*) but determined by the assembly; yet because the speaker before the people needed to appear spontaneous, there was no acknowledged preparation or later record of his words. None of these speeches seems to have been published before those circulated by Demosthenes in the crisis of Athens' collapse before Macedon.[4] There were also ceremonial public speeches, especially the official *logoi epitaphioi* at public funerals (such as Pericles' funeral speech as reported by Thucydides), and display speeches at festivals or cultural displays.

Litigants in Athenian civil cases and defendants on serious charges before the huge democratic juries were expected to present their own case, but regularly employed speechwriters (*logographoi*). Socrates, who conducted his own defence in terms that may have ensured his condemnation, supposedly refused the speech offered him by Athens' best contemporary writer, Lysias, as he refused also to make the standard appeal for pity expected of a defendant (reported by Cic. *De Or.* 1.231; cf. Pl. *Ap.* 34c, 37a). These speechwriters were often disqualified from a career as a public speaker by lack of citizenship or weakness of voice. On the other hand, even the most gifted advocate would speak in court only if he himself were a prosecutor, a defendant, or a litigant.

THE SCOPE OF THE ROMAN ORATOR: CICERO AS EXAMPLE AND SOURCE

In republican Rome's more hierarchical world the two main forms of public speaking, political and judicial, were relatively open to members of the governing class, just as they were virtually closed to the ordinary citizen. This discussion will consider roughly three hundred years of public life from the long career of the elder Cato (*cos.* 195 BCE) through the career of Cicero (*cos.* 63 BCE) in the republic to Tacitus (*cos.* 97 CE) and the younger Pliny (*cos.* 100 CE) in the early empire. But evidence for the second century BCE comes mostly from Cicero and his contemporaries. Indeed, modern knowledge of Roman politics and rhetoric of all kinds has been shaped by Cicero's speeches, theory and letters.

Cicero's study of rhetorical education, *De Oratore*, retains the

Greek division of types of public speaking between political, judicial and ceremonial, but acknowledges their unequal importance: he gives priority to the two major contexts of political speaking (i.e., assembly and senate; cf. *De Or.* 2.333–40) – which I shall consider first – while recognizing the importance of at least the major public trials to a political career. Other texts, such as the anonymous manual for Herennius (around 85 BCE), pay far more detailed attention to lawcourt rhetoric, confirming its predominance as (what we would call) a profession in the daily life of Rome and Italy. As for the third category, it was primarily associated with funeral eulogy, but became a miscellaneous catch-all covering military harangues and moral exhortation in many semi-private contexts.

In Roman political life the assembly had less power than in Athens but offered more scope for official eloquence. Public assemblies were summoned to meet in the open *comitium* in the north-east corner of the Roman forum when one of Rome's major magistrates wished or needed to address the citizens. Normally the consul whose turn it was to preside over the senate[5] would summon the assembly on one of the authorized days[6] to present senatorial policy or to submit new proposals (*senatus consulta*) for ratification. The same word, *contio* (from *conventio*, 'causing to come together'), described both his speech and the preliminary meeting, but on this occasion the audience could not vote: there was a statutory waiting period of three market 'weeks' before citizens could assemble in their official divisions for the formal *comitia* or voting assemblies. The orator, however, could use his eloquence only at a *contio* and only if he were either the magistrate presiding over the meeting or invited to speak by him. There was no provision for amendment or challenge from the crowd. In such planned and disciplined public meetings stage management was not only possible but normal. Unauthorized public gatherings were illegal, but the consul might have to deal with negative rumours and popular discontent, even potential rioting, by calling an emergency meeting: Cicero did this in 63 BCE to deal with a potential theatre riot at the games of Apollo.[7] In such a context the magistrate's attendants would have to impose order and designate a meeting place before the consul could make his eloquence felt. It is no accident that one of Vergil's most powerful similes compares Neptune's benevolent intervention to calm a storm to the wise statesman who appears to quell a riot when stones and torches are already flying and soothes the mob by his sheer authority and eloquence (*Aen.* 1.148–53).

We have some idea of the skill this entailed from Cicero's surviving (i.e., published) speeches to different assemblies. When he entered office as consul he faced the challenge of persuading the assembly to vote against an agrarian law that could have benefited many of the voters. Cicero objected to this law both on principle, from conservative disapproval of allocating public land away from its occupants, and also more strongly on pragmatic grounds, for the power and influence it would give the appointed commissioners. His strategy in the *De Lege Agraria* was to convince the crowd that any land they might receive would not be worth farming and that the law was in some mysterious way aimed against Pompey, whose conquests in the East had made him a popular hero. Cicero faced a worse challenge at the end of the year when he had to justify emergency measures against the radical Catiline; it had been relatively easy to obtain senatorial approval for his first measures (*Cat.*1), but the two speeches to the people (*Cat.* 2, 3) show how he depended on stressing the immediate risk to themselves, their families and livelihoods, and on invoking patriotic religious fervour. By superb stage management he organized the replacement of a damaged statue of Jupiter *optimus maximus* for the evening before his third speech in order to exploit the physical setting of the open-air meeting by pointing out to the people the renewed presence of their protecting god, who was blessing the order restored by Cicero to Rome.[8]

In contrast the senate met within walls, but not always the walls of the senate house. It would often meet in a temple, at times that of Apollo or Bellona, outside the official walls of Rome, to receive reports from foreign envoys or from a returning commander who could not enter the walls while holding military *imperium* and awaiting a triumph. In the Catilinarian crisis of 63 BCE Cicero convened the senators in the temple of Concord. When Caesar was assassinated in 44 BCE, the senate had been summoned to a meeting in the temple attached to Pompey's theatre complex. While speeches to a *contio* in the open forum needed all the speaker's authority and dramatic skill, senatorial speeches were given with less parade; not only was the audience experienced (Cicero calls it a 'wise advisory body', *De Or.* 2.334–7),[9] but the speaker was only one of many giving his *sententia*, a word denoting both opinion and actual vote. Priority went to the dozen or so ex-consuls who formed the senate's senior ranks, then magistrates in descending order, but after elections each year these followed the incoming magistrates; many senators would have no chance to speak.[10]

Thus, all of Cicero's senatorial speeches were delivered as *sententiae* to initiate or respond to a motion. They might take the form of a personal attack, such as his denunciation of the ex-consul Piso or of Mark Antony, which was delivered in the last year of his life, but they had to support or oppose a concrete proposal: that Piso's provincial command be terminated (to be reassigned to an outgoing magistrate), Mark Antony be declared a public enemy, Servius Sulpicius receive a public funeral and monument, or the senate confer special rank on young Octavianus Caesar to command an army against Antony.[11] Speeches that seem to resemble each other in content, such as the encomium of Pompey's generalship in 66 BCE and of Caesar's generalship in Gaul ten years later, could be quite different in circumstance. The speech 'On the Command of Gnaeus Pompey', also called 'In Support of Manilius' Law', was delivered by Cicero as one of several magistrates invited by the tribune Manilius to address a public assembly. It was a *suasio*, whose purpose was to ensure the passing of the law conferring an extraordinary command on Pompey. But the speech 'On the Consular Provinces' was a two-part motion proposed in the senate to recall Piso and Gabinius from their commands and to renew the command that Caesar had exercised so successfully in Gaul, honouring him with a public thanksgiving of fifty days.

EARLY DEVELOPMENTS: THE SECOND CENTURY BCE

These examples, taken from the better-known generation of Cicero, can help us to reconstruct political life in the second century around Rome's earliest known statesman–orator, Marcus Porcius Cato. An outsider to Rome, he is said to have begun his career as an advocate in private cases in his own Sabine country before serving in the Hannibalic war. Between 205 and 184 BCE, he held every magistracy from *quaestor* to *censor*; almost uniquely he made his opinion heard in the senate as an ex-consul for over forty years.

It is very unlikely that anyone else other than Cato produced written texts of his own speeches during this period. Certainly nobody left behind so many as Cato. Their variety can serve as an index for some of the contexts and types of speech we have not yet considered. As magistrate Cato delivered policy speeches to both the senate and assembly. Outside Rome and Italy he harangued his soldiers as provincial commander in Spain and addressed the

Athenian assembly as a Roman envoy. He would have made many diplomatic speeches, for example, when he was sent to Carthage in his last years to convey Rome's official policy to the assembly; on his return, determined to see this dangerous rival eliminated, he ended his recorded vote on every topic in the senate with the proposal that Carthage must be destroyed. Cato was a master of invective, a mode of speech not limited to any one context. Besides prosecuting and denouncing rival politicians, he resorted to invective as *censor* in 184 BCE when he demoted an ex-consul, Lucius Flamininus, from the senate for the wanton killing of either a prisoner or a deserter. Livy, who seems to have read Cato's speech with other censorial speeches justifying demotion, declares that Cato's invective was so damaging that if he had made this speech as a prosecutor before Lucius Flamininus was demoted, instead of as *censor* after the demotion, not even Lucius' famous brother could have kept him in the senate (39.42.6–7). After Cato's campaigns in Greece and the East, there are records of other speeches in the senate and (probably) the assembly reporting the corruption of rival commanders. In 171 he acted as *patronus* for communities of his former province, Nearer Spain, suing former governors for extortion. But he was also sued in his turn: he had been obliged to defend his own governorship of Spain on his return in 195 BCE. He was prosecuted forty-four times in all but was acquitted in each case. For Cato, as for other statesmen, public speeches and court speeches often served the same political purpose.[12]

Indeed, Cato's three most controversial speeches represent each of the three politically important categories: a consular *contio* to prevent the repeal of moral legislation, a senatorial vote on foreign affairs, and a speech to the assembly in its judicial capacity in support of the prosecution of a sadistic and corrupt provincial governor. The first is Cato's public address against the repeal of the Oppian law, a wartime austerity measure limiting women's clothing and vehicles. Agitation against the old law provoked an unprecedented female demonstration in the forum. Livy includes an imaginative reconstruction (34.2–5) of Cato's speech rallying Roman husbands to control their wives as a basis for order in the community.

In 167 BCE Cato rose in the senate to oppose a demagogic motion to declare war on the Greek commercial state of Rhodes, a Roman ally that had tried to mediate between Rome and her enemy Perseus. His argument was that if not only Rhodes but many other states were afraid of Rome's victory, this was no offence against Rome but brought on by her overweening behaviour. Regarding this warning as of national importance for future statesmen, Cato included this speech in his own narrative history. It so impressed Livy that he openly renounces offering his own version, which would be 'a mere ghost of this powerful man' (43.25), and its main arguments are still quoted three hundred years later (Gell. *NA* 6.3). In his last year of life Cato denounced Servius Sulpicius Galba's massacre and enslavement of a disarmed Spanish tribe, in support of a popular tribune bringing Galba's prosecution before the assembly. This too Cato incorporated into his own narrative history because it embodied principles of imperial morality that he wanted his countrymen and readers to follow.

Cato prevented the unjustified war, but lost his battle in the assembly for the *lex Oppia*, as he did in the judicial assembly when he sought justice for Rome's Spanish enemies. The term judicial assembly (*iudicium populi*) describes the assembly functioning in another capacity: not in election or legislation but in the cumbersome procedures of the popular trial. Until the beginning of the first century BCE, any magistrate could be accused by a tribune of capital offences springing from abuse of power. The assembly itself represented the Roman people as jury; it could also serve as jury in lesser cases brought by the aediles for breach of public order. These potentially huge crowds giving the verdict are the nearest Rome came to the Athenian Heliaea. Eyewitness accounts by Cicero of the last full-dress popular trial include organized heckling by partisans of the presiding aedile Clodius.[13] This called for oratory, whether in prosecution or defence, of the man under investigation. Thus, when Cato supported restitution of status to the enslaved Lusitani and the prosecution of Sulpicius Galba on his return from Spain, the eloquent Galba secured his acquittal by appealing to the people's pity and parading his son and his ward, threatened with orphanhood (Cic. *De Or.* 2.227–8). We may wonder how much the randomly gathered citizens cared about a Spanish tribe against whom many had fought and more were afraid to fight.

Such trials required three hearings on different days and an adjournment, after which the people were summoned to vote either by tribal divisions in the *comitium* or by class and century on the election grounds of the Campus Martius.[14] The expense, the delay, the risk of disorder, the impossibility of ensuring that the jury consisted of even roughly the same crowd who had actually heard the evidence, all accumulatively brought this procedure into disuse.

Powerful men could vitiate justice, making fools of the prosecuting magistrate. A tribune or aedile would normally preside from the *rostra*, raised slightly above the assembly, and would be reinforced by attendants to keep order. But in one famous episode of 187 BCE, when tribunes launched a public prosecution of the great general Scipio Africanus, Scipio appeared with a huge escort of friends and supporters and marched up to the dais to speak uninvited. He told the crowd that it was the anniversary of his great victory over Hannibal at Zama, an occasion for thanksgiving to the gods when there should be no petty litigation, and invited them to follow him to the Capitol to give thanks to Jupiter. Scipio was almost certainly guilty of irregularities, both in the expenses of his recent campaign and his negotiations with the king of Syria. But he led the entire assembly away from the *comitium* like a pied piper, leaving the tribunes and their secretaries and attendant slaves deserted and impotent (Livy 38.50.10–51.7).

It was probably the scandal of Galba's acquittal (or failure to come to trial) in 149 that provoked the new senatorial legislation replacing this kind of popular trial of political figures by a regular standing court. It may have been in the interest of the senate rather than of justice itself that Calpurnius Piso Frugi proposed in this year a permanent court for claims by the provinces against abusive governors, based on a panel of senators serving as jury to award damages under a senatorial presiding officer. This was in every sense a trial by peers. In this new standing court *de repetundis* ('for compensation with damages') the provincials were represented by senatorial orators and their suit was assessed by members of the senate. In addition, the trial was modelled on civil procedure, exempt from appeal to the popular tribunes, so that many aspects favoured the senatorial defendant. As J. A. Crook has pointed out, criminal law is

> the most obvious interface of law and politics, since it is bound
> to impinge frequently on public policy. That was all the more
> so in the Roman case, in that the statutory criminal law of the
> *quaestiones perpetuae* arose out of public policy considerations
> – *repetundae, ambitus, peculatus* and so on.[15]

A number of specialized standing courts dealt with other offences of magistrates at home and on military service: abuse of power (*maiestas*), embezzlement, bribery and political violence. Such was the power of these courts, especially the one dealing with provincial governors, that the senate's control of the jury panels was a bitterly contested issue, dominating the rhetoric of Roman political life until a compromise was arrived at in 70 BCE.

For part of the controversy lay in the expectations of the companies who contracted to farm provincial taxes. In the period when the *equites*, the social class including these tax companies, were serving on the court *de repetundis*, at least one honourable assistant governor, Rutilius Rufus, suffered malicious prosecution by friends of the tax contractors whom he had prevented from bleeding his province. His unwarranted condemnation caused a revulsion that returned the jury into senatorial hands. But senators too were concerned with the profits of tax farming and overseas financial interests and a speaker before them had to tread carefully: he could not assume they would support criticism of the tax companies.

Most important for our immediate concern, these courts increased the demand for skilled oratory and boosted its prestige. Cicero explains the increasing importance and power of judicial oratory at Rome in the period before 130 BCE by two changes: the new permanent courts and the introduction of the secret ballot for large popular trials (Cic. *Brut.* 106). About this time, too, the increasing complexity of private and public law led to a gradual separation between the expertise of legal advisers (*jurisperiti*) and that of advocates.

We have looked so far only at political trials involving either criminal procedure or the civil procedure of the board of assessors (*recuperatores*). But a far larger proportion of Roman legal activity consisted of civil lawsuits in which considerable property or money was often at stake. Rome had originally entrusted to the annual *praetor urbanus* the preliminary hearing of all civil suits *in iure*: first the contesting parties set before him their version(s) of the facts; then he appointed an arbitrator (or a group of judges) acceptable to them before whom they could bring their witnesses and documents (the procedure *apud iudicem*). The *praetor urbanus* officiated in the *comitium* until lack of space led him to move to the other side of the Roman forum by the temple of Castor. Here, in the open, he conducted his hearings, as the *praetor peregrinus* did nearby for lawsuits between Romans and foreigners. By the time of Cicero there was a permanent tribunal, the *tribunal Aurelium*, for the *praetor urbanus*, but his business and the secondary procedure before one or more judges still continued in the open without use of the basilicas now flanking the forum. And by the 70s BCE, the limited forum space was filled by an increasing number of standing courts. In his speech defending Cluentius against a charge of murder, Cicero seems to be claiming that five other courts are taking place simultaneously in the space between the Regia and the Comitium (Cic. *Clu.* 147).[16] The published prosecution of Verres describes the forum as full of trials (*Verr.* 2.5.143).

How would a professional orator make his name in the courts, winning glory and discreetly indirect financial reward?[17] Minor lawsuits only called for influential men to serve as character witnesses or to use their legal expertise on behalf of their humbler friends; yet arguments about equity could easily be used to confuse a private judge into going against the letter of the law. The evidence of Plautus early in the second century suggests that patrons could find themselves hard pressed to defend the business practices of the wealthy clients they had taken up (*Men.* 576–96):

> When they are summoned to court, so are their patrons, since they are obliged to defend the client's offences: they must plead either before the people or in the praetor's court or before the aediles. It was just like that today; a client gave me a bad time and I couldn't get any of my own business done: he hung on to me and held me back so. I pleaded his case before the aediles and offered twisted and knotty terms of agreement. I stated the case neither more nor less than I should to secure an agreement. And what did he do after giving surety? I never saw a man caught so red-handed. There were three sharp witnesses to every one of his misdeeds.

This kind of lawsuit required more legal than oratorical skill, but in major private cases, for example testamentary disputes before the centumviral court with its large jury panels, there was more room for grandstanding and more reason to enlist the most powerful speakers. Indeed, this court continued to be a focus for public excitement in the imperial period, when political life had waned and criminal trials of importance had become less frequent.

Speakers gained the most publicity, however, from criminal trials. In the absence of public prosecutors, any respectable man could go to the *praetor* with a request to prosecute another, and once accepted by the *praetor*, file a charge summoning the accused to appear at an agreed time. Many a young man made his name by accusing a public figure, as Cicero's student Caelius did by his successful prosecution of Antonius Hybrida for provincial misgovernment. Indeed, it was virtually a duty for a young Roman to lay a charge if there was a family vendetta and to prosecute the man who had laid charge against his father. The reward went beyond the political silencing and exile of his enemy and could include promotion to the defeated enemy's status.[18] Even so, there was a greater reward in prestige and recognition. Yet only outsiders repeatedly used their eloquence to prosecute: men advancing in politics had too much to lose by making enemies, so that their reluctance to prosecute increased the ill odour of those who accused their fellow citizens.[19]

The key to glory was to defend the influential and to acquire a share of their influence. This service was expected of the best orators, who might find themselves under pressure to defend in several simultaneous trials. Lesser figures competed to demonstrate association with the élite, with the result that in some show trials of the fifties BCE four to six advocates defended one man. The network of family and career loyalties might bring sworn enemies like Cicero and Clodius to speak for the same personally undeserving defendant, such as Marcus Aemilius Scaurus, whose best feature was his famous father (Asc. Sc.).[20] But this was just before the breakdown of order led to Pompey's emergency legislation in 52 BCE. This imposed a shortened procedure to get through the mass of charges of public violence, eliminating adjournment to a second session, and fixing a maximum of two hours for the prosecutor's speech and three for the defending counsel (Asc. Mil.).

The Roman public played as large a part in these trials as the formal jury. Repeatedly Cicero speaks of the need to move the anger or sympathy not only of the upper-class jurors but also of the surrounding common citizens, whose hostility could affect and intimidate the jury. Quite apart from disturbances in the forum, such as passing funeral processions,[21] speakers had to cope with the competing noise of other trials and, in 52, squads of soldiers brought in to keep order in face of rioting.

One of Cicero's last speeches breaks all precedent: it is the *Pro Rege Deiotaro* of 45 BCE, spoken before Caesar as sole judge in his private house and in defence of a client king accused by a pretender to the throne of disloyalty to Caesar. This might more properly be called a *cognitio extra ordinem* (private legal hearing) than a court and is very close to the justice of the bedchamber described by Tacitus when emperors like Tiberius and Claudius heard charges of aristocratic disloyalty within their private suite. The chief difference lies in Caesar's shrewdness, as opposed to Tiberius' neurotic suspicions, and the blunders of Claudius, notorious for allowing his wives

121

and freedmen to manipulate the evidence and falling asleep while hearing it.[22]

THE PRINCIPATE: ORATORY IN AND OUTSIDE POLITICAL LIFE

With the principate there came a reduction of independent political oratory, which a traditionalist like Tacitus can both justify and deplore. His *Histories* show how the traditionalist senator Helvidius Priscus challenged a Neronian informer at the beginning of Vespasian's principate, affirming the senate's right to choose the representatives sent to the new emperor. On two occasions the informer put Helvidius in the wrong by accusing him of insulting and provoking the emperor and of trying to dominate the senate in the emperor's presence (4.7–8; 13). The natural insecurity of both senate and emperor led to the silencing, exile and later death of Helvidius.

Imperial power also affected judicial oratory: the new tendency was to move away from the major public courts to more private imperial hearings (*cognitiones*), which demanded a more technical kind of advocacy. The situation in an imperial *cognitio* can be compared with long-standing practice in Roman provinces during the republic: within their own provinces governors functioned autocratically, deciding both civil and criminal cases with a *consilium* that had only advisory capacity. Their absolute power meant that verdicts could be arbitrary personal reactions rather than inferences based on previous edicts or precedent. With a bad governor like Verres advocates could rely only on influence, bribery or appeals to mercy.

The evolving principate continued the growth of decision by decree in the provinces and brought an increase in the emperor's personal hearings at Rome. Indeed, the emperor was the court of first resort for offences committed by his freedmen or officials, the court before which came any offences against the emperor himself, and the court of last resort for appeal against the verdict of a regular magistrate or jury. Given the emperor's absolute authority and busy schedule, the procedure had to become more flexible. Fergus Millar notes that imperial hearings involved 'not only speeches on either side but verbal exchanges between [the emperor] and the parties'.[23] Quintilian cites instances of mutual accusation before the emperor and Suetonius remarks that Nero required disputants to argue point by point, thus eliminating continuous *actiones* (Quint. *Inst.* 7.2.20;

Suet. *Nero* 15; cf. Pliny *Ep.* 6.22.2). Professional advocates could speak for the defendant at any of these hearings, especially when senators were accused of treasonous activity or offences committed as governors; they also conducted the more complex lawsuits, and Crook rightly stresses the mass of low-profile cases in which Romans and provincials alike resorted to advocates to present their plea.[24]

Advocates were also needed to represent communities and corporations. Athens had been using its cultural leaders as envoys to Rome since at least 155 BCE;[25] in the sophistic revival of the second century CE civic ambassadors like Herodes Atticus of Athens or Polemon of Smyrna won fame by their eloquence as advocates as well as by their elegant public lectures. In the imperial province of Egypt petitioners for citizenship or those appealing against tax assessments could represent themselves like regular litigants, but regularly chose advocates to put their case.[26] Such private and domestic pleas could be appealed as far as the emperor. We get an inside view of the mixture of business coming before the emperor Trajan from the letters of Pliny, who served as an assessor at his judicial hearings: not only mutual accusations of fraud between officials but even cases of adultery came before the emperor (*Ep.* 6.22), who had to discourage the natural tendency of citizens to appeal to him over the heads of the regular courts.

But judicial eloquence still enjoyed a more public arena in civil and criminal cases, and two vignettes from Pliny's career as a lawyer reflect the negative and positive side of its changing circumstances. In one letter he complains of trivial cases and incompetent speakers 'mostly unknown young men who have arrived in our midst to practise rhetoric', and 'audiences no better than the speakers, being hired and bought for the occasion' (2.14). Another letter describes a cause célèbre: his speech for a daughter contesting her father's will before 180 judges, the grand combination of all four jury panels, with public seating packed with supporters and onlookers, and crowds overflowing the basilica, while spectators hung from the galleries above trying to hear (6.33 1–5).[27] Justice has moved indoors but the disturbances continue, like the shouting of the hired claque of Larcius Licinius that interrupted Pliny's pleading. Several of Pliny's letters describe his performance before the senate sitting as court over an offending provincial governor. It was a showcase trial, especially as the emperor Trajan, being consul, was presiding. Both Tacitus and Pliny were prosecuting (for the honour of the senate) and Pliny was allocated four extra water-clocks besides the twelve large ones. He is proud of speaking for almost five hours, even after Trajan had sent Pliny a message that he should spare his throat (2.11.10, 14–15). The outcome was probably a foregone conclusion, but Pliny polished his speech for publication as if it had the controversial impact of a Verrine oration.

Pliny's proudest day was another performance before the senate: his speech of thanks to Trajan, the *gratiarum actio*, known to posterity as the *Panegyricus*.[28] This was given in the first year after the new emperor returned from a campaign in the East to hold office as consul and to inaugurate the year. Trajan's recent return to Rome and Pliny's seniority as statesman and orator[29] gave an additional impact to the words in which he ostensibly praised but actually helped to determine the emperor's behaviour towards the senate, his supposed partner in government. But Pliny's extraordinary and elaborate speech[30] foreshadows the later imperial panegyrics, two forms of encomium with ancient roots in Hellenistic eloquence: the congratulation of a new ruler on his accession and the welcome given on his ceremonial arrival (the *adventus*) from abroad.

Let me end by focusing on the individual orator statesman in the period we have discussed. Pliny was atypical of his time: he represents the literary side of oratory and worked as hard on the written versions of his speeches after delivery as he had before the event, expanding them to clarify their context to an external audience and inviting his friends to criticize successive drafts. But this was not how the Romans judged oratory. Cicero echoes Demosthenes: performance was the first, second, and third most important factor of any speech (*De Or.* 3.213; *Orat.* 56). The good orator needed powerful lungs to make himself heard in the open, a commanding presence and eloquent gestures to convey his meaning to those at a distance, and a sense of theatre. The first-class speaker would know his client's case with both its strengths and weaknesses: he would have prepared not only an outline but most probably a verbatim text of at least his introduction and his final appeal; yet he would know how to deliver a prepared speech as if it were spontaneous and to improvise in response to the unexpected, turning a gesture or a witness's incidental comment against his opponent (*De Or.* 1.149–53; 2.99–103). Once in front of his audience he would play on it like an instrument, sensing its mood, entertaining it with humour or placating it with sympathy if the jury were weary from the ranting of the prosecution; he would conciliate it at the beginning, seize its attention by a clear and lively narrative of the facts, and wait until it was under his control before pulling out the stops of indignation or compassion (*De Or.* 1.153; *Brut.* 192–3, 322).

Two passages from Cicero's *Brutus* convey the scene in the forum, first when there is a poor speaker (200):

> The intelligent critic can often judge an orator at a glimpse in passing. . . . If he sees the jurors yawning, talking to each other, even getting up and walking round, asking to know the time and urging the presiding officer to adjourn, he will know without hearing a word that the case has no pleader who can apply his speech to the jurors' hearts, playing on them like the strings of a lyre.

Then the ideal. 'This' says Cicero, 'is what I wish for the orator' (290):

> When people hear he is going to speak, every place on the benches is taken, the judges' tribunal full, the scribes earning goodwill by assigning or giving up seats, a huge listening crowd, the jury eager and alert; when the speaker rises the whole crowd will ask for silence; then there will be frequent 'hear hears!' and cries of admiration; laughter when he wants it, or tears, so that the distant onlooker . . . will know a real star is on stage.

When Pliny commented that even the passer-by could be sure that 'the man who raises most cheers is the worst speaker' (*Ep.* 2.141), he was contrasting the taste of his own times with the age of Cicero. Both his and other voices suggest a coarsening of taste and a loss of critical attention.[31] Commenting on the death of the unscrupulous and flashy prosecutor Regulus, Pliny regrets that courtroom orators and audience alike now seem only concerned to get the case over; such is the disrespect for oratory and the defendant's fate (*in-reverentia studiorum periculorumve, Ep.* 6.2). The modernist orator Aper in Tacitus' *Dialogus de Oratoribus* claims that sophisticated contemporary audiences could not sit through the leisurely flow of Cicero's generation, but needed the stimulus of striking turns of phrase, the ancient equivalent of the sound-bite.[32] There were no burning political issues, only hope of entertainment. Even his adversary Maternus seems to agree that eloquence is becoming superfluous (*Dial.* 41.4):

What need is there for long senatorial speeches when the best policy is quickly agreed? What need for many harangues to the people when it is not the ignorant crowd that determines matters of state but a single wise man? What need of spontaneous accusations when offences are so few and so modest? What need of excessive and odious defence speeches when the mercy of the judge reaches out to those at risk?

Scholars have long debated how far Tacitus endorses Maternus' ironic portrait of a paradise where no voices need be raised or his vivid denunciation of the disordered public life of the crumbling republic, where the glory of eloquence was fostered by individualism beyond control.[33] For better or for worse this world with all its complexities could not be recalled. Pliny's world, if not more honest, seems at least nearer to our own, and certainly offered scope for workmanlike advocacy, but already the grandeur of high eloquence had little public function beyond the adorning of ceremonial. Henceforward all oratory would be in the service either of gods or the emperor. And in its dissemination and persistence the Christian sermon would outlast even panegyric.[34]

NOTES

1 Cf. Plaut. *Amph*. 38; *Mostell*. 1124–5; *Poen*. 358, 384; *Stich*. 291, 495 with Plautus' older contemporary Naevius using *orator* in the Greek political sense of *rhetor*: 'There was a crop of new-style speakers, silly young men' (Naev. fr. 107 [Warmington 1937: 110]).

2 For the *rhetores*, the regular speakers, cf. *Ach*. 38, 680.

3 Glaucon is not yet twenty years old.

4 The 'speeches' preserved in the corpus of Isocrates were texts in speech form composed for dissemination in writing, while the speeches of statesmen in Thucydides (as in other historians) are either pure invention or reconstruction. On 'improvised speech' in the assembly, see Williams 1951.

5 Regular meetings of the senate were presided over by the consuls of the year in alternate months, but could be held by a praetor. More exceptionally tribunes of the plebs could also summon the senate to present it with decisions of the assembly.

6 Days lawful for voting assemblies were fixed in the calendar and marked as *comitiales*: meetings were probably freer but not allowed on days that excluded public business (*nefasti*), public holidays, or whenever the senate was in session. All adult male citizens could attend assemblies, but in practice they were chiefly attended by politicians and their humbler partisans.

7 This is the context of Cicero's (now lost) speech *Pro Othone* in defence of the magistrate who had legislated privileged seating for the equestrian

upper class. When Cicero called the rioting audience away from the theatre to address them in the nearby temple precinct of Bellona, he must have used his lictors to stop the performance; see Coarelli 1968.

8 See Vasaly 1993: 81–7 (*signum Iovis*).

9 Cicero does not add that most senatorial debates would be preceded by private factional lobbying that would determine their outcome.

10 See Greenidge 1901: 269–70. The clearest evidence for this is the senatorial debate of December 63 reported by Sall. *Cat.* 50–3.

11 Cicero's corpus of fourteen *Philippic Orations* included one that was not delivered (*Phil.* 2).

12 See Malcovati 1975: 16 no. 4, 20–1. Cato's advocacy of the Spanish provincials' claims for compensation is described in Livy 43.2.1–12. For the forty-four prosecutions see Pliny *HN* 7.100.

13 See Jones 1972: 1–39. For eye-witness accounts see Cic. *QFr.* 2.3.3, 2.5(6)4 (Jones 1972: 8–9).

14 For the physical context of these assemblies, see David 1992: 18–41.

15 Crook 1995: 47.

16 For this and much of the ensuing discussion, see David 1992: 18–41.

17 Direct reward for a speaker from his client was forbidden at Rome by the *lex Cincia*, but during the republic speakers would be rewarded for their services by 'loans' and legacies from grateful clients. By the time of the emperor Claudius (41–54 CE), the only issue was the scale of reward permitted.

18 See Alexander 1985.

19 Gentlemen did not prosecute; cf. Cic. *Off.* 2.49–51 and *De Or.* 2.220–3 on the ill-famed prosecutor Brutus. In Cicero's only prosecution – that of Verres when he was a 35-year-old candidate for the aedileship – he presents his role largely as defensive, championing the victimized Sicilian provincials and vindicating the honour of the senate.

20 His six *patroni* were Cicero, Hortensius, Milo, Faustus, Memmius and Clodius. Only the first two were orators, and Cicero and Clodius were sworn enemies. In *Brut.* 108 Cicero points out the flaws of a system in which a defending counsel might not have heard either his fellow advocates or the accusers.

21 See Cic. *De Or.* 2.225 and 288 for speakers' witty exploitation of these solemn distractions.

22 Cf. Sen. *Apocol.* 12; Tac. *Ann.* 10–12 (the surviving Claudian books of Tacitus).

23 Millar 1977: 236–40, 517–27, here 236.

24 Crook 1995: 53–4, 60–1.

25 In that year the Heads of the Academic, Peripatetic and Stoic schools were sent to Rome to represent Athens' case against Oropus before the senate and people (Cic. *De Or.* 2.155, Gell. *NA* 6.14).

26 On papyrus evidence for advocacy, see Crook 1995: 58–118; on traditional legal documents see Crook 1995: 119–71. A bilingual inscription in *SEG* 17 no. 759 (discussed by Crook 1995: 91–4) records in Latin the dispute of the people of Gohara in Syria with their tax collector before the emperor Caracalla, but both sides employ Greek-speaking advocates, whose speeches are recorded in Greek (cf. Millar 1977: 535).

27 The case, a *querela inofficiosi testamenti* ('protesting an undutiful will'), was an élite scandal, since the 80-year-old father had left his estate to a new young wife.

28 The recent study of Bartsch 1994: 148–87 shows how difficult the previous practice or necessity of insincere praise had made Pliny's task.

29 Pliny would not be the first to thank Trajan for his honour, since all incoming consuls now offered thanks to the emperor who had nominated them, just as they had once thanked the gods for their election.

30 Pliny's *Epistles* (3.13, 18) show that the written text is a deliberate expansion of the original performance with an eye to posterity, remodelled and tested by the orator in a series of private readings to his patient friends.

31 For William Dominik's more favourable estimate of the change that had taken place in both audience and speaker since the rise of the declamation schools and the loss of occasions of relative political substance, see Chapter 4.

32 The *Dialogus* is a subtle and complex discussion of the changes in the orator's career and the public role of oratory since the coming of the principate; its dramatic date in Tacitus' youth conceals a later date of composition, probably just after the assassination of Domitian. Murgia 1980 suggests 97 CE (after Quintilian's *Institutio Oratoria* but before the *Panegyricus* of Tacitus' friend Pliny).

33 See, e.g., Köhnken 1973; Williams 1978: 26–49; Heldmann 1980: 12–19; Fantham 1989a: 282–6; Luce 1993; Bartsch 1994: 106ff.

34 I would like to thank Gualtiero Calboli and Emmanuele Narducci for the stimulus I have received from their work and in discussion with them.

Part III

RHETORIC AND GENRE

8

Towards a rhetoric of (Roman?) epic

Joseph Farrell

My aim is to examine the context in which the rhetorical aspect of Roman epic is discussed and to suggest that a widening of that context is in order. The title expresses a particular view of the matter: not 'rhetoric *in* epic', that is, elements of an alien discursive system that have somehow made their way into the epic genre, but rather 'the rhetoric *of* epic', something intrinsic to the genre that is nevertheless cognate with the 'communications protocols' that operate in other genres as well. This approach is intended to advance a growing reaction against the still not uncommon belief that most Roman epic has indeed been adversely influenced by external elements and as a result is 'too rhetorical' and so 'unpoetic'. I will begin by examining some of the factors commonly used to articulate the histories of epic and of rhetoric, respectively, then move on to consider the methods by which influential scholars have framed the relationship between epic and rhetoric, and conclude by calling for a somewhat different approach. The direction of this approach is suggested in part by my treatment in the title of the word 'Roman', by which I mean to cast doubt on whether the rhetoric of epic can be neatly divided into familiar national or linguistic categories. It is with this point that I begin.

GREEK AND ROMAN, 'GOLD' AND 'SILVER': THE NOT-QUITE-PARALLEL HISTORIES OF EPIC AND RHETORIC

The distinction between Greek and Roman seems like a natural one, but in practice it is very difficult to draw clearly. This is especially true in the realm of literature – where, however, the obvious and

irreducible difference between the Greek and Latin languages apparently inspires a false confidence in the success of the effort.

In both areas of immediate concern, the distinction between Greek
and Roman has sometimes been figured approximately as one
between 'primary' and 'secondary' phases, a formulation applied first
to epic poetry and then to the history of rhetoric.[1] Primary epic is
folk epic or oral epic, secondary epic a self-conscious literary
imitation of the oral variety. By the same token, the business of
primary rhetoric is direct persuasion of an audience via the spoken
word. In secondary rhetoric it is not, or not only, persuasion that the
speaker or, more commonly, the writer has in mind. He also wants
the audience (or readership) to savour his handling of the means of
persuasion themselves. His product might be characterized as an
imitation of an utterance intended to persuade. As in the case of epic,
so with rhetoric, the secondary phase, whatever its excellences, is
often felt to be a less authentic than and, in some respects, even a
debased form of the original.

Of course the great oral epics of classical antiquity and the first
application of rhetorical theory to the business of persuading one's
fellow citizens belong to archaic and classical Greece; the corresponding literary versions one associates with imperial Rome. But the
distinction between primary and secondary phases of both rhetoric
and epic does not conform to a simple distinction between Greek
and Roman culture. The conditions necessary to produce a culture
of secondary rhetoric certainly existed in the Hellenistic period. The
Asianist movement would seem to be one manifestation, 'tragic
history' another.[2] It is clear, moreover, that Hellenistic poetry
displays a kind of fascination with the technologies of writing and
the possibilities that arise from translating a once oral art into scribal
form.[3] George Kennedy is undoubtedly correct in observing that the
writers of imperial Rome went well beyond their Hellenistic predecessors in cultivating technical rhetoric as a literary art form.[4] At
the same time, it seems obvious that the intellectual climate of the
Hellenistic period had more in common with the culture of 'secondary rhetoric' that prevailed under the Roman empire than with the
culture of 'primary rhetoric' that obtained in the classical *polis*.

What, then, of the epic? In a study of speeches in Greek epic, Peter
Toohey draws a clear distinction between Homer and Apollonius on
the grounds that they use and represent formal speeches in very
different ways. Briefly, Toohey finds that in Homer speeches are (1)
frequent, (2) often lengthy, (3) formally and technically elaborate in

ways that anticipate later, technical rhetoric, (4) 'positive, outwardly directed, and expectantly ameliorative',[5] that is, they generally represent speakers as trying to influence in definite and productive ways the actions of some other character(s). In sharp contrast to all this, speeches in Apollonius are (1) relatively rare, (2) generally brief, (3) clearly structured, but otherwise unprepossessing in formal respects, (4) reflective of 'an interiorisation typified by hesitance, inwardly turned anger, guile and passivity'[6] illustrating a belief that words have little power to effect change and that events merely happen as a result of forces outside human control. These findings are based on an acute, untendentious reading of the evidence and accord well with what is generally known about these two poets. On these grounds, Toohey's argument seems reliable.

Pressing the evidence a bit harder, Toohey raises some troubling questions to which no easy answers are forthcoming. First, he attempts to correlate his findings with the distinction between primary and secondary epic, which he (as others have done) frames explicitly as a difference between 'orality' and 'literacy'. Toohey suggests that literacy actually begets the attitude that he labels 'interiorisation' and so correlates Apollonius' tendency to avoid representations of speech with both literacy and 'the possibly related change in *mentalité*' of the Hellenistic world.[7]

Avoidance of representing direct speech, Toohey notes, persists beyond Apollonius to the Greek epic of the imperial period, just as one would expect if literacy were its cause; but 'it does not [persist] in Roman epic (which, curiously enough, is probably the result of the Roman taste for rhetoric)'.[8] Curious, indeed. The conditions of literacy that obtained during the Hellenistic period were surely duplicated and perhaps exceeded in Roman times.[9] Evidence from Roman epic lies beyond the scope of Toohey's essay, but because this evidence bears on the idea that orality and literacy are important factors in distinguishing between the primary and secondary phases of both epic and rhetoric, it seems worthwhile to take up the comparison here.

The evidence involves us in a double conundrum. If it is valid to distinguish between Greek and Roman epic with respect to rhetoric, then we ought to find resemblances involving Homer and Apollonius, but excluding Vergil, Lucan, and other Roman poets. As Toohey shows, however, the differences between Homer and Apollonius are pronounced. His results do not encourage one to speak of 'the rhetoric of Greek epic'. If on the other hand rhetorical analysis can distinguish between primary (oral) and secondary (literary) epic, then we ought to find similarities involving Apollonius and Vergil (and Nonnus, Quintus, Statius and the rest), but excluding Homer. Such a finding would discourage one from speaking of 'the rhetoric of Roman epic' as well, though the case against this idea would be slightly different from the one that Toohey implicitly makes against the corresponding Greek category.

A few such similarities do in fact exist, but there is conflicting evidence as well. First, representations of speech occupy almost twice as much of the Homeric poems as they do of the *Argonautica*, and second, they occur almost twice as frequently in Homer as compared with Apollonius.[10] With these striking differences Toohey convincingly correlates the differences in purpose or attitude – 'interiorisation', 'guile', and so forth – that I mentioned above. If however we take the measure of later epics, Greek and Roman, the result is rather more miscellaneous. Quintus is like Apollonius, only more so: speeches occupy an even smaller amount of his text and occur less frequently than in the *Argonautica*. But Roman epic on the whole seems to 'move back' in the direction of Homer, at least part of the way: about one-third of the text of all Roman epic from Vergil to Silius is given over to speeches. On this basis one might form a preliminary hypothesis that Roman epic, unlike Hellenistic and imperial Greek epic, resembles Homer in the representation of speech, either in spite of its literary character or because of 'the Roman taste for rhetoric'. But the frequency with which these epics represent speech differs greatly from Homer and very little from what we find in Apollonius and Quintus.[11] On this basis, one might form the opposite hypothesis, that Roman epic, *like* Hellenistic and imperial Greek epic, *differs* from Homer in the representation of speech, either *because of* its literary character or *in spite of* 'the Roman taste for rhetoric'.

One additional fact stands out. Nonnus and Lucan differ sharply from all other epic poets in two respects. First, they introduce speeches only about half as frequently as do all the others; second, whereas the average length of a speech in all other epic poets from Homer onwards is between eleven and thirteen lines, in these two poets speeches average twice that length, or twenty-five and twenty-two lines, respectively. Because the speeches in Nonnus and Lucan are half as frequent, but twice as long, the proportion of text that the two poets devote to them is about the same as we find in most of their fellows. But in their predilection for fewer, longer speeches, they stand out from the rest and, just as obviously, resemble each other. Further, if we move on from bare quantitative measures to a more critical characterization, it is debatable whether Nonnus resembles Apollonius in showing the quality of 'interiorisation typified by hesitance, inwardly turned anger, guile and passivity'; but there is no question about Lucan. These are in fact Lucan's defining characteristics; the formulation might have been penned specifically to describe not the *Argonautica*, but the *Pharsalia*. Lucan displays this quality not, however, like Apollonius, in short, 'unrhetorical' speeches, but in long, florid, highly impressive set-pieces – just the opposite of what one finds in the *Argonautica*.

Taking all this into account, we find that the rhetorical differences among the epic poems of antiquity do not conform neatly to the categories 'Greek' and 'Roman' or 'oral' and 'literary'. Some Greek epics differ sharply from one another, as do some Roman ones. Some Greek and Roman epics resemble one another in expected and unexpected ways. Some literary epics resemble oral ones in certain ways more than they resemble other literary epics. In general, it seems that the rhetorical similarities and differences between individual epics – if for the moment we define 'rhetorical' as 'having to do with the representation of speech' – are more pronounced than any that may exist between groups, such as Greek and Roman or oral and literary epic.

There is an additional factor that challenges the idea of a Roman epic defined by rhetoric, one that is nearly ubiquitous in the secondary literature – a factor that drives a wedge between the various poems commonly defined as 'Roman epic' in much the same way that Apollonius differs from Homer. 'The Roman taste for rhetoric' may be taken to refer chiefly to the taste of the so-called 'silver age'. Most handbooks and histories of literature regard the development in this period of 'the first truly rhetorical literature' as anything but a glowing achievement. Instead, they habitually blame the pervasive influence of rhetoric for the supposedly inferior quality of the poetry produced at that time. Censure is distributed unevenly, of course, and perhaps unfairly. Juvenal, for all his 'excesses', was much admired by later satirists. Martial, though lacking most of the qualities associated with poetry in modern times, is admitted to have been the consummate master of a minor form, the epigram. Even Seneca, roundly abused by many, has his admirers and wins points for his decisive influence on the formal structure of later European tragic drama. Epic, however, is another matter.

Of the four epic poets who lived in the first century CE, only two, Lucan and Statius, enjoyed much of a *Nachleben*. In the Middle Ages, they became curriculum authors and into the Renaissance they had their admirers and imitators. But in modern times, they have become almost unknown except to scholars, and even in the academy their reputation always seems to need defending. The most common charge is that they are not true poets, but mere rhetoricians. While they are perceived to share this fault with the other poets of their age, there are apparently no circumstances sufficient to mitigate the judgement against them, as in the case of Juvenal, Martial, and Seneca. Thus the poetry of the 'silver age' most belaboured by the charge of being 'too rhetorical' is, undoubtedly, the epic.

The 'pernicious' influence of rhetoric on Latin poetry is generally accounted for as follows. Under the empire, opportunities for free speech disappeared. At the same time, and perhaps as a consequence, the educational system, largely based on rhetoric to begin with, turned its attention from the goal of persuasion to the elaboration of the art itself. Trained minds naturally demanded some outlet for their talents. For some, poetry was the first choice, but rhetoric had become an almost reflexive mode of expression and overwhelmed their poetic sensibility. Others would have preferred to speak in the forum and the curia; but because political oratory was so dangerous, they turned to various literary forms such as tragedy and epic, to which they brought formidable, even overdeveloped, rhetorical powers, but little feeling for poetry.

In this view we find vestiges of several different theories of cultural development. Kennedy remarks on the apparently automatic tendency of primary rhetoric to mutate into secondary rhetoric, and notes that this process is abetted when the conditions that favour open public discourse disappear or are curtailed.[12] On this view, the Roman republic should be characterized as a culture of primary rhetoric, the precursor of an imperial period characterized by a culture of secondary rhetoric. And the history of rhetoric is usually written in just these terms. It is certainly true that the republic was characterized by *libertas* (free speech), and that critics of imperial culture, notably Tacitus, contrasted the conditions under which they lived with those of republican times in precisely this way. But according to Kennedy, primary rhetoric is characteristic of an oral culture. Can we maintain that the Roman republic of the first century BCE was in some sense an oral culture and that the secondary rhetoric of the empire was a symptom of literacy?

Obviously we are now dealing with orality and literacy in a different sense than the absolute one employed by, for example, some Homerists. It is at least theoretically possible to maintain that the Homeric poems can only be the product of a preliterate culture. But it is in fact very difficult to maintain that there exists an absolute difference between oral and literate cultures. The technologies of orality and literacy may be employed in varying combinations for many different purposes and by different groups within a single cultural milieu, and this raises serious questions both about the 'oral' or 'literate' character in general of any given culture, and even about whether such distinctions can be made.

Tying primary rhetoric to speech virtually necessitates some effort to make this distinction. The birthplace of classical rhetoric was, in effect, fifth-century Athens, where writing had been in use for centuries and which has been adduced as the prime example of a culture moving from 'orality' to 'literacy' thanks to increasing use of the technologies of writing.[13] Lately, however, arguments have been made with increasing frequency that the use of writing at Athens, though by no means unusual, had not by the end of the fifth century given rise to an exclusively or uniformly 'literate' culture and that aspects of an 'oral' culture continued to exist.[14] The standard historical accounts of rhetoric at Rome require that we view the culture of the late republic in much the same way.[15] If we do so, at least some of the difficulties we have encountered in distinguishing on rhetorical grounds between primary and secondary epic might be removed. It is thus worth asking whether the Roman poetry we have from the first century BCE can plausibly be regarded as the product of a culture that is predominantly oral rather than literate.

Such a view of course would be difficult to maintain. True, the Roman tradition of free speech had not yet died, but by the late republic Latin poetry had begun to cultivate an intricate, cunning aesthetic that owed at least as much to Hellenistic Alexandria as to the atmosphere of the Roman forum. Indeed, the poetry of the late republican and Augustan periods is universally regarded as a poetry of reflection and meditation, one that does not strive for immediate impact but instead discloses meaning through repeated exposure, often eluding decisive interpretation. Ovid, on the other hand, is frequently regarded as ushering in an era during which poetry was emptied of any meaning apart from immediate effect. Seneca and Lucan are the other poets most frequently cited as examples of this phenomenon, which is held to be emblematic of the entire 'silver age'.[16] Indeed, one scholar has advanced a novel theory according to which the poets of the so-called 'golden age' employed a variety of specific rhetorical figures that lent their poetry a distinct character and a level of quality that neither earlier nor later poetry could match.[17] It does not matter whether this contribution to the history of rhetoric is correct. But I would say that it represents accurately the fact that republican and Augustan poetry may in some ways be even 'more rhetorical' or, at least, more deviously rhetorical than the poetry of the early empire, eschewing direct persuasion and demanding iterative exposure, meditation, and reflection. And if this is so, I would ask, which sort of poetry would seem to be more representative of an oral, which of a literate, culture?

The terms of our discussion are dissolving before our eyes. Rhetorical considerations have disrupted the apparent unity of the categories 'Greek epic' and 'Roman epic' and have complicated the apparently clear distinction between 'oral epic' and 'literary epic'. Indeed, the supposed dichotomy between orality and literacy raises serious questions about using the history of rhetoric as an instrument of generic analysis. I would be willing to conclude from the discussion so far that the history of the epic cannot be written in terms of the history of rhetoric. Beyond this I would observe that the effort to do so is, despite its impossibility, extremely instructive in that it raises significant questions about the validity of distinctions commonly drawn between primary and secondary phases in the histories of both epic and rhetoric on the basis of a distinction between orality and literacy. Specifically, the evidence from epic lends support to those who have questioned the technological determinist approach.

SIC ORE PROFATUS, ETC., OR STUDYING SPEECHES IN EPIC POETRY

In the previous section, I provisionally defined 'rhetorical', for the purposes of the student of epic, as 'having to do with the representation of speech'. In this respect I was following most others who have written on 'epic and rhetoric', especially those who have studied the Roman material. It is obviously in some respects a valid and indeed valuable approach. But it is surprising to find that there exists no book, no article dealing with the relationship between epic and rhetoric *in toto*. What we do have is a number of monographs devoted to speeches in the individual epic poems. Many of these studies are instructive in all sorts of important ways, but one must ask: is the subject 'epic and rhetoric' best framed as 'representations of speech making and persuasion in particular epic poems'?

The author most intensively studied from this angle is Homer; the impulse behind this type of investigation, however, is concerned with Homer not as an epic poet, but as a proto-rhetorician. Greek rhetoric developed as a formal *technê* in the classical period. Our sources for the kind of speeches that the Greeks actually made before this period are few. Homer, who frequently represents his characters as speaking publicly and privately in a variety of circumstances, is our most important single source for those traditional habits of speech that contributed to the formal systems of rhetoric developed in later times. Thus the study of speeches in Homer can make a significant contribution to the history of rhetoric and, indeed, to European intellectual history.

To study speeches in the Roman epics is quite a different matter. The approach most scholars have taken involves assessing epic speeches in terms of the fully developed rhetoric that we know had characterized the Roman educational system for generations before any of these poems was written. Thus studying speeches in, say, Lucan differs greatly from studying speeches in Homer. The history of rhetoric in the Roman period, unlike the history of rhetoric in preclassical Greece, can be written on the basis of much better and more plentiful sources than are provided by epic poetry. Unlike 'the speeches in Homer', 'the speeches in Roman epic' occupy no more than a small and relatively unimportant chapter in a history of rhetoric.

One might, of course, study the speeches in later epic to illustrate how specific developments in rhetoric or rhetorical culture influenced their form, content, or purpose. This is the basis of the handbook bromide characterizing Roman epic as 'too rhetorical'. But among specialists, the most common reason for studying the speeches in Roman epic points in exactly the opposite direction. These scholars are aware, and painfully so, that extensive training in formal rhetoric is common to all the Roman epic poets, and that it is largely for this reason that these poets have been scorned. In fact, most if not all who have studied 'the speeches in . . .' have done so in order to prove that their author is not *merely* a rhetorician, but is in fact a poet. This procedure is perfectly understandable as a response to a significant body of opinion that condemns the poets in question for their rhetoric. The findings reached often illuminate the poems themselves. But a defense of these poems based on the study of the speeches that they contain seems to me incapable of achieving what is intended. The modern feeling that Roman epic became too rhetorical has nothing to do with the number or kinds of speeches found in the individual poems. To revert momentarily to statistical measures, we know for instance that far more of the *Iliad* than of the *Pharsalia* consists of direct speech.[18] This information is unlikely to persuade a modern reader that Lucan is less rhetorical than Homer. As for the argument that the speeches in, say, Statius are handled appropriately, and therefore serve poetic ends, this is to invoke a consummately rhetorical criterion, that of *to prepon* ('propriety'). On this basis one might argue that an author is a better or worse rhetorician, but not whether he is more a rhetorician or a poet.

At this point it becomes necessary to face up to a complicating issue. In discussing any aspect of Roman epic, one has to deal somehow with the Vergil factor. Whatever we say about Lucan, Statius, Silius, or Valerius, Vergil is usually felt to belong in a slightly, or even a radically, different category. Rhetoric is no exception.

The most ambitious modern study of Vergilian rhetoric remains Gilbert Highet's study of the speeches in the *Aeneid*. Highet was perhaps the first to frame a study of any epic poet as a defense against the charge of being a rhetorician, his point of departure being the opinion of ancient scholars who actually did regard Vergil not just as a rhetorician, but as an orator. This trend evidently began early: indeed, the title of Highet's concluding chapter is borrowed from the second-century dialogue of P. Annius Florus, *Vergilius Orator an Poeta?*[19] How Florus answered the question is unknown; but by the time of Servius and Macrobius, as Highet documents, Vergilius Orator was very much in the ascendant, and for Donatus he had won the field.[20] This conception was long-lived, and has recently been studied via the reception of the *Aeneid* in the Renaissance.[21]

In spite of this impressive continuity, however, ancient opinion regarding Vergil's status as an orator is not the same as modern anxiety about the excessively rhetorical nature of Roman epic. Highet is in a sense tilting at a straw man, arguing against scholars like Donatus because he could find no contemporary classicist whom he could saddle with the opinion that Vergil is a 'mere rhetorician'. Modern critics do not worry so much that Vergil in particular is 'too rhetorical' and therefore not sufficiently 'poetic'; it is the later epic poets who labor under this charge. Indeed, Highet is happy to contrast Vergil with Lucan (and especially Ovid) on just this score.[22] But here continuity between ancient and modern opinion may be only apparent. Quintilian, for instance, remarks that 'Lucan is fiery, impetuous, and really outstanding for his epigrams – more a model, to state my own opinion, for orators than for poets' (*Lucanus ardens et concitatus et sententiis clarissimus et, ut dicam quod sentio, magis oratoribus quam poetis imitandus, Inst.* 10.1.90). Mark Morford takes him to mean that 'the antithesis between poets and orators implies that he who is the one forfeits claim to be the other as well'.[23] But it is not at all clear that Quintilian places poetry and rhetoric in a hierarchical relationship, as so many modern critics have done. Nor, if he did, would he necessarily agree with modern critics in according poetry the higher place.[24] In fact Quintilian's thumbnail sketches of the poets, though they provide perennial fodder for final examinations and the like, tell us very little, and it is wrong to put much weight on them – particularly when Quintilian's interest in poetry as such is so limited. In the present case, I would be tempted to argue that the judgment pronounced on Lucan by the world's first professor of Roman rhetoric is high praise indeed: the *Pharsalia* is an even better model for orators than it is for poets. What greater compliment could Quintilian bestow?

Is it, then, in fact the case that our modern perception of a difference between, say, Vergil and Lucan receives warrant from Quintilian? If so, the warrant is highly qualified, since Quintilian actually admires Lucan as a model for orators; but not more than he admires the author of the *Aeneid*. Against more than 100 citations of Vergil in the *Institutio Oratoria* (no one but Cicero himself appears more frequently), Lucan is *mentioned* only in this one passage! Many reasons besides Quintilian's personal opinion help to account for this, not least the fact that at the time of Lucan's death there existed almost a century's worth of Vergilian scholarship on which to draw; and on the evidence of Quintilian alone, a good deal of this scholarship must have concerned Vergil's excellence in oratory. It was, furthermore, not long after Quintilian wrote, and not long after the 'rhetorical' epics of Statius, Valerius, and Silius had appeared, that Florus posed the question whether Vergil was more a poet or an orator. Was Florus' essay inspired by a perception that epic after Vergil had become too much like oratory? If so, are the later poets being defended against this charge by the argument that Vergil himself was more an orator than a poet? Or is the inquiry actually a defense of the old master, who must be argued to have written an epic every bit as oratorically spectacular as those of his fashionable successors? The fact is we simply don't know. What we probably do know is that, while ancient critics did draw some sort of distinction between poetry and oratory, they almost certainly did not do so to the detriment of either. The question is 'academic' in the vulgar sense; and to imagine that Quintilian or any other Roman critic would have devalued Vergil, Lucan, or any other epic poet for being 'too rhetorical' also depends on the modern Romantic notion that poetry must be a truthful or at least a sincere utterance, as well as on another vulgar usage, one that equates 'rhetoric' with 'lies'.

Thus the habit of distinguishing Vergil from his epic successors on the grounds that he is a poet, while they are mere rhetoricians, receives little if any support from the ancient critics, and a good deal of opposition. If anything, it was apparently felt in antiquity that Vergil was more of a rhetorician than they. Thus the tendency to distinguish later epics from the *Aeneid* on rhetorical grounds, while practically universal and apparently founded on ancient criticism, upon inspection is found open to question.

The final point to be made under this heading is that rhetoric in the epic is not confined to speeches. Whatever we find 'too rhetorical' in Roman epic appears in narrative and descriptive passages as well as in direct speech. This is an obvious point, but it needs making because it is not adequately reflected in the existing scholarship. The only real exception is Morford, who studies the speeches in Lucan's *Pharsalia* as only a part of the poem's overall rhetorical character. Why more students of Roman epic have not followed this approach is a great mystery. The rhetoric of historical writing appears not just in set speeches, but in narrative and descriptive passages as well, to name only the most plentiful components of the genre. Students of historiography have come to appreciate this fact.[25] Epic poetry also consists not merely of direct speech, but of narration, description, and other elements, all of which are composed on rhetorical principles. It is true that most of the rhetorical handbooks we possess concern themselves with oratory, and with judicial oratory at that. But even if we confine ourselves to the ancient handbooks, the importance of *narratio* is clear. Despite the bias of these sources, the basic materials from which one might piece together a facsimile of an ancient rhetoric of Roman epic lie ready to hand.

142

CONCLUSIONS

The most obvious conclusions that suggest themselves are negative. First, it is not clear that Greek and Roman epic differ categorically with respect to rhetoric. Second, the same is true of the distinction between 'oral' and 'literary' epic, which is to say, between Homer and everyone else. Third, it is not at all clear that received notions concerning Vergil's superiority as a poet over his epic successors who labored under the pernicious influence of rhetoric run wild receives any support from an examination of ancient attitudes; scholarly expressions of such opinion in fact reflect nothing other than simple modernist prejudice. Fourth, those who study the rhetoric of epic should look beyond formal aspects of the representation of speech in order to account fully and accurately for the rhetorical aspects of epic precisely as constitutive generic elements.

How may this be accomplished? In general, it seems far from clear that the historical study of the ancient *ars rhetorica* affords the most useful perspective. Whatever scholars say about the rhetorical qualities of epic poetry in Latin does not differ substantially from what they say about other genres of prose or poetry. Imperial epic in particular is commonly held to be 'too rhetorical'; but so in varying degrees are imperial tragedy, satire, historiography, epistolography, and so on. I have argued that critical assessment of the epic has been less favorable than in the case of other genres for specific historical reasons, but negative judgments about the influence of rhetoric pertain to the entire period, not just to any individual genre. If adverse judgments about the literature of the early empire need to be questioned, then the study of rhetoric in the epic will be only a part of this effort. But maintaining the idea that the supposedly inferior quality of this literature is the result of developments in the history of rhetoric can only be an obstacle to any critical re-assessment of epic in particular.

Rather than seeking answers from the history of rhetoric outside the genre, it seems more profitable to direct our attention to the genre itself. I noted at the beginning of this chapter that I prefer to frame the subject not as 'rhetoric in the epic' but as 'the rhetoric of epic', that is, as the study of something intrinsic to the genre rather than (as I regard the study of specific types of speech in the epic) the study of something possessing an independent existence imported into the genre from without. I propose that we begin by eliminating, or at least de-emphasizing, the parameters that have received such prominence heretofore. The evidence we have seen suggests that this study should be stretched to include, at the least, both Greek and Roman epic. It is to this body of literature, I believe, rather than to so narrow (and prejudicially defined) a sample as 'silver Latin epic' that a rhetorically informed approach would best be applied. In addition, a synchronic perspective – which is nothing other than a generic perspective – ought to form the basis for studying the rhetoric of epic. Only from this perspective can a rhetoric internal to any given genre be discerned. It is true that the synchronic approach fails to address the questions that have dominated this field so far, questions that can be articulated only on a diachronic axis. The problem, however, is that the diachronic approach has traditionally – as is true, by the way, in the study of classical rhetoric as a whole – taken only one form, one that is admittedly important, but hardly all-important. This form involves the historical development of technical rhetoric as an independent discipline and the search for traces of its 'impact' or 'influence' on various aspects of classical culture of various times. If we regard rhetoric as a discrete discursive system with its own technical basis and historical development, then Roman epic obviously ought to differ from Greek, mainly for the banal reason that it is later. But in fact, as we have seen, it is not easy to demonstrate that this is in fact the case.

It follows also that a synchronically framed study of rhetoric in epic poetry or any other ancient literary genre need not be limited to the rhetorical systems actually articulated in antiquity. Like any other tool of literary criticism, rhetoric may be used to study the historical circumstances under which the literature in question was produced, or it may be used ahistorically to answer questions formulated with the critic's own interests primarily in view. Modern rhetorical theory is built largely on ancient foundations, but addresses itself to aspects of communication that are only dimly adumbrated or even ignored by ancient theorists. Both approaches are valid, and the insights of some modern rhetoricians actually suit the study of ancient poetry more closely than their ancient counterparts. It is true, as Brian Vickers has recently lamented, that the name of rhetoric is often invoked illegitimately by writers seeking to borrow prestige for what is often a highly idiosyncratic type of literary study.[26] But some modern rhetorics are in fact systematic, rigorous efforts to articulate important aspects of the structures within which communication takes place.[27] To be sure, some first steps have been taken, but a thoroughgoing 'Rhetoric of Epic' remains to be written.[28]

NOTES

1 Epic: Bowra 1945: 1–32; Lord 1960: 3–12; Finnegan 1977; Zumthor 1990; rhetoric: Kennedy 1972 xv *et passim*; Kennedy 1987: 3–6, 108–19.
2 Asianism: Kennedy 1963: 301–2 with further references; 'tragic history': Walbank 1972: 32–65.
3 Bing 1988.
4 Kennedy 1987: 111–13.
5 Toohey 1994: 154.
6 Toohey 1994: 169.
7 Toohey 1994: 170.
8 Toohey 1994: 170.
9 Hellenistic Greeks: Harris 1989: 325; Rome: Harris 1989: 325–6; cf. Harris 1989: 283–4. Note that Harris makes a (convincing) 'pessimistic' case against the existence of anything approaching mass literacy in the ancient world. For a somewhat more 'optimistic' approach see Beard *et al.* 1991.
10 The statistics that follow are based on Elderkin 1906: 6 and Lipscomb 1909: 15, where exact figures may be found.
11 In Homer speeches occur once every 21 lines (47/1000) as against once every 41 lines (25/1000) in Apollonius, once every 50 lines (20/1000) in Quintus, once every 37 lines (27/1000) in Vergil, Lucan, Statius, Valerius and Silius.
12 Kennedy 1987: 5, 110–19.
13 Goody and Watt 1963.
14 Havelock 1963; cf. Havelock 1982; Havelock 1986. The case is developed further, with greater sensitivity to the problem of technological determinism, by Thomas 1989 and 1992, with an excellent summary in the latter of scholarship in this field on pp. 15–28; cf. Robb 1994.
15 Harris 1989: 326–7; Thomas 1992: 158–70 emphasizes the similarity of rhetorical practices in both Greek and Latin linguistic milieux in the republican and imperial eras (pp. 159–61).
16 More recent work on Ovid (Hinds 1987a; Hinds 1987b), Lucan (Henderson 1987; Masters 1992) and Statius (Ahl 1986; Dominik 1994) in particular suggests that adverse assumptions about the depth of reading and reflection that these texts will support have been made much too easily.
17 Williams 1980.
18 The figures are 44 per cent for the *Iliad* (according to Elderkin 1906: 6) as against 32 per cent for the *Pharsalia* (according to Lipscomb 1909: 15).
19 Edited and translated by Jal 1967: 97–120.
20 Highet 1972: 3–8.
21 Kallendorf 1989.
22 Highet 1972: 47, 280–2, 346.
23 Morford 1967: ix.
24 Kennedy 1987: 114–16.
25 Woodman 1988 offers intelligent general commentary on the rhetoric of

historiography, exemplary analyses of individual texts, and references to further studies.

26 Vickers 1988: 435–79, esp. 438–69. I do not agree with Vickers' blanket condemnation of the titular formula 'The Rhetoric of . . .'. I do agree with him, however, that such a title leads the reader to expect a work of a particular rigor and scope, and that one is often disappointed in the result.

27 Booth 1961; cf. Booth 1974a; Booth 1974b. Within classical studies one can point to Conte 1986; Leach 1988.

28 duBois 1982; Wofford 1992; Johnson 1994.

9

Declamation and contestation in satire

Susanna Morton Braund

Have I got to stay on the receiving end forever? Won't I ever
get my revenge? . . .

Juvenal, Satire 1.1

What makes the speaker of Juvenal's opening satire so angry and so
intent on revenge is the continual outpouring of poetry that is (he
claims) inflicted on him everywhere he goes. The situation is so bad
that he has decided to join in. His qualifications (15–18):

> I too have felt the master's cane on my hand. I too
> have given Sulla advice, to retire into a deep
> siesta. No point in sparing paper (it's already doomed to
> destruction) when you run into all those 'bards' everywhere.

According to Juvenal's speaker, a training in rhetoric is the sole
qualification for be(com)ing a poet. The reference to rhetoric is
specifically a reference to the education received by Roman school-
boys, an education in which corporal punishment (the 'cane' here)
clearly played a part. The final stage of this education was devoted
to public speaking, which followed the Greek system on which it
was modelled in dividing public speaking into three types of oratory:
judicial, deliberative and epideictic. Judicial oratory, also called
forensic oratory (because the Roman law-courts met in the forum),
consisted of speeches of prosecution and defence in cases being heard
in the courts. Deliberative oratory involved making speeches advising or urging or rejecting a proposed course of action in the Senate,
for example, or any other body making such decisions. And epideictic (Greek: 'display') oratory consisted chiefly of speeches of
praise (also called panegyrical and encomiastic speeches) about a god
or an individual or a city or about a public building such as a temple.

The training in all three kinds of public speaking was done through a combination of exercises and the study of specimen speeches. Students had to compose practice cases on specific or general themes. The earliest Roman handbook that survives, the *Rhetorica ad Herennium*, which dates from the mid- to late 80s BCE, shows the set topics that were thought likely to crop up in senatorial debates and in the law-courts. But our fullest source is the writings of the elder Seneca of the first half of the first century CE. Seneca's works are memoirs of famous rhetorical teachers and famous orators of his time. This body of Roman declamation (i.e., public speaking) is divided into *suasoriae* (persuasions) and *controversiae* (disputes). In a *suasoria*, the pupil had to compose a speech delivered by or addressed to a mythological or historical character. In a *controversia*, the pupil had to act as prosecutor or defending counsel in a fictitious lawsuit: the subject-matter of *controversiae* typically involved pirates and tyrants and magicians, and the pupil's task was to bring some novelty to his handling of his theme.

In the Juvenal passage quoted above, the speaker claims to have delivered a *suasoria* addressed to Sulla the dictator, advising him to resign from public life. Sulla was a popular theme (Quint. *Inst.* 3.8.53). So too was Cato, whose speech before he committed suicide in 46 BCE was a standard school exercise, as the Neronian satirist Persius tells us (3.44–7):

Often when I was little, I remember, I dabbed my eyes with oil,
if I didn't want to learn the magnificent words of Cato facing
    death –
a speech that my lunatic teacher would praise lavishly,
while father listened in a sweat, with the friends he'd brought
    along.

And so was Hannibal – which accounts for the resounding close of the section in Juvenal's *Satire* 10 in which the speaker demonstrates the futility of military glory (166–7):

On you go, you madman, race through the savage Alps
to make school-boys happy and become a theme of declamation!

This training in declamation certainly had its critics.[1] The part of Petronius' *Satyricon* that survives begins in the middle of a debate about the efficacy of rhetorical education. The narrator, Encolpius, is in full flight, delivering a savage attack on the teachers of rhetoric (1–2):

The only result of these pompous subjects and this empty thunder of platitudes is that when young speakers first enter public life they think they've landed on another planet. I'm sure the reason our schools produce young idiots is because they have no contact with anything of use in ordinary life. All they get is pirates standing on the beach with chains, tyrants writing orders for sons to cut off their fathers' heads, oracles advising the sacrifice of three or more virgins during a plague – a mass of cloying verbiage, every word and every move sprinkled with poppyseed and sesame. People fed on this diet have as much chance of learning sense as dishwashers have of smelling clean. If you'll forgive my saying so, you teachers are the main cause of the destruction of good speaking. By getting a few laughs with your smooth and empty sound effects, you took the guts out of real oratory, and that was the end of it.

Agamemnon, a teacher of rhetoric, responds by blaming the pupils and their parents (3–4):

The fact is, the teachers are not to blame for these exhibitions. They have no choice but to humour the madmen. If the speeches they make do not win the approval of their young pupils, as Cicero says, 'they will be the only ones in their schools'. . . . The teacher of rhetoric is like a fisherman: he has to bait his hook with what he knows the little fishes will rise for, or else he'll be sitting on his rock with no hope of a catch. What's the answer? It's the parents you should blame. They won't allow their children to be properly disciplined. . . .

The same debate is later replayed in Juvenal's *Satire 7*, which provides the source and context for the famous phrase *crambe repetita* ('rehashed cabbage'; 150–4, 158–64):

Are you a teacher of rhetoric? Poor Vettius! You need a steel chest   150
when your huge class slaughters its cruel tyrants.
They recite it sitting down, then standing up rehearse precisely
the same stuff, chanting the same stuff in precisely the same way.
The cabbage rehashed again and again does the poor teachers to death.
                      . . . I suppose   158
it's the teacher's fault that our young Arcadian

bumpkin's heart isn't set racing when he pounds
his 'Hannibal the Terrible' into my poor head every five days,
no matter what the question set was: should he strike straight
    at Rome
from Cannae, or after the torrential thunderstorm should he
    play safe
and order his rain-drenched cohorts to turn around?

The satirical twist is that the parents are reluctant to pay for their
sons' tuition, with the result that the teachers abandon their 'rehashed
cabbage' of wicked tyrants and other staples of declamation to go to
court to extract their fees (168–70):

> ... the 'sophists'
> pursue *real* law-suits, abandoning the Rapist;
> the Poured-Out Poison goes quiet and the Bad Ungrateful
>   Husband;
> so too the Drugs that Cure the Chronic Blind.

Whatever its merits and demerits, rhetoric was a central and crucial
element in the training of the Roman élite of the early imperial
period. Accordingly, the influence of rhetoric is palpable in the
literary products of that élite. Even the most cursory glance at
Juvenal's *Satires* reveals that influence, even without his speaker
pointing the way so explicitly. In fact, what is remarkable about
Juvenal is that he obtrudes the rhetorical tropes and figures that he
uses in order to draw attention to his own rhetoricality and to the
satirical tricks and turns he executes. In E. J. Kenney's words:
'rhetoric, and specifically declamatory rhetoric, the rhetoric of the
schools, is Juvenal's *idiom*'.[2] Some of the ways in which this is
manifested are investigated thoroughly in the work of Josué De
Decker, Inez Scott and William Anderson. In his monograph entitled
Juvenalis Declamans, De Decker quantifies in detail the presence
of rhetoric under the headings of *inventio* (broadly speaking,
subject-matter), composition and expression.[3] Scott in her monograph shows how features of the 'grand style' assumed at times in
oratory are found in abundance in Juvenal's *Satires*, for example,
enargeia, rhetorical questions and exclamations, hyperbaton, hyperbole, repetition and apostrophe.[4] Anderson in his essay on 'Juvenal
and Quintilian' demonstrates the importance of rhetorical theory to
Juvenal in his creation of a character who is (or at least believes
himself to be) the ethical rhetorician, the combination of good man

and good orator, posited by Quintilian (*vir bonus dicendi peritus*, Quint. *Inst.* 12.1.1, quoting the words of Cato *Libri ad M. Filium*;[5] cf. Quint. *Inst.* 1 *pr.* 9).[6]

Rhetoric *is* Juvenal's idiom, in a way that had not applied to earlier satirists. To a large extent, this reflects the rise of enthusiasm for the schools of declamation under the early empire. Accordingly, this essay will focus primarily upon Juvenal. But it does not mean that earlier satirists are excluded from consideration. The rhetoric of earlier periods was part of the cut and thrust of Roman political life in which the stakes could be very high: even death, if you consider the result of Cicero's invective against Antony in the *Philippics*. And that is reflected in the satirists. Juvenal is the first satirist to embrace rhetoric as his idiom, but rhetoric in other manifestations informs the writings of the earlier satirists, as we shall see. In this essay I shall show how Roman rhetorical theory and practice pervade Roman satire from Lucilius onwards and I shall argue that the familiarity of the Roman audience with the rhetorical frameworks and conventions exploited by the satirists equipped them to appreciate the satirists' twists and parodies. Finally, I shall suggest that satire replays the contestatory function of rhetoric in Roman society by its staging of conflict in pseudo-forensic, pseudo-deliberative and even pseudo-epideictic contexts.

I shall begin with the longest surviving fragment by Lucilius, the second-century BCE aristocrat who is credited with founding the genre of Roman satire (1196–1208):[7]

Excellence, Albinus, is being ready to pay what is truly due
in our business dealings and in life's dealings;
excellence is knowing what each situation involves for an
    individual;
excellence is knowing what is right, useful and honourable,
what things are good and what are bad, what is useless,
    shameful and dishonourable;
excellence is knowing the end and limit of acquiring an object;
excellence is the ability to pay what is due from our resources;
excellence is giving what is truly owed to honour,
is being an enemy and no friend of bad people and ways,
and on the other hand being a defender of good people and ways,
valuing *them* highly, wishing them well as a life-long friend;
and, besides, putting first the interests of our country,
then our parents' interests, thirdly and lastly our own.

In English, this 'Virtue' passage too readily sounds rather pious, perhaps because of the Christian overtones of the word 'virtue' (or even 'Virtue') – and this line of interpretation was established very early, in the very preservation of the fragment by the Christian writer Lactantius. It is not about 'virtue' but about 'man-ness': being a man, being a Ro-man, being a true Roman aristocrat, which the addressee Albinus clearly has failed to do.[8] As Wendy Raschke observes, Lucilius' language is the language of Roman political life in the second century BCE.[9] This view of Lucilius as highly politicized on behalf of his friend and patron Scipio is borne out by the vignettes of the satirist provided by his followers in the genre, Horace (*Sat.* 2.1.62–74) and Persius, who mention his attacks on, for example, Scipio's enemy Lupus (Pers. 1.114–15):

> Lucilius ripped into Rome –
> you, Lupus, you, Mucius, and smashed his back tooth on them.

What is more, Lucilius utilizes the battery of rhetorical concepts by which a (Ro)man's conduct was measured, concepts such as honour (*honestum*), right (*fas, rectum*), fairness (*aequum*), advantage (*utile*), obligation (*necessarium*) and duty (*pium*) and so on. In this passage of Lucilius, we meet *rectum, utile, honestum, bona, mala, inutile, turpe* and *inhonestum*. It is clear that Lucilius is using satire as a weapon of political engagement, rather as oratory was used in the late republic.

But satire derives from rhetoric more than its terminology of approbation and criticism. On the largest scale the influence of declamation is evident in the choice of subject and framing of ideas. Satire exhibits a number of the standard topics of the training in rhetoric and of the slants put upon those topics. Juvenal even makes an explicit reference to the declamatory term for 'slants' or 'lines of argument', *colores*, when he has one of his catalogue of dreadful Roman wives in *Satire* 6 defend herself to her husband against a charge of adultery (279–84):

> But she's lying in the arms of a slave or a knight. 'Come on,
> Quintilian, please tell me how to excuse myself (*dic . . .*
> *colorem*) now.'
> 'I'm stuck. Find an excuse yourself.' 'We agreed a long time
> ago,'
> she says, 'that you'd behave as you wanted and that I'd be able

to suit myself. You can roar all you like and turn the world upside down. I'm a human being as much as you.'

Although Quintilian, the professor of rhetoric, could not (or would not!) supply a *color* to the wife caught committing adultery, he *can* provide a useful insight for us into the topics that were most popular in the 'curriculum' of the schools of declamation (*Inst.* 2.4.24–5):

> *Theses* [general questions] ... deal with comparisons with questions such as, 'Which is preferable, country or city life?' 'Who deserves the greatest praise, the lawyer or the soldier?' These provide plenty of attractive practice in public speaking and offer the greatest pleasure whether directed at deliberative oratory or at forensic debate.... There are *theses* too that relate entirely to the deliberative class of oratory, for example, 'Should a man marry?' and 'Is high public position a worthwhile aim?'

Many of these questions feature in satire. The very opening of Horace's first satire consists of a comparison of different choices of profession and life-style: the trader, the soldier, the lawyer and the farmer, the country-dweller and the city-dweller (Hor. *Sat.* 1.1.1–12). Juvenal's incomplete *Satire* 16 presents the advantages of the military life. Both Horace and Juvenal compare and contrast city and country life, most obviously in the poem that closes with the tale of the Town Mouse and the Country Mouse (Hor. *Sat.* 2.6) and in Umbricius' tirade against Rome (Juv. 3, the model for Samuel Johnson's *London*). A study of the satirical texts that deal with city and country reveals that the city is generally depicted critically while the country is idealized to provide a foil to the criticisms of city life. That is, of the four possible debating positions, satire tends to present just two: the disadvantages of city life and the merits of country life.[10] For the élite Roman audience, these positions and the arguments wielded to support them would have been familiar from rhetorical exercises they themselves had had to compose in their school-days.[11] Juvenal's *Satire* 3 reflects this conventional presentation of material with its condemnation of the greed, corruption and selfishness of the urban rat-race punctuated by occasional glimpses of life in the country where traditional morality still prevails: an eloquent counterpoint. More specifically, Umbricius' speech can be read as the inversion of a standard type of speech practised in the schools of declamation, the speech termed the *syntaktikon*, that is, the farewell speech of a departing traveller.[12] Such speeches contained praise of the place that the traveller was leaving; in this case, the inversion consists of the substitution of attack for praise.

Another familiar and standard set-piece exercise (*progymnasma*) was 'Should a man marry?' Juvenal offers a satirically inflated version of this in his huge *Satire* 6.[13] The specific position adopted here is an anti-marriage position. The speaker is attempting to persuade his addressee Postumus not to marry, chiefly because of women's infidelity, of which he provides many and lurid examples in this overgrown poem. In short, *Satire* 6 is an example in poetry of a dissuasion from marriage (*logos apotreptikos gamou*). Again, Juvenal's audience would have been familiar with the theme and the arguments from their school exercises (*progymnasmata*), which Francis Cairns describes as 'the minimum formal rhetorical equipment of any literate person from the Hellenistic period on'.[14] This particular topic was especially popular, it seems. According to the treatise of 'Pseudo-Dionysius' (possibly dating from the third/fourth century CE), the subject of the desirability of marriage was set as an elementary exercise in *thesis* writing more often than any other topic (Dion. Hal. *Rhet.* 261).[15] This is confirmed by a study of Aelius Theon's *progymnasmata* (second century CE) in which marriage occurs prominently among *thesis* titles. And when Quintilian distinguishes between indefinite and definite questions at *Institutio* 3.5.8, his use of questions concerning marriage as examples suggests the prominence of such questions in the schools: 'Should a man marry?' (*an uxor ducenda?*) and 'Should Cato marry?' (*an Catoni ducenda?*). This language is reflected in *Satire* 6 at lines 201–2 where the words 'there seems to be no reason for marrying' (*ducendi nulla videtur causa*) indicate the rhetorical *thesis* that forms the backbone of the poem. We can go still further in our assimilation of satire to declamation. *Satire* 6 is an example not of the indefinite question, 'Should a man marry?' but of the definite question, here, 'Should Postumus marry?' (*an Postumo ducenda?*). The framework is borrowed from rhetoric and so too much of the content.[16] In short, *Satire* 6 is a satirical reworking of a standard rhetorical set-piece – and this would have been obvious to Juvenal's audience.

Satire 13 delivers a satirical parody of another rhetorical set-piece, the consolation (*consolatio*). In *Satire* 13 the addressee Calvinus has suffered a minor financial loss caused by fraud and perjury and as a result is angry; the speaker delivers to him an ironic *consolatio* in which the crime of fraud compounded by perjury is equivalent to the death of a loved one and the addressee's reaction of anger is equivalent to a bereaved person's reaction of grief. That is, the passion of anger replaces the passion of grief. When *Satire* 13 is set against the background of the *consolatio* tradition, this again illuminates Juvenal's choice of topics and the way in which he structures the poem.[17] What emerges is that *Satire* 13 is a consolation for a trivial case of anger and a parody of conventional consolations for distressing circumstances that do merit consolation. Again, Juvenal is playing with the conventions of a rhetorical set-piece highly familiar to his élite audience in a way that could only enhance their enjoyment of his satirical *consolatio*.

The structure and content of Juvenal's *Satires* is shaped by rhetoric. To these three examples – *Satire* 3 as an inversion of the farewell speech of the departing traveller (*syntaktikon*); *Satire* 6 as an inflated 'dissuasion from marriage' (*logos apotreptikos gamou*); and *Satire* 13 as a parody of the rhetorical *consolatio* – we can add several more. *Satire* 5 can be seen as a dissuasion from the life of a parasite, with its opening and closing addresses to the servile client Trebius. *Satire* 8 is a dissuasion from reliance upon inherited 'nobility' addressed to a Ponticus whose name suggests he is likely to do precisely that. *Satire* 12 is a satiric version of the *prosphonetikon*, the speech of welcome, offered to a shipwreck survivor; the satiric twist is that the poem turns into an attack on legacy-hunters. *Satires* 1 and 2 perhaps have more in common with forensic oratory in their presentation respectively as the self-defence of the satirist and as an invective on the theme of deviant sexuality, which featured prominently in legal speeches, but these poems nonetheless exhibit many of the hallmarks of declamation. The fact that Juvenal's audience of élite men had all shared in the experience of the declamation schools makes it likely that they would have understood immediately Juvenal's rhetorical framework and would have appreciated the divergences from that framework introduced for satirical purposes. On a smaller scale, the influence of rhetoric determines the kinds of choices the satirists make in matters of detail in content and style, for example, in the deployment of *exempla* (stories presenting role-models), *loci communes* (commonplaces) and *sententiae* (pithy epigrams).

One of the most prominent features of the declamatory education was the presentation of material in terms of exemplarity. Conduct was frequently described in terms of role-models, *exempla*, both positive and negative, for protreptic and apotreptic purposes.

Quintilian discusses the use of *exempla*, which he regards as a kind of proof, at *Institutio* 5.11, and a handbook of such *exempla* survives from antiquity in the *Facta et Dicta Memorabilia* ('Deeds and Sayings Worthy of Record') of Valerius Maximus, writing under Tiberius. This is a collection of 967 stories about named individuals taken from various authors and organized into categories to illustrate various characteristics, for example, 3.4 and 3.5 on people who rise from humble origins and on the decadence of the nobility, 5.4–6 on *pietas*, and 9.3 on anger. Satire differs from oratory, not surprisingly, in its predominance of apotreptic *exempla*: the extremes of bad conduct. Horace provides a vivid (if idealized) picture of education through *exempla* when he depicts the moral education he claims to have received from his father (*Sat.* 1.4.105–15, 121–6):[18]

> My good father gave me the habit; to warn me off   105
> he used to point out various vices by citing examples.
> When urging me to practise thrift and economy and to be
>   content
> with what he himself had managed to save he used to say:
> 'Notice what a miserable life young Albius leads and how Baius
> is down and out – a salutary warning not to squander
> the family's money.' Steering me away from a squalid attach-
>   ment
> to a whore he would say: 'Don't be like Scetanus!' To stop me
> chasing another man's wife when legitimate sex was available:
> 'It isn't nice to get a name like that of Trebonius – he
> was caught in the act.' . . .
>   . . . Recommending something he'd say: 121
> 'You've a good precedent for that,' and point to one of the
>   judges
> selected by the Praetor; or by way of dissuading me: 'How can
>   you doubt,'
> he'd say, 'whether this is a wrong and foolish thing to do
> when X and Y are the centre of a blazing scandal?'

Juvenal's *Satires* are teeming with negative *exempla*; the fewer positive *exempla* function as a foil, for example, towards the close of *Satire* 2 where Juvenal uses characters from the republican era as *exempla* of pristine virtue (2.153–5). *Satire* 1 is a striking case of the phenomenon of exemplarity on a larger scale: the catalogue of the wicked people who populate Rome presents an inversion of a parade of the finest and most glorious *exempla*, such as the parade of Aeneas' descendants in Vergil, *Aeneid* 6.756–853. Perhaps the most sustained parade of *exempla* in Juvenal is that in *Satire* 8 on the theme of true nobility. For most of the poem, the speaker castigates the degeneracy of the descendants of the great and heroic republican families with a series of lurid vignettes of their disgusting behaviour, for example, patricians performing as clowns on stage and Nero singing and strumming on the lyre (185–98). In the closing section, he demonstrates that true nobility can be shown by those of humble origins: Cicero, Marius, the Decii and Servius Tullius (236–68). Juvenal's material corresponds precisely to two consecutive categories in Valerius Maximus' handbook for orators (3.4 and 3.5). But typically he does not produce a straightforward replica of Valerius' in-built morality; Juvenal's speaker in *Satire* 8 is a clever cynic who parades these *exempla*, negative and positive, only to throw out the baby with the bath-water at the end of the poem by insisting that there is no point in relying on family trees because everyone is descended from a herdsman or a criminal (272–5):

> And yet however far you backtrack and rewind your
> name, your family derives from the 'haven' of ill repute.
> The first of your ancestors, whoever he was,
> was either a shepherd – or something I'd rather not name.

This is the *reductio ad absurdum* of the rhetorical staple, the *exemplum* – the role model drawn from the parade of past Roman heroes.

The *exempla* were designed to be memorable. So too were the *sententiae* with which Juvenal's text is laden. These *sententiae*, pithily framed points, formed an important element in Roman rhetorical technique.[19] Several of Juvenal's are so memorable that they are still used today, by politicians and others in the media, as well as by academics, usually without the slightest awareness of their original context or authorship. The three most famous are *panem et circenses* ('bread and circuses', 10.81), *mens sana in corpore sano* ('a healthy mind in a healthy body', 10.356) and, best of all, *quis custodiet ipsos custodes?* ('Who will guard the guards themselves?', 6.347–8). Such phrases readily sound moralistic – and that is why they get quoted. But, when taken in their full context, a slightly different picture emerges. Juvenal undoubtedly uses such rhetorical flourishes to shape his satires, but not without a twist. For example, the 'healthy mind . . .' *sententia* has an irreverent lead-up (10.354–6):

Still, to give you *something* to ask for, *some* reason to offer
in the shrine those holy sausages and white piglet's guts,
what you should ask for is – a healthy mind in a healthy body.

That is, the *sententia* plausibly belongs to 'rhetoric' but in the hands
of the satirist is put to a parodic use. Similarly, his speaker who
sounds so very moral frequently turns out to be a flawed character.
That is evident in *Satire* 6, where Juvenal presents a misogynist raging
against marriage. His fine-sounding warning, 'Who will guard? . . .',
apparently about the guardians of morality, is actually drawn from
a racy passage in which he savagely attacks the propensity of Roman
wives to seduce or suborn their slaves in order to keep their sexual
antics secret. Again, a potentially moralizing *sententia* takes on a
different complexion in the mouth of this misogynist, who sees
himself as the upholder of old-fashioned Roman morality but is out
of control in his lurid and lubricious condemnation of Roman wives.

Another element of the training in declamation was the use of *loci
communes*, literally 'commonplaces', stock themes that might use-
fully be inserted in a variety of contexts. The elder Seneca lists four
chief types of commonplace as *de fortuna, de crudelitate, de saeculo,
de divitiis* (*Controv.* 1 *pr.* 23), that is, (1) changes in luck, (2) human
cruelty and pity, (3) contemporary decadence and praise of former
times, and (4) the advantages and inconveniences of wealth. To these
can be added the *loci philosophumeni* (Sen. *Controv.* 1.7.17) on
conscience, remorse, true nobility and similar ideas. All of these *loci*
are present in Roman satire, above all in Juvenal, as De Decker shows
in detail.[20] For example, he incorporates the *locus de saeculo* in the
form of signs of luxury and decadence in the subject of over-
ambitious building that occurs at 3.190–6 and the topic of gluttony
that occurs at 1.135–41 and 5.93–6.

More specifically, certain *loci* were considered especially appropriate for the arousal of *indignatio* by the orator in his audience. Now
indignatio is, famously, the mode of presentation that Juvenal
chooses for his early *Satires*. A list of such topics that an orator can
use to arouse indignation or pity in his audience in the conclusion of
a speech (*peroratio*) is provided by Cicero at *De Inventione* 1.100–5.
If we set this list alongside Juvenal's angry satire, this will demonstrate the extent to which rhetoric is Juvenal's 'idiom'. Cicero's
extensive list of fifteen topics that can fire the audience's indignation
(cf. the discussion of *amplificatio* at *Rhet. Her.* 2.48–9, which has the
first ten topics of Cicero) shows a striking similarity to the kinds of

things Juvenal's angry speaker says throughout *Satires* 1–6. The closing passage of *Satire* 6 (627–61) is particularly rich in these marks of indignation. The message here is that women are capable of the worst crimes. This general message corresponds to the following topics in Cicero's list of anger-rousing topics: (2) *Passionate demonstration of the parties affected by the act that is being denounced: all people or superiors or peers or inferiors*; (7) *Demonstration that the deed was foul, cruel, wicked, tyrannical.* Juvenal's passage starts with a warning addressed to wards and to children about their stepmothers and mothers (627–33):

> They hate the children born to a mistress. No one would oppose
>   or forbid that – it's long been lawful to murder a stepson.
> Orphans, I'm warning you too: if you own a decent fortune,
>   watch out for your lives and don't trust anything served at table.
> Those blackening cakes are seething with mother's poison.
> Let someone else taste before you do what is offered you by
>   the woman who bore you; get your trembling tutor to sip the drinks first.

This corresponds to topic 11 in Cicero: *Demonstration that the crime was committed by a person who least of all should have committed it and who might have been expected to prevent it happening.* The vivid picture created by the details of 6.631–3 is typical of the graphic descriptions that abound in Juvenal and that put into practice Cicero's advice to the orator: (10) *Enumeration of the attendant circumstances to make the crime as vivid as possible.* Juvenal's speaker proceeds to appeal to the Roman state (6.634–7):

> You think this is fiction? That my satire has put on the boots of
>   tragedy? That I have gone beyond the limits and law of earlier writers,
> that I am ranting in grand Sophoclean style a song sublime,
>   unfamiliar to the Rutulian hills and Latin skies?

This connects with Cicero's first piece of advice to the orator, that indignation may be aroused by: (1) *Consideration of the great concern shown by the relevant authority – the gods, ancestors, rulers, states, Senate, authors of laws – about the matter under discussion.* Juvenal's next lines make it clear that the woman's murder of her children was premeditated (6.638–42):

I wish I were talking nonsense. But Pontia cries 'It was me!
I confess! I gave some aconite to my children.
The deed was detected and everyone knows it, but the mur-
derer is me!'
Two, you say, at a single meal, you savage viper,
you killed two? 'Yes, and seven, if there'd been seven!'

This exactly puts into practice item 6 on Cicero's list: *Indication that
the act was premeditated*. By calling her a 'venomous viper' (641) the
speaker places the murderess on a bestial level, fulfilling another
element of Cicero's advice: (8) *Demonstration that the deed is unique
and unknown even among savages, barbarians and wild beasts,
typically acts of cruelty committed against parents or children or acts
of injustice towards people who cannot defend themselves*. The
remainder of *Satire* 6 introduces a comparison between the horrific
heroines of Greek tragedy and modern women, which is designed to
show how much worse modern women are (643–61):

Let's believe what tragedy says about Procne
and the cruel woman of Colchis; I won't dispute it. They too
dared to commit monstrous crimes for their day –
but not for cash. The worst atrocities cause
less shock when the female is driven to outrage
by fury and when, with hearts inflamed by madness, they are
carried
down like boulders torn from a mountain ridge as the ground
collapses
and the vertical face falls in from the overhanging cliff.
I cannot stand the woman who assesses the profit and coolly
commits a major crime. They watch Alcestis enduring
death for her man, but if they were offered a similar choice
they would rather let their husband die to preserve a pet dog.
Every morning you meet dozens of daughters of Danaus
and Eriphyles; every street has a Clytemnestra.
The difference is this: Tyndareus' daughter wielded an oafish
and awkward two-headed axe with both her hands,
but now the job is done with the tiny lung of a toad –
though it may need steel too, if your son of Atreus is now
immune
from taking the Pontic drugs of the thrice-defeated king.

This is an excellent case of Cicero's ninth recommendation: (9) *Comparison of the deed with other crimes to enhance the horror*. And, finally, it is clear that Juvenal's speaker expects his audience's sympathy throughout, just as the orator trying to simulate and provoke indignation does, according to Cicero: (14) *Request to the audience to identify with the speaker*. It seems likely that Juvenal's audience, who had received the same grounding as the poet, would have appreciated the convergence of rhetorical theory and practice in this passage – and throughout Juvenal's *Satires*.

Finally, it is useful to remind ourselves that Cicero's recommendations are directed at the orator who has to face a real engagement, debating an issue before a decision-making committee or arguing a case in court. The training in rhetoric was above all a preparation for argument and debate, for a context of two clearly demarcated sides, the ancient equivalent of the adversarial politics of the British House of Commons and legal system. Satire too stages conflict – both in and out of court. In his second book of *Satires*, Horace stages a range of disputes in dialogue form, some of them more fiercely contested than others. His mock-legal consultation of the eminent lawyer Trebatius in *Satires* 2.1 concerning the 'laws' of satire is conducted in a bantering tone. This is epitomized by the concluding pun on the words *mala . . . carmina*, which in the ancient legal code known as the Twelve Tables meant 'evil spells', but which Horace here twists to mean 'bad poetry'.[21] Satire specializes in such humorous dismissal or side-stepping or closure.

But it is in his first book of *Satires* that Horace presents most vividly the kinds of conflict that connect most closely with the rhetorical background of Roman public life. Several of the poems in this book stage conflicts and in one of them, *Satires* 1.7, that conflict has a court setting. This poem presents a vivid narrative of a quarrel (*litis*, 5) between two men in Brutus' camp in Asia in 43/2 BCE, Persius the half-Greek, half-Roman businessman of Clazomenae, and Rupilius Rex of Praeneste, who has been proscribed by Antony. This pair, 'the Outlaw vs. the Half-breed',[22] are unable to resolve their quarrel and so, like a pair of gladiators (*par*, 19), into court they go for Brutus' adjudication. There they provide a spectacle (*magnum spectaculum*, 21) as they continue to hurl abuse at one another until Persius in exasperation appeals to Brutus to maintain his and his family's habit of regicide by slaughtering *this* King (*Rex*, 33–5). And so he wins his case, as we have known from the beginning, since Horace tells us straightaway that this is the story of how Persius got his revenge on Rex (*ultus*, 1–2). In other words, this poem dramatizes a violently contested legal case and demonstrates the power of words. In this case, Persius uses his words to appeal successfully to Brutus, the man with the power. This he does by a combination of flattery and panegyric of Brutus (23–5), invective against Rex (25–7) and, finally, a witty appeal to precedent (33–5) – always a good bet in a Roman argument.

This is not the only poem in *Satires* 1 in which Horace dramatizes a conflict. He presents a foretaste of the slanging-match of *Satires* 1.7 in *Satires* 1.5, the famous 'Journey to Brundisium'. At the centre of this poem occurs a verbal 'fight' (*pugnam*, 52) between the slave Sarmentus and the Oscan Messius Cicirrus staged for the entertainment of the city-slickers accompanying Maecenas on his mission of political reconciliation (1.5.51–70). Despite a mock-epic invocation of the Muses (53), their quarrel (*litis*, 54) turns out to be a fierce bandying of personal insults. By making this contest the centre-piece and longest single episode in the poem, Horace perhaps creates a rustic equivalent of the virulence of rhetorical invective that was so central to Roman public life.[23]

Another battle of words takes place in *Satires* 1.9, in which 'Horace' is assailed by 'The Pest', a social climber who wants Horace to engineer an introduction to his patron Maecenas (43–8). In this duel Horace is on the losing side because of his lack of assertiveness or aggression towards the pest, who continues to dog him through the city despite the fact that he is bailed to turn up in court that day; he sacrifices his case (*litem*, 35–7) to pursue Horace. Horace is only saved because the pest's adversary at law appears and drags him off to court (74–8). This poem represents an interesting twist on the theme of conflict in satire. On the surface, this is a battle of words that Horace loses thoroughly. But at the same time he is on the winning side in the war: he is the survivor, preserved by the 'divine intervention' of Apollo (78), an allusion to his intervention in the fighting in *Iliad* 20 and to his role as the god associated with the law-courts. Horace gets his revenge.

Satire, then, readily incorporates scenes of conflict that reflect the contexts in which Roman rhetoric was exercised. Scenes of debate are another staple of satire. Take, for example, Lucilius' council of the gods in his book 1, although the debt to epic generally and specifically to book 1 of Ennius' *Annales* is obviously the primary feature here. Another example is the meeting that takes place on Olympus in Seneca's *Apocolocyntosis* when the gods debate the dead

Claudius' eligibility for admission to their divine 'Senate' in speeches laden with the formulae of senatorial procedure (Sen. *Apoc.* 8–11).[24] The presence of a debate scene here and the numerous debates and dialogues in the works of the second-century CE Greek satirist Lucian suggest that for Menippean satire (i.e., prose satire) the debate was a standard setting. If more of Varro's prose satires (first century BCE) survived, we would find ample reflection of the influence of Roman rhetorical theory and practice there. In *Satire* 4 Juvenal provides a satirical version of the *consilium principis*, the emperor's cabinet of advisers. Not that the quality of the rhetoric there is remarkable, but that is the point. Juvenal's *consilium* is a parody, designed to castigate the abuse of his advisers by the tyrannical emperor Domitian.

I shall close with a device inculcated through training in declamation that serves as a final reminder of the adversarial and contestatory basis of both rhetoric and satire: the fictitious adversary or interlocutor.[25] All the satirists from Lucilius to Juvenal use this device to create a vivid opponent. A prime example is the close of Juvenal's first satire where the speaker engages in a dialogue with an interlocutor who warns him of the dangers of satire (1.149–71). But it is the earlier satirist Persius, writing under Nero, who characteristically produces the ultimate satire on this rhetorical technique. In his first satire, his interlocutor rebukes him and he replies (1.40–7):

> 'You mock,' he says, 'and let your nostrils
> sneer too much. Is there any poet of cedar-oil-grand compositions
> who would deny the desire to be the talk of the town and to leave
> behind him poetry that need not fear mackerels or frankincense?'
> You, whoever you are, my home-made devil's advocate –
> when I write, if something rather good happens to pop out,
> and that would be a rarity, if, though, something rather good pops out,
> I have no fear of praise.

That is, Persius here takes part of the standard rhetorical fabric that satire regularly borrows and reduces it to tatters by exposing its flimsiness: *quisquis es, o modo quem ex adverso dicere feci* ('You, whoever you are, my home-made devil's advocate', 44).

All the satirists in their different ways reflect the pervasive presence of rhetoric and declamation among the Roman élite and react to that presence by producing satirical twists upon standard elements. Juvenal above all draws attention to his own rhetoricality by replaying (with satiric twists, of course) some of the forensic, deliberative and epideictic forms and contexts of oratory. His awareness of the power of rhetoric as central to the contestatory ideology of Roman society emerges nowhere more powerfully, perhaps, than in his speaker's condemnation of prayers for eloquence in *Satire* 10, 'The Vanity of Human Wishes', as Samuel Johnson entitles his imitation. Of Cicero he says (120–6):

> Because of his genius his hand and neck was slit – never
> was the rostrum stained with the blood of a petty pleader.
> 'O state of Rome so fortunate, dating from my consulate!'
> He could have scorned Antony's swords if he had always
> spoken like that. So – better to write laughable poems
> than you, immortal Philippic number two
> of conspicuous fame.

Juvenal typically has it both ways: he demonstrates the dangers of virtuoso oratorical display in real life while parading his own virtuosity in his satires.

NOTES

1 On ancient critics of declamation, see Bonner 1949: 71–83.
2 Kenney 1963: 707.
3 De Decker 1913.
4 Scott 1927: 18–45; cf. Braund 1996: 24–9 for analysis and tabulation of Juvenal's style in *Satires* 1–5.
5 Jordan 1860: 80 n. 1.
6 Anderson 1982: 396–486.
7 Warmington 1938: 391–3.
8 For a convincing interpretation of this fragment as part of Roman aristrocratic ideology, see Raschke 1990.
9 Raschke 1987: esp. 317–18.
10 On city and country in Roman satire, see Braund 1989b.
11 Cf. Sen. *Controv.* 2.1.11–12, 5.5 (criticism of country life); 1.6.4, 2.1.8 (praise of rustic ancestors); see Braund 1989b: 23.
12 Cairns 1972: 38, 47–8.
13 As I have argued in Braund 1992, developing the suggestive comment by Cairns 1972: 75.
14 Cairns 1972: 75.
15 Translated in Russell and Wilson 1981: 362–81.

16 As argued in detail in Braund 1992.
17 For full argumentation see Braund (1997).
18 Translated by Rudd 1987: 58–9.
19 Significantly, Quintilian devotes an entire section (*Inst.* 8.5) to *sententiae*.
20 De Decker 1913.
21 See Cloud 1989 on the satirists' engagement with the law.
22 Henderson 1994: 151.
23 On Roman rhetorical invective see Richlin 1992a: 96–104.
24 See also Eden 1984.
25 On arguments with a real or an imaginary *adversarius*, see Quint. *Inst.*
     5.11.3–5.

10

Melpomene's declamation
(rhetoric and tragedy)

Sander M. Goldberg

In the late summer of 55 BCE, Cicero sweltered through the inaugural ceremonies for Pompey's new theater complex in the Campus Martius. The vast structure itself was in many ways a marvel: Rome's first stone theater, designed to hold perhaps 40,000 spectators, incorporated a temple of Venus Victrix above the *cavea*, flanked by four ancillary sanctuaries to revered abstractions like Honos and Virtus, while behind the stage building stretched an elaborate portico and formal garden connecting the theater with a new senate-house some 200 meters to the east. It was all very impressive, but not the surroundings nor the awnings nor the innovative water-courses of the new building itself could relieve the heat of that Roman August or the tedium of that inaugural display.[1] Cicero described the program with wry distaste in a famous letter to his friend Marcus Marius, himself comfortably installed in a villa on the Bay of Naples.

The entertainments staged in the new theater included mimes, plays, and farces. Performances were in Greek as well as Latin and employed both local and imported talent. Some distinguished veterans of the stage had also been invited out of retirement for the occasion, and some, says Cicero, unwisely accepted the invitation: old Aesopus, the famous tragic actor of the late republic, actually lost his voice in mid-sentence, to the embarrassment of all. Related shows in the Circus included races and wild animal displays performed over a five-day period – memory of an elephant hunt there lingered down to Pliny's day – but the most notorious spectacle on the program, or at least the spectacle that most exasperated Cicero, was the lavish staging of two classic Roman plays, Accius' *Clytemnestra* and the *Equus Troianus* of (we think) Naevius (*Fam.* 7.1):[2]

166

What pleasure is there [groused Cicero to Marius] in getting a
Clytemnestra with six hundred mules or a *Trojan Horse* with
three thousand mixing-bowls or a variegated display of cavalry
and infantry equipment in some battle or other? The public
gaped at all this; it would not have amused you at all.

Within a generation, similar complaints over the ostentatious pomp
of Roman tragic revivals had become a critical *topos*. Horace, for
example, would soon be writing in the same vein to Augustus (*Epist.*
2.1.187–93):

Nowadays even the knights have stopped listening, and all their
interest is taken up with inane and ephemeral pageants.
The curtain is up for four-hour periods, if not longer,
as squadrons of cavalry and hordes of infantry hurtle past;
fallen kings are dragged across with their hands pinioned;
chariots, carriages, wagons and ships rumble along,
carrying works of bronze and ivory taken from Corinth.

Theatrical Art, we may think, has surrendered unconditionally
to Show.

Testimony like this certainly suggests the assimilation of tragic
performances in the late republic to different (and less literary) kinds
of public spectacle, in particular the triumph with its elaborate
procession, deliberately breath-taking ostentation, and related side-
shows. The crowd that gathered to watch 'tragedy' under such
circumstances must surely have come to the theater with different
expectations from those of the notoriously loud but knowledgeable
audiences of classical Athens or even the expectations of Roman
audiences a century before them. Interest in tragedy now lay, as
William Beare remarked, 'not so much in the essential dramatic
qualities of the performance as in externals – impressive staging,
violent utterance and action, lines that might be taken as topical, the
arrival of distinguished spectators, and of course any mishap that
might befall either the actors or any members of the audience'.[3] All
these forms of disruption are well attested for the late republic. The
tragic genre seems to have lost its intellectual bearings and surrendered its integrity to stage managers and politicians on the make.

Yet there were Romans who never lost a serious interest in tragedy.
Cicero disliked extravagant revivals precisely because he liked the
old plays themselves, and there were eventually new plays to like as
well. Accius, who died about 90 BCE, was the last professional

tragedian at Rome, the last poet to make his literary reputation on the strength of his dramatic scripts. Yet he was not the last to write tragedies of note. Varius, one of the better poets of the Augustan age, wrote a tragedy of more than passing success, and so did Ovid. In fact, Melpomene's footprints (if not always her actual songs) may be traced through at least the next century of Roman literary history. The genre did come to change profoundly, however, in this period. To understand how it survived the loss of professional playwrights and the extravagances of public performance in the late republic to emerge under the principate with a new style and new sense of purpose means taking the measure of those changes. The task involves social as well as literary history, and it centers on one of the great social and literary phenomena of the Roman aristocracy: rhetoric.

1

The first thing to understand about Roman tragedy is that in the course of the first century BCE it underwent the same process of gentrification common to all Roman poetry. The earliest record of the transition lies with the aristocrat Julius Caesar Strabo, an aedile in 90 and an orator of note until his death in the Marian proscriptions of 87. Strabo not only wrote tragedies; he attended meetings of the professional *Collegium Poetarum*, where Accius once refused to rise in deference to his superior social position (Val. Max. 3.7.11). Despite this deliberately insulting verdict on his talent, Strabo's plays survived for Cicero to read, and they circulated long enough for excerpts from them to enter the grammatical tradition over a generation later through the work of Augustus' learned freedman Verrius Flaccus. And Strabo was just the first significant example of a republican aristocrat who dabbled in tragedy. Others include an *eques* named Gaius Titius; Cicero's brother Quintus, passing away a winter in Gaul by writing four tragedies in sixteen days; his commander Caesar, whose juvenilia included an *Oedipus;* Octavian, who wrote an *Ajax*; the two sons of Horace's Piso; and the Augustan literary lion Asinius Pollio.[4] The point is not that such people wrote, much less staged, good tragedies. These tragedies were almost certainly not good. They were not produced, and most never even circulated. Augustus expressly forbade publication of his uncle's poetry and, as he told Varius, he preferred his own Ajax to fall upon his sponge (Suet. *Iul.* 56.7; *Aug.* 85; Macrob. *Sat.* 2.4.2). Yet the aristocracy clearly remained interested in the form, at least as a literary exercise. And the two efforts by serious poets were much more than exercises. Varius' *Thyestes* and Ovid's *Medea* became canonical texts – Quintilian thought the *Thyestes* equal to the best Greek tragedies (10.1.98) – and by the later principate something still called tragedy remained a viable medium for Curiatius Maternus to arouse the passions and the concerns of his friends (Tac. *Dial.* 2–3, 12.6).

What kept tragedy alive in the aristocratic imagination, however, was not that tendency toward lavish public spectacle we saw in Cicero's day. Varius' play was probably performed either in conjunction with Octavian's triumphal celebrations of 29 BCE or at the restored *ludi Apollinares* of 28, but we do not know how lavish and how public its production was.[5] Ovid claimed in a different context that he had never staged a play (*Tr.* 5.7.27), and the appeal of his *Medea* was in any case somewhat bookish. It contained Vergilian echoes that, as the elder Seneca comments, sought to proclaim rather than conceal his debt (*Suas.* 3.7). Pomponius Secundus, who was *consul ordinarius* under Claudius and widely respected as a tragedian by his peers, was nevertheless booed in the public theater when one of his works was performed (Tac. *Ann.* 11.13). Tragedy was losing its place in the large, open theaters of Rome. These were increasingly dedicated to mimes, pantomimes, and even less literary forms of public entertainment, while literary drama moved to more intimate (and more aristocratic) confines, whether in smaller roofed halls or private homes, with recitation rather than fully staged performance becoming increasingly common. Maternus' plays were apparently written for recitation before friends, as most poetry of the time was, and small-scale performances are attested in the early empire.[6]

Meanwhile, back in the study, the expanding repertoire of old plays continued to be mined for literary tags and purple passages. As early as Sulla's day, rhetoricians were culling tragic scripts for effective maxims and elegant turns of phrase (cf. *Rhet. Her.* 4.4.7). Cicero introduces a discussion of diction in the *Orator* (36) with a comparison of Ennius, Pacuvius, and Accius, and he has Crassus of *De Oratore* illustrate different styles of delivery with a long series of tragic quotations (3.217–19). In his philosophical mode, he illustrated the expression of anger at *Tusculan Disputations* 4.77 by quoting Accius' *Atreus*. Nearly two centuries later, Quintilian was still doing the same. He illustrates the point that nobody wants to appear as bad as he is with a passing allusion to Sallust's Catiline, but also includes an explicit quotation from Varius' *Thyestes*: *iam fero infandissima,*

169

iam facere cogor ('Now I endure, now I am compelled to commit outrageous deeds', *Inst.* 3.8.45). But those were, for the Romans, already classical or at least neo-classical allusions. Why did Roman aristocrats *keep* writing tragedies, and what did they come to think a tragedy was?

The fragments of republican tragedy are often sufficiently colorful to hint at the genre's extraordinary capacity for depicting violent and pathetic emotion. It also displayed a keen taste for argument, which rhetorical writers soon put to use – and not just for the occasional stylistic flourish. In Cicero's youth, the anonymous author of the *Rhetorica ad Herennium* mined tragic texts for illustrations of good and bad argument (e.g., 2.34–42), and we eventually find Quintilian, who praised Roman tragedy highly within the context of rhetorical education (10.1.97–8), extolling the thrust and parry of Accius' combative dialogue. Yet Accius, he reports, also knew the difference between the stage and the courtroom (5.13.43):

> They say that Accius, when asked why he did not plead cases since his tragedies showed such skill in repartee, gave this explanation, that the things said in his plays were what he wanted to say, while in court his opponents would say what he did not want them to say.

This was precisely the distinction that Gaius Albucius Silus, one of the great Augustan declaimers, learned to his cost when he unwisely entered the rough-and-tumble of the centumviral court. He proposed an extravagant oath, a well-known rhetorical figure, only to have the opposing counsel take him at his word and express his client's willingness to swear it (Sen. *Controv.* 7 *pr.* 6–7; cf. 9 *pr.* 2–5). That miscalculation cost Albucius both the case and his self-respect. No such mishap was possible in the declaimers' artificial debates. Nor could it happen in tragedy, which the Romans had long since made the verse equivalent of declamation.

The ubiquity of recitation as the preferred medium for bringing literature to its audience doubtless encouraged the assimilation of poetry to the demands of rhetorical display. This may well have been the secret of Ovid's success with his *Medea*: he was an accomplished declaimer, whose surviving poetry bears ample evidence of his accomplishments in that form. It is certainly the case with Seneca, whose plays are not just generally rhetorical in style but specifically declamatory in conception. As Friedrich Leo, the great pioneer of modern Senecan studies, observed, 'These are not really tragedies,

170

but declamations patterned after tragedy and divided into acts.' Leo rightly insisted on reading them against the background of the Roman rhetorical tradition. Yet because Leo thought rhetoric had exerted a negative effect on Roman literature (rhetoric was certainly a major factor in making Latin works unlike their Greek models), he treated Seneca's *tragoedia rhetorica* as a thing apart from 'real' tragedy. He and his descendants generally confined their inquiries to matters of style and then faulted Seneca for fulfilling their expectations.[7] This could be a rather dry exercise, and the more sympathetic criticism that has since emerged understandably looks in other directions. Attention to Seneca's philosophical roots, for example, has shown not just how Stoic vocabulary underlies his diction, but how Stoicism furnished a powerful intellectual foundation for his tragic constructions and insured their lasting appeal.[8] Senecan drama, however, is not only philosophical: rhetorical criticism should also have something to say about the substance of his tragedy.

Leo's basic perception about rhetorical tragedy remains true. His only mistake was to dislike rhetoric and therefore to confine his investigation of its influence to stylistic matters, as if to suggest that the plays are *only* style. In fact, the influence of rhetoric on tragedy extends far beyond the tropes, figures, and *sententiae* that Leo's disciples went on to catalogue. Nor is that influence necessarily baneful. Rather than simply observing, and then dismissing, rhetoric as the source of mannerisms and verbal pyrotechnics, we might productively argue that rhetoric – in particular declamation – was a positive influence on tragedy because it asserted the primacy of language over spectacle. The declamatory model that shaped Seneca's idea of tragedy thereby brought the genre out of the intellectual doldrums that had so exasperated Cicero and Horace. To argue this case requires only some sympathy for the declamatory enterprise and its effect on both the writing and the reception of tragedy.

2

Consider, by way of example, one of the great Senecan moments. As we begin the last act of *Thyestes*, Thyestes has been fed his own children's flesh. Now Atreus, eager to claim the reward of his infamy, is ready to display his handiwork. He orders his servants to unbolt the palace doors and reveal the scene of feasting within (901–7):

turba famularis, fores
templi relaxa, festa patefiat domus.
libet videre, capita natorum intuens,
quos det colores, verba quae primus dolor
effundat aut ut spiritu expulso stupens
corpus rigescat. fructus hic operis mei est;
miserum videre nolo, sed dum fit miser.

The curious expression *quos det colores* (904), says Richard Tarrant in his commentary on the play, means 'what complexion he shows (i.e., how his face turns red and pale by turns)'.[9] Atreus thus is saying:

Servants, loosen the palace
doors, let the festive house lie open.
I want to see, as he inspects his children's heads,
what complexion he shows, what words his first
sorrow pours out or how, gasping and shocked,
his body stiffens. This is the reward of my work:
I want to see him not wretched, but becoming wretched.

Tarrant's gloss is certainly correct, but it is not complete. The word *colores* can refer not only to facial complexion.

Those schooled in rhetoric, which most assuredly means Seneca and his audience, would also hear in *color* its technical sense, that is, the kind of plea a speaker makes, the line of argument, the 'complexion' he puts on the case at hand. Though never more than a loose assemblage of attitudes, postures, and rationales, the *colores* were nevertheless fundamental to declamation, where success often depended on the apt and inventive twists given to familiar topics.[10] Atreus, as he awaits Thyestes' appearance, thus wonders what *color* he will assume and how original its application will be. We may thus also hear his words like this:

I want to see, as he inspects his childrens' heads,
what face he puts on this: what words his first
sorrow pours out or how, gasping and shocked,
his body stiffens.

The entire audience doubtless shared this curiosity, for Thyestes' condition was a famous *topos*. By the first century CE, not only had his banquet become emblematic of tragedy, but his impassioned response to its horror had become a rhetorical cliché.[11] Seneca's father, for example, represents anger as the distinctly Thyestean *color* (Sen. *Controv.* 1.1.21):

colorem ex altera parte, quae durior est, Latro aiebat hunc sequendum, ut gravissimarum iniuriarum inexorabilia et ardentia induceremus odia Thyesteo more.

Latro said that on the other side, which is more difficult, we should follow the *color* of representing unremitting and passionate hatred, arising from the gravest injuries, Thyestes-wise.[12]

Small wonder that Atreus should wonder – or at least Seneca's audience should hear him wondering – what *colores* this new Thyestes will employ.

Such conscious and even metatheatrical allusion to the content and technique of declamation has two important ramifications for the appreciation of Roman tragedy. The first involves the audience. Modern readers, encouraged in part by the parodies and sneers we find in Petronius and Juvenal, tend to regard declamation as a dry and stale exercise, or at best as a source of effete and even immoral sophistries. Think, says Juvenal (6.279–85), of the unfaithful wife:

> sed iacet in servi complexibus aut equitis. 'dic,
> dic aliquem sodes hic, Quintiliane, colorem.'
> 'haeremus. dic ipsa.' 'olim convenerat', inquit
> 'ut faceres tu quod velles, nec non ego possem
> indulgere mihi. clames licet et mare caelo
> confundas, homo sum.' nihil est audacius illis
> deprensis: iram atque animos a crimine sumunt.

> She is lying in the arms of a slave or (worse!) a banker.
> 'Please, Quintilian, give me some *color*.'
> 'We're stuck. Speak for yourself.' 'We agreed long ago',
> she says, 'that you could do as you like, and I could please
> myself. Rant on until you bring heaven down to earth.
> I am human.' Nothing is brasher than women
> caught in the act. Crime feeds their anger and their energy.

This example is not wholly fictitious. The elder Seneca reports what was apparently a real case in which a woman was found with a handsome slave in her bedroom. Her husband divorced her and prosecuted the slave for adultery. The wife defended the slave.[13] 'There was need for some *color*', says Seneca in discussing the ensuing arguments, 'since she had been seen in the bedroom with a slave by her husband' (*Controv.* 2.1.34–6). He preserves several of the *colores* employed on the occasion, not all of them as brazen as Juvenal's, along with the spirited exchanges that followed. The victorious pleader (for the husband, apparently) was Vallius Syriacus, whose wit earned great applause.

The case is interesting not only for the opportunity it affords to compare the handling of a *topos* in both literary and rhetorical contexts. Seneca's admiring analysis of the declaimers' art is a good antidote to Juvenal's cynicism, for the spectators' keen and enthusiastic response to the advocates' performance belies the poet's charge of tedium. Rhetorical education forged a common bond between declaimers and audiences. Laughter, shouts, applause, sharp retorts, and sudden interruptions were everyday occurrences in the declamation hall. Declamation before adult audiences – school exercises were something different – was a spectator sport for engaged and experienced spectators. To watch Cestius and Latro perform was not just like watching masters take the stage, but like watching them play the piece you played yourself last week or had struggled to play when you were young.

In recalling that bond, Atreus' allusion to his brother's *colores* encourages a similar tie between the play and its audience. Reading Seneca rhetorically requires us not just to recognize certain mannerisms and their sources but to set his plays against a background of shared experiences that unites speakers who are reaching as far as they can with spectators fully prepared to applaud their successes and mock their failures.[14] The atmosphere would thus have been lively and highly charged. Viewed in this way, rhetoric reveals itself to be a source of energy, not tedium. Let us then rejoin Atreus and his audience as they discover what *colores* Thyestes does in fact employ.

It is not the *color* of 'unremitting and passionate hatred'. When Thyestes appears, he at first persists in thinking he has shared a banquet of reconciliation, and he is therefore perplexed and confused by his own sense of foreboding (965–9). This weakness extends throughout the revelation of catastrophe. Though never at a loss for words – he will have three emotional speeches in the scene to come (1006–21, 1035–51, 1068–96) – his words consistently lack power. Appeals to heaven are unanswered, and his brother is of course unmoved. Atreus himself speaks comparatively little (his one longish speech at 1052–68 is an aside), but his words are vicious in their taunting, riddling style:

THYESTES

      redde iam natos mihi!   997

ATREUS

reddam, et tibi illos nullus eripiet dies.   998

      Expedi amplexus, pater;   1004

venere. natos ecquid agnoscis tuos?

THYESTES

agnosco fratrem . . .   1006

      frater hic fratrem rogo: 1027

sepelire liceat. redde quod cernas statim

uri; nihil te genitor habiturus rogo,

sed perditurus.

ATREUS

      quidquid e natis tuis

superest habes, quodcumque non superest habes.

THYESTES

utrumne saevis pabulum alitibus iacent,

an beluis scinduntur, an pascunt feras?

ATREUS

epulatus ipse es impia natos dape.

THYESTES

Give me back my sons!   997

ATREUS

So I shall: no day will ever take them from you. 998

     Prepare your embrace, Father. 1004

They have come. Do you recognize your sons?

THYESTES

I recognize my brother . . .   1006

    I ask my brother this as a brother: 1027

Allow their burial. Return what you will straightaway see

burned. As a father, I ask you not for something to have

but to lose.

ATREUS

      You have what remains of

your sons, and what does not remain you have.

THYESTES

Do they lie exposed as food for savage birds,

or are they torn apart by beasts, or nourish wild things?

ATREUS

You have yourself made an impious banquet of your sons.

Atreus' desire to see Thyestes not just wretched but *becoming* wretched *(miserum videre nolo, sed dum fit miser,* 'I want to see him not wretched, but becoming wretched', 907) necessitates this slow, deliberate, and inexorable progress toward the truth. Thyestes is almost childlike in his dependence and pitiful in the ignorance that Atreus so cruelly mocks. His one potentially great retort, *agnosco fratrem* ('I recognize my brother', 1006), is founded on error: he does *not* yet know his brother. He will not know him fully until Atreus spells out the extent of his crime boldly and unequivocally at line 1034. And what happens then? Still no *ardentia odia* ('passionate hatred'), but only more vain appeals and a strikingly weak *sententia*: *genitor en natos premo / premorque natis* ('I oppress those I have begotten and am oppressed by those begotten', 1050–1). And there are more turns of the screw to come until Atreus, satisfied at last, proclaims his satisfaction: *perdideram scelus, nisi sic doleres* ('I would have wasted my crime were you not grieving this way', 1097–8).

All this anguish and all this horror are brought about entirely by Atreus' ability to manipulate speech. What could have been a culminating action, the display of the children's heads and hands at line 1004, is deliberately undercut by Thyestes' ignorance of all that these relics imply. The bare fact of kindred murder is not the issue of maximum importance: this is only half the expected revelation. We are still waiting for Thyestes' discovery that he has himself committed the final outrage against nature. Yet Seneca deliberately postpones that decisive moment. The effect on Thyestes of his children's death remains incomplete at line 1004 and is for this reason decidedly unclassical. Consider, by way of contrast, two other possible orchestrations of the discovery.

Aristotle had pointed out that the most effective recognitions combine objects and actions to reveal simultaneously both a fact and its full significance: *anagnorisis* then brings about *peripeteia*, to use the technical terms (*Poet.* 55a20). The ghoulish display of *Thyestes* could certainly have worked this way. That is how Herodotus orchestrated a similar revelation in telling the story of Astyages' revenge on Harpagus for saving the infant Cyrus. Harpagus is entertained at dinner and then ordered to lift the lid of the remaining dish, which conceals the head, hands, and feet of his only son: 'As he kept control of himself and did not lose his head at the dreadful sight, Astyages asked him if he knew what animal it was whose flesh he had eaten. "I know, my lord", was Harpagus' reply. . . . He said no other word, but took up what remained of the flesh and went home' (1.119). Ovid in the *Metamorphoses* replaced the quiet poignancy of Harpagus' anguish with something more energetic. When Tereus, having completed his equally horrid meal, asks for his son Itys, Procne replies with a riddle and Philomela with an action (6.655–6, 658–9):

> 'Intus habes, quem poscis' ait. circumspicit ille
> atque ubi sit quaerit . . .
> prosiluit Ityosque caput Philomela cruentum
> misit in ora patris . . .

> 'You have inside whom you seek', she says. He looks
> around and asks where he is . . .
> Up jumped Philomela and hurled Itys' bloody head
> into his father's face . . .

Tereus at once leaps from the table, clutching his middle. His recognition and reversal of fortune are simultaneous and complete.

Seneca doubtless had this second example in mind: Atreus' riddle (*quidquid e natis tuis superest habes*, 'you have what remains of your sons', 1030–1) is but a heightened version of Procne's. The pace of discovery in Seneca is nevertheless very different. The poet separates the pitiful remnants of the crime from the banquet they supplied, and his Thyestes, unlike Tereus, is too slow-witted and ineffective to see unaided the connection between them. He remains, like the phantom opponent of a declaimer's debate, only a foil. Atreus alone controls the pace of recognition. He is very much the impresario, and he is helped immeasurably by the fact that his victim, like that declamatory phantom, says only what suits his purpose. Though the exercise of real power was what enabled Atreus to punish his brother by killing Thyestes' children, it was rhetorical power that granted his true wish, which was to watch Thyestes become wretched in consequence of that act. This formidable contrivance insures that the horror will lie not in the deed but in its revelation.

What we are seeing at work here is not just a choice of *colores* and skill in manipulating language to create them, but Seneca's special confidence in the power of that manipulation. Rhetoric taught him how to subordinate action to language: he can put the emphasis on how his characters react through speech to what they see done. The *Thyestes* offers clear proof of this emphasis, but an even more striking example of confidence in the power of language over spectacle is the famous, some would say notorious, ending of the *Phaedra*, where

Theseus first contemplates and then reassembles the shattered remains of his son.

Theseus begins by facing squarely the consequences of his rash condemnation of the boy (*Phaed.* 1247–52).

> huc, huc, reliquias vehite cari corporis
> pondusque et artus temere congestos date.
> Hippolytus hic est? crimen agnosco meum:
> ego te peremi; neu nocens tantum semel
> solusve fierem, facinus ausurus parens
> patrem advocavi.

> Here! Carry the remains of that beloved body here, and
> set down the burden of its randomly piled limbs.
> Is this Hippolytus? I recognize my fault.
> I destroyed you, and as if one crime were not enough
> or committing it alone, I called upon my father's help
> to perpetrate this wrong against my son.

To wonder why Theseus here has difficulty recognizing the corpse when Phaedra could see the face clearly (1168) or to turn his despairing question into a statement is to miss the point and power of the scene.[15] What Theseus is really contemplating is not the body of his son but the magnitude of his own error. The horrific ruin of Hippolytus has become both the proof and the symbol of Theseus' moral destruction. The thing he values most lies (all too literally) in pieces before him, and his pathetic effort to reassemble those pieces is an attempt to restore a semblance of moral order by fulfilling the one parental obligation left to him (1256–8).

> disiecta, genitor, membra laceri corporis
> in ordinem dispone et errantes loco
> restitue partes.

> Parent, set the scattered limbs of this broken corpse
> in order and restore the wandering fragments
> to their place.

This is why the physical identification of the pieces echoes the language of moral recognition (e.g., *crimen agnosco meum*, 'I recognize my fault', 1249; *laevi lateris agnosco notas*, 'I recognize his left side's ruin', 1260). We may find the effect bizarre, but Seneca's point is not ghoulish display or mere rhetorical excess. The audience does not necessarily see or need to see what Theseus sees. The scene might even be more effective – whether fully staged or only recited hardly matters – if it does not. The emphasis is in any case on Theseus, an emphasis created less by what he does than by what he says while doing it. Rhetorical tragedy means, above all, verbal tragedy.

Senecan tragedy demands careful listening. Daring to make language the prime vehicle of meaning was a decision with important consequences. It reversed the tendency toward action and spectacle we saw developing in Cicero's day. The balance between seen and unseen action characteristic of Greek drama had tilted significantly by the end of the republic as technical capabilities grew and popular tastes changed. This was the tendency that encouraged the immense mule train of Accius' *Clytemnestra* and eventually the staging of seafights in a flooded orchestra, not to mention the gory excesses of Nero's mythological tableaux (Suet. *Ner.* 12.2). In the process, tragedy – or what *we* would like to call tragedy – ceased to be popular entertainment, and its more recondite successor abandoned the public world for the private one. It was this remnant of the past that reclaimed its literary heritage when Seneca discovered how to describe effectively what could then, perhaps mercifully, remain unseen.

The resulting scripts preserved tragedy as a vehicle for serious literary endeavor, which is what Renaissance dramatists would in turn discover when erecting their new tragic aesthetic on Senecan foundations. The intellectual tension they found there, the power that makes *Thyestes* and *Phaedra* plays to reckon with, develops out of Seneca's struggle to understand the forces he observed at work in the world, in the terms his education provided. This of course meant employing the language of poetry as well as the substance of philosophy: his plays are as rich in poetic allusion – especially to Ovid and Vergil – as they are in Stoic metaphysics. His creative process is essentially a literary one as he experiments with the application of poetic language to new tasks. Yet though our first allegiance may remain to Seneca as literary man and philosopher, we must never forget that the catalyst for his literary experiment with tragedy is rhetoric, and that his laboratory was the declamation hall.[16]

NOTES

1 For Pompey's theater see Hanson 1959: 43–55; Richardson 1987; and Gleason 1994. Pliny puts its capacity at 40,000 (*HN* 36.24.115), and there is no compelling reason to doubt that figure. For the running water see

Val. Max. 2.6. Theatrical awnings were apparently first introduced at the *ludi Apollinares* of 60 BCE (Plin. *HN* 19.23; cf. Lucr. 4.75–83, a much-argued passage).

2 Cic. *Fam.* 7.1 is the primary testimony. Cf. Plin. *HN* 8.7.20; Dio Cass. 39.38. *Ludi* traditionally extended over several days, with different sites for the different kinds of activity: Cic. *Leg.* 2.15.38; Livy 42.10.5.

3 Beare 1964: 71. For the politicization of theatrical productions in the later republic, see Nicolet 1980: 154–63; Beacham 1992: 363–73. Contrast the Athenian evidence gathered in Pickard-Cambridge 1968: 272–8. Given the recurrent presumption of fifth-century models for Roman tragedy, it remains worth pointing out that Romans necessarily brought Hellenistic sensibilities to their reading of *all* tragedy. For what such sensibilities entailed see Tarrant 1978 and, for a nice example of the problems involved, Frank 1995: 16–27.

4 The sources are Cic. *Brut.* 167 (Titius) and *QFr.* (Q. Cicero); Suet. *Iul.* 56.7 (Caesar) and *Aug.* 85 (Augustus); Hor. *Epist.* 2.3 (*Ars P.*) 24ff., 366–90 (the Pisones); Verg. *Ecl.* 8.9 with Serv. *ad* Verg. *Ecl.* 8.9 (Pollio). There is helpful discussion of this evidence in Fantham 1982: 5–6.

5 Fantham 1982: 6–7; esp. Cova 1989: 9–27. A lavish public performance should not be deduced from the million sesterces Augustus is said to have paid Varius. The gift may have been not a *quid pro quo* but the reward for long service, rather like Horace's Sabine farm. See Coffey 1986: 46–7.

6 For recitation as an aristocratic entertainment, see in general Mayor 1872: 173–82 (*ad* Juv. 3.9). For recitation of specifically dramatic verse by Romans, see Zwierlein 1966: 156–66, and for the stylistic effect of recitation on poetry, Williams 1978: 303–6. The spread of roofed theaters in the empire suggests small-scale public performances as well as the private recitations recorded, for example, by the younger Pliny (*Ep.* 1.15.2, 5.3.2, 9.36.4), whose taste apparently ran toward comedy. On the spread of small public theaters, a topic that merits further study, see Izenour 1992.

7 Leo 1878: 158. Of the studies directly fostered by Leo's ground-breaking work, Canter 1925 remains most valuable for its comprehensive examination of Seneca's debt to rhetorical practice. Bonner 1949: 160–7 provides a useful overview. For Ovid's *Medea* in this context, see Leo 1878: 148–9; Currie 1981: 2702–4.

8 I think in particular of Braden 1985; Rosenmeyer 1989. For the more specific Senecan instance to come, see Lefèvre 1985.

9 Tarrant 1985: 219 *ad* 904.

10 For the role of *color* in declamation, see Bonner 1949: 55–6; Fairweather 1981: 166–78.

11 Cf. the 'Thyestean imprecations' of Hor. *Epod.* 5.86. *Epist.* 2.3.91 (*Ars P.*) makes the *cena Thyestae* ('dinner of Thyestes') stand for tragedy itself (cf. 186); Cic. *Tusc.* 4.77, quoting Accius, makes Thyestes the epitome of *ira* ('anger').

12 Translated by Winterbottom 1974.

13 For the slave-defendant in such a case, presumably under the *lex Iulia*

de adulteriis coercendis, see Mette-Dittmann 1991: 50 n. 132. I owe both the legal explanation and the reference to Thomas McGinn.

14 Whether this audience was notional or real and whether the plays were written with full stage performance in mind hardly matter, though (as far as I can see) nothing much is added to the effect of a Senecan play by a visual component or lost by its absence. For sensible roasting of this Senecan chestnut, see Fantham 1982: 34–49; Braden 1985: 230–1 n. 14; the issue is examined from a different perspective by Sutton 1986: 57–62.

15 Thus Zwierlein 1966: 17–19; Sutton 1986: 52–3. I agree with Sutton that the question is rhetorical, but not 'merely' rhetorical. The most recent commentary, Coffey and Mayer 1990: 195 (cf. 17–18), is surprisingly deaf to the pathos of this scene.

16 I thank Routledge for allowing me to publish a longer version of this chapter in *TAPhA* 126 (1996). This essay owes much to the advice and criticism of Richard C. Beacham and Robert A. Kaster.

11

Inter tribunal et scaenam: comedy and rhetoric in Rome

Joseph J. Hughes

In 160 BCE, the veteran actor and producer Ambivius Turpio presented himself as an *orator* seeking a fair hearing for Terence's *Hecyra*. It was not the first time Ambivius had played *in propria persona* the role of Terence's advocate. To be sure, protatic characters of various descriptions had been pleading for audiences' good will since the invention of drama, but Terence's choice of an orator represents much more than an attempt at literary novelty. If we are to believe the prologues, the *Hecyra* had already flopped twice before churlish audiences more interested in pugilists and ropewalkers than in the restrained Menandrean pleasures Terence brought them. Ambivius' appearance is a characteristic Terentian conflation of Greek and Roman: the pleader speaking words written out beforehand by a *logographos* and the venerable, well-connected *patronus* pleading for a client of lesser status. It also illustrates the topic of this chapter: the interaction between comedy and rhetoric in the late Roman republic.

Few would disagree that Terence here and elsewhere persuaded his audience to be entertained by his comedies, just as Roman orators entertained their listeners in order to persuade them. The nature of the evidence, however, complicates this formulation. There is no shortage of testimonia. The second-century BCE comic poet Afranius borrowed freely from Menander (Macrob. *Sat.* 6.1.4) and modelled his style on that of the orator/tragedian Titius (*Brut.* 167). Roscius, the great comic actor of the first century BCE, not only gave lessons in voice and gesture to orators such as the youthful Cicero, but also attended the speeches of the florid Asianist orator Hortensius to cull tricks he might employ on the stage (Val. Max. 8.10.2). According to Macrobius (*Sat.* 3.14.16), Roscius also competed with Cicero occasionally in expository technique, the actor 'expressing' a maxim in gestures, and the orator in words, with Roscius' successes prompting him to write a book comparing his art to that of the orator. Roman rhetoricians, early and late, were obviously familiar with comedy. The youthful Cicero expected the jury in his first public case, the *Pro Roscio Amerino*, to understand a detailed reference to three characters from a comedy nearly one century old.

But in all too many cases the evidence is too sketchy, or deprived of its proper context, or both. For instance Quintilian praises Menander for his oratory, but the comedies he cites as evidence are all but totally lost. Social and literary considerations have also helped confuse the picture. The Romans never totally overcame their ancient ambivalence toward Greek innovations; rhetoric and philosophy ultimately became respectable, but the fine arts always inspired contempt regardless of their undeniable public utility. Moreover, a strict *lex operis* governed Greek and Roman authors alike, constructing strict boundaries of theme and form around genres. Necessarily the *lex operis* was violated constantly from Greek times onward, as oratory took on theatrical tones and vice versa; even so, the authors seldom if ever called attention to such deviation.[1] In light of these factors, it is small wonder that a systematic study of the interaction between comedy and rhetoric in ancient Rome has never appeared. Exhaustive catalogues of direct references and semi-veiled allusions to comedy in Cicero's rhetoric and oratory have been available for roughly a century, as have rhetorical analyses of Terence's prologues.[2] More recent scholarship has taken more account of the parallel duties of the playwright and the orator, and how each borrowed from the other.[3] This chapter will sketch out the interaction between Roman comedy and rhetoric in its full scope, offer original illustrations of Cicero's oratorical practice in light of this outline, and, finally, suggest possible reasons why the Romans themselves found it difficult to explain the relationship between the tribunal and the stage.

RHETORIC IN PLAUTUS AND TERENCE

The peoples of Italy seem always to have preferred farcical humour.[4] What little we know about the pre-literary comedic forms of the mime and the *fabulae Atellanae* indicates broad, physical humour enacted by a small repertoire of exaggerated stock characters. While the Roman *comoediae palliatae* (comedies set in the Greek world, with ostensibly Greek characters involved in ostensibly Greek adventures) and their Romanized variant, the *comoediae togatae*, are rightly considered the continuation of Greek New Comedy, the farcical aspect never disappeared entirely. Farce was a staple of the comedies of Plautus, whose mixture of extravagant language and action, Greek dramatic convention and Roman *mores* made him a commercial success; Terence's unwillingness to indulge in these one generation later created friction between playwright and audience. New Comedy, both Greek and Roman, was largely formulaic, with stock characters and a plot depending on thwarted love, deception, mistaken identity or any combination thereof. The most popular theme was deception, and the most uniquely Roman character was the *servus callidus* ('clever slave'), a braggart who wheedles and lies, fixated on obtaining the money to buy the object of his master's affections. The *servus callidus* also gleefully usurps the language of almost every profession and social standing to glorify himself or worry about his next move. But references to public discourse or seemingly 'rhetorical' language are neither lengthy nor frequent. For instance, Pseudolus appoints himself (*Ps.* 606) the *precator et patronus* ('intercessor and patron') for a battered door; in *Amphitruo*, the prologue speaker Mercury uses forms of the adjectives *iustus* ('just') and *iniustus* ('unjust') seven times within three lines (34–6). The first is simply a metaphor, while the second is a mere parody of 'the argument from justice'. On the other hand, Plautus expected his audiences to appreciate references to legal arcana. At line 23, Pseudolus parodies the ancient marriage-formula 'for begetting children' (*quaerendorum liberorum causa*) by claiming the letters on a wax tablet are climbing one another and 'begetting children' (*quaerunt liberos*). Later, he imitates a praetor addressing a public assembly (125–8). The Roman audiences clearly possessed the sophistication in public discourse to enjoy these and other even more recondite jokes, but the scarcity of explicitly rhetorical jokes among all the other references to everyday Roman life seems to indicate that Hellenistic rhetorical theory had not yet saturated the Roman consciousness by Plautus' day.[5]

Terence faced a far different situation. By his time, the gulf between the upper and lower classes was widening rapidly, and the rift was reflected in their entertainments: an inauspicious time for a brave experiment in returning to the carefully crafted realism of Greek New Comedy. A recent study of the prologue to Terence's *Heauton Timoroumenos* and its difference from its Plautine counterparts shows Terence using the same 'rhetorical' tools that Cato the censor was employing offstage.[6] Not all of the *nobilitas* were philhellenic, nor would all of them have recognized Simo's impersonations of his son Pamphilus' conversation in the *Andria* (134, 139–41) as *prosopopoeia*, or Simo's inference that if Pamphilus rescued a stranger from a fire, he must love his father even more (110–12; cf. Cic. *De Or.* 2.172) as a syllogism. But as a whole the Roman upper class was replicating enthusiastically the sort of intellectual milieu in which Menander had worked, and will have appreciated Terence's studied refinement. Whether these rhetorical flourishes were taken directly from Menander's original or Terence's own is impossible to tell; it is worth noting that at least one fragment of Afranius, the self-admitted borrower from Menander, contains an allusion to a point of school rhetoric.[7] Terence was certainly hard pressed to win over an audience conditioned to more robust entertainment. Still, his audiences, even allowing for the wide spectrum of people who attended the productions, could not possibly have been the rollicking vulgarians Ambivius alludes to in the prologue of *Hecyra*. According to Suetonius' *De Poetis*, Terence's comedies actually enjoyed considerable success, at least in the long run, which indicates that his pleas for a fair hearing were granted. Thus Terence's prologues clearly were more than schoolbook rhetoric trotted out to edify a small circle of aesthetes. They represented Roman rhetoric in action, and contributed to its dissemination among Romans of all classes.[8]

The *comoediae palliatae* officially died with Turpilius in 103 BCE, and the *togatae* a quarter-century afterward. Although especially popular *palliatae* and *togatae* were occasionally revived long after originals had ceased to be written, the New Comedy was defunct by the time Cicero began his career in the courts. Schoolboys studied the works of the poets, and the erudite continued to dabble in writing purely literary drama. The mime and the Atellane farce had reclaimed their primacy on the Roman stage, in a scripted form to be sure, but with their traditional subject matter of sex, violence, and slapstick. The victory of the lower comedic forms had consequences for our understanding of the relationship between rhetoric and comedy. Connection with the comic stage in any form had always carried a stigma. The Romans had always considered the subject matter of comedy alien to the *gravitas* and *dignitas* upon which they prided themselves: after all, the antics of a Pseudolus and his hapless masters were fit for public viewing primarily because they were understood to be Greeks. The degeneration of the Roman viewing public's tastes in the first century BCE only exacerbated the situation. The rare exception might be made for a Roscius, but as a whole, comedy and comic actors became associated with the demimonde. Even the Greeks, who were more appreciative of their playwrights and actors, had been careful not to make their borrowing from comedy too blatant. Although Demosthenes borrowed brilliantly from Old Comedy in the *Philippics*, as did Lysias in *For the Handicapped Person*, there is little indication that borrowing from comedy was acknowledged in the received Hellenistic theory, much less integrated into it.[9] Roman comedic borrowing would develop along Roman lines.

COMEDY IN REPUBLICAN ROMAN ORATORY BEFORE CICERO

Our best sources for the state of technical rhetoric at the beginning of the first century BCE are the teenaged Cicero's unfinished *De Inventione* and the anonymous *Rhetorica ad Herennium*. Predictably, there is no direct encouragement to study comedy or to use comedic technique in one's oratory. Both treatises (*Inv. Rhet.* 1.27; *Rhet. Her.* 1.13) mention in their discussion of *narratio* a declamatory exercise designed to amuse and to develop skill at handling narrative, which I will term the *narratio in personis* ('narrative based on persons'). Cicero illustrates this exercise with a passage from Terence's *Adelphoe* (60–4) in which the *pater mitis* ('kindly father') Micio recounts the criticisms of his sterner brother, the *pater durus* ('stern father') Demea.[10] In a schema that will recur in his mature rhetorical works, Cicero explains that the exercise should express the conversation (*sermones*) and mind-set (*animi*) of the characters involved, but stops short of advocating the study of Terence's works in the hopes of matching him at *ethopoeia*.[11] The operative word for this sort of exercise is *festivitas* ('liveliness'; *Inv. Rhot.* 1.27):

> This sort of narrative should possess great liveliness, to be drawn from a number of factors: dissimilarity of characters, severity, gentleness, hope, fear, suspicion, desire, dissimulation, error, pity, change of fortune, unlooked-for disaster, sudden joy, and a happy ending to the affair.[12]

Cicero's discussion of the *narratio in personis* ends on this note. He never completed the section on ornamentation in which he promises to expand on the exercise's efficacy. Although he makes no such claim, all of the factors contributing to *festivitas* are present in the *Adelphoe* and the other surviving *comoediae palliatae*, as an examination of the *Rhetorica ad Herennium*'s extensive treatment of stylistic ornament demonstrates. Each of a series of 'figures of thought' related to *ethopoeia* is described and illustrated with a passage of the author's own composition: 'portrayal', including physical description (*effictio*, 4.63), 'character delineation' (*notatio*, 63), 'dialogue' (*sermocinatio*, 65), and 'personification' (*conformatio*, 66). The passage that illustrates *notatio* is a lengthy character sketch (63–5) of the *ostentator pecuniosi* ('vaunter of money'), a variant on the traditional *alazon* ('braggart', 'impostor') whose incessant boasting and brushes with comeuppance strongly recall the spirit of comedy and – in all likelihood – the influence of the *narratio in personis*. The young Cicero's failure to finish *De Inventione* is unfortunate: his illustrations of these figures would have come from the Latin poets. But the expressed connection between comedy and rhetoric is not particularly strong in the early handbooks. The study of comedies was seen as conferring skill at *ethopoeia* and at handling of *narratio*; in other words, it contributed more to style than to function.[13]

Careful examination of the evidence shows that Cicero was not the first Roman orator to draw upon comedy in his orations.[14] In *Brutus* he singles out two of his mentors, Crassus Orator (*cos.* 95 BCE) and Caesar Strabo, the aedile of 90 BCE, as particularly witty and stylish. The oratory of the latter, who discourses on humour in *De Oratore*, is all but lost, but he alone is singled out for his *festivitas* in the *Brutus* (77). We learn also that Caesar Strabo wrote tragedies and declaimed in public; he could treat tragic subjects 'almost comically'. The remarks attributed to him in *De Oratore* further show a more than passing acquaintance with the mime; given his reputation as both orator and wag, it would be odd indeed if Caesar Strabo did not use comedic techniques in his orations. Happily, there is more evidence about Crassus Orator. Speaking in *De Oratore*, Caesar Strabo cedes first place in wit to him, comments on the *festivitas* of one of his invectives (2.227), and sketches out an anecdote Crassus told about his adversary Memmius in his *De lege Servilia* of 106 BCE (2.240–2). Elsewhere Cicero claims (*Brut.* 164) that this speech was the culmination of Crassus' oratory and that it was studied as a textbook. The anecdote, about the brawl of Memmius and one Largus over a woman from Tarracina, has achieved a notoriety of its own. For years references to this fascinating passage have dotted footnotes and commentaries, but it has not yet been studied exhaustively in its proper context: the Rome of 106 BCE. A brief indication of its comedic affinities is in order.

The *lex Servilia* was directed against the senatorial monopoly on jury service, and the *optimate* stalwart Crassus was speaking out against it at an assembly of the people. Cicero provides a hint of comedic content and style (*Brut.* 164) when he says that the speech was delivered *populariter*. The political connotation ('in the manner of a *popularis*') is possible, but the meaning 'in language tailored to the *populus*' is more appropriate. Supposedly the brawl was over 'a little lady friend' (*amicula*) and it ended with the letters L.L.L.M.M. splattered on walls all over town. The inscription was actually a formulaic campaign slogan on the order of *lege laetus lubens merito Memmium* ('Vote cheerfully for Memmius – he deserves it.'). In Crassus' interpretation, though, an old duffer from the town (*senex quidam oppidanus*) interprets it as *lacerat lacertum Largi Mordax Memmius*, which means 'Munching Memmius Lunched on Largus' Limb'. Harding has well noted that such physical slapstick action was demeaning for an upper-class Roman.[15] It is worth noting in addition that there are signs of comedic plot (the 'adultery mime' was a popular type of low popular entertainment), stock characters (the 'little lady friend', the 'old duffer from town', and the two brawling lovers), and even hints of comedic diction: the supposed translation of L.L.L.M.M. is an iambic *senarius*, and it is referred to as a *clausula*, which is the technical term for the conclusion of a play. Of course, the anecdote cannot be reconstructed in its entirety, but it is impossible not to posit some of the characteristics that create *festivitas* in Cicero's description of the *narratio in personis*. Like the narrative exercise, anecdotes such as Crassus' are said to depend on character delineation (*sermo*, 'way of speaking'; *mores*, 'character') and, in this case, a liberal admixture of humour – regardless of its factual content or the lack thereof. Although Cicero endorses the use of such narratives, the *lex operis* intrudes. This passage is literally surrounded in *De Oratore* by injunctions against using humour that smacks too strongly of the mime: a disclaimer, as it were, that the boundaries of dignity must be maintained. Consequently the connection is not nearly as explicit as one would like. Yet this glimpse of Crassus Orator at work in the forum hints in no uncertain terms at where Cicero developed his instinct for using comedic technique.

COMEDY IN CICERO'S ORATORY

As the groundbreaking works of Geffcken, Dumont, and Axer have demonstrated and subsequent studies have confirmed, comedic characterization, diction, and plot structure occur in all phases of Cicero's career as an orator.[16] Although it is an overstatement to say that *Pro Roscio Comoedo*, *Pro Caelio*, or any other oration *is* a comedy, I am greatly indebted to their sensitive studies of Cicero's use of comedic themes, characters, and diction toward the much more practical end of securing acquittal for his clients. Examination of Cicero's use of comedy in three of his earliest orations – *Pro Roscio Amerino*, *Pro Roscio Comoedo* and *Pro Cluentio* – will narrow the scope of my investigation while providing an overview of Cicero's strategies and techniques that represents fairly his practice throughout his career. The analysis of *Pro Cluentio* will further provide an entirely original interpretation of an oft-remarked (yet never completely appreciated) passage.

In Cicero's first public case, the *Pro Roscio Amerino* of 80 BCE, his client is a rural landholder charged with parricide. As the junior Roscius' motive, the prosecutor Erucius alleged his resentment of his father for leaving him in the backwater of Ameria, while taking another, better favoured, brother to Rome. Cicero's riposte (47) is a direct reference (without any quotation *per se*) to the fragmentary *Subditivus* of Caecilius Statius. As best as the plot can be reconstructed, the unnamed father takes his son Chaerestratus to the city and leaves his son Eutychus in the country, but is a loving father to both. In this way, Cicero presumes upon the jurors' familiarity with the stage to define the *ethos* of both Roscii and to demolish the prosecution's alleged motive: Roscius junior is the fundamentally simple, but good, rustic youth while his father is the likeable *pater mitis* ('kindly father') of comedy. A thoughtful recent study further suggests that Erucius may also have used comedic stereotyping to buttress his own argument, attempting to portray Roscius senior as the much less sympathetic *pater durus* ('stern father').[17] Amusingly, Cicero indicates elsewhere in the oration that the Roscii were both well heeled and well connected in Rome, which hints at his confidence in the power of comedic stereotyping to convey a positive picture of his client – even if it contradicted something he had said earlier. Aloud, however, he comes off as hesitant, pretending not to recall Eutychus' name and referring to his citation from a comedy as *ineptiae* ('trifles'). His strongest justification betrays a concern about the general applicability of poetry to real life (*Rosc. Am.* 47): 'Indeed, I believe the poets contrived these productions to show us, in other characters, our own customs and a picture of our everyday life.' This apologetic tone is undoubtedly caused by a combination of the stigma against fine arts and the equally pervasive *lex operis*, but the jurors seem not to have faulted Cicero for resorting to *ineptiae*, as they voted to acquit.

In his defence of the actor Roscius, Cicero had much wider scope for borrowing from comedy, and perhaps less to lose; the case is generally regarded as a tough one. Traditionally dated to the mid-seventies, there is now some evidence for a date of 66 BCE, which would set it at the same time as the *Pro Cluentio*.[18] As does the *Pro Roscio Amerino*, the oration Cicero delivers for his old tutor in elocution refers directly to Roman comedy without any direct quotation. This time, the plaintiff Fannius Chaerea is compared to one of Roscius' most popular roles – Ballio, the pimp from Plautus' *Pseudolus*. Comparing Chaerea's appearance to Ballio's, Cicero paints a vivid word-picture to go along with the recollection of this most unsavoury of all stock characters. The effect is constantly reiterated and refreshed through subtle allusions to comedy and what Axer terms 'comic stylization', a number of effects that include the frequent use of dialogues, colloquial expressions (e.g., diminutives and compounds of *per*), repetition of significant words, and assonance.[19] The effect is to suggest in a subtle and engaging fashion that Roscius was ethically incapable of defrauding Chaerea, while the Ballio-figure Chaerea was capable of literally any misdeed.[20]

The *Pro Cluentio* of 66 BCE likewise represents a step beyond the technique of direct reference, as Cicero uses comedic plot structure, characterization, and language to help sell a revisionist version of the notorious series of three trials in 74 BCE called the *iudicium Iunianum*, after the name of the president of the court that tried all three. The challenge was daunting. Statius Oppianicus had been convicted in that year of attempting to poison his son-in-law Aulus Cluentius Habitus. Although the same jury had already convicted two of Oppianicus' alleged apprentices, Fabricius and his freedman Scamander, a persistent rumour maintained that Cluentius had purchased the guilty verdict via the notorious Gaius Staienus. As late as 69 BCE, *popularis* orators scored points by lambasting the whole affair as a travesty of justice (i.e., Oppianicus had been the innocent victim of Cluentius and his henchman Staienus), and as an example of senatorial jurors' venality. One particularly vocal critic was

Cicero, whose outrage was undoubtedly stoked by his failure to get Scamander acquitted. By 66 BCE, Oppianicus was dead, and Cicero was defending Cluentius against charges of judicial murder. His new affiliation in the affair caused Cicero to readjust his view on the *iudicium Iunianum*; the problem lay in convincing the jurors of his new interpretation. Most likely, both Cluentius and Oppianicus had offered bribes to the jurors, but Cicero offers a dazzlingly fallacious argument from probability. Of course the jury had been bribed, but if he could prove Oppianicus had committed bribery, Cluentius had to be innocent of bribery and therefore innocent of judicial murder. For all of the scholarly effort devoted to explaining Cicero's success in – as he put it – 'casting fog in the jurors' eyes', the fashion in which he cloaked this ridiculous argument has not yet been completely explained.[21]

The key to Cicero's strategy in this portion of *Pro Cluentio* is his depiction of Staienus as a character from Roman comedy. Although the dramatic overtones of Cicero's narrative have been remarked, the nature of Staienus' characterization has not: a strange concoction of the *servus callidus* ('clever slave') and the *alazon* ('braggart' 'impostor') with a dash of the pompous, thieving cook thrown in for good measure.[22] Promising not to violate the jurors' sense of decorum or their cultivation (in terms strongly recalling his apologies for citing Caecilius Statius in *Pro Roscio Amerino*), he starts with the first trial, that of Scamander. Suspecting danger, Oppianicus starts (*coepit*, 68) to cultivate Staienus, here described as 'needy, audacious, and adept at fixing juries'. After the convictions of his accomplices, Oppianicus starts (*coepit*) to seek Staienus' help as if he were 'most clever at planning, most audaciously impudent, and most vigorous at getting the job done'. The words 'as if' are crucial. Cleverness, audacity, and impudence are all hallmarks of the *servus callidus*, which is exactly the role Oppianicus sees for Staienus. These qualities also characterize the *alazon*, who, like the handicapped man of Lysias' speech and the *ostentator pecuniosi* ('vaunter of money') of the *Rhetorica ad Herennium*, specializes in passing himself off as what he is not. Cicero warns the listeners that Staienus possesses these qualities to a certain extent, but beyond that he is all show. His *modus operandi* is that of the *suppressor*, a go-between who agrees to dispense bribes but keeps the money for his own purposes. He boasts that nobody else can get the job done; he starts (*coepit*, 69) to drag his feet preparatory to demanding a huge sum of money (*permagnam pecuniam poposcit*, 69). This combination of alliteration and a colloquial *per*-compound is the first taste of the Plautine language that figures so prominently in *Pro Roscio Comoedo*. Even at this point in the anecdote, Cicero's audience must have anticipated the fixings of a very familiar comedic subplot involving a swindler, a dupe, and a large amount of money. They were not disappointed.

In the next section of the anecdote, Staienus takes centre stage. At home with the money he has promised to dispense among the jurors, he starts (*coepit*, 69) to pose himself a dilemma. If Oppianicus is acquitted, he will either have to pay off the jurors or return the money to Oppianicus. At this point Cicero interrupts the narrative to remind the jury that Staienus is 'needy, a spendthrift, audacious, clever, and untrustworthy', and that these character traits alone should serve as evidence. But Cicero has not finished. Staienus starts (*coepit*, 70) to turn his mind to trickery, and delivers a direct-discourse soliloquy in which he rehearses in more agitated language the dangers he runs if Oppianicus is acquitted, resolving, in a second barrage of plosives, to 'push him from his precipice ... and propel him to perdition' (*praecipitantem igitur impellamus ... et perditum prosternamus*, 70). The plot proper is introduced with the same sort of wordplay. Now Staienus is 'twisted and wrong-side-up' (*praeposterus et perversus*, 71) because he starts with a juror cognominated Bulbus ('the Onion') and then recruits one Gutta ('Salad Oil'), in violation of the Roman custom of serving salad as an early course and onions as a dessert. The sustained association of Staienus' activities with those of a professional – in this instance, a cook (*conditor*, 71) – is a particularly Plautine touch.[23] Staienus next 'sprinkles the Onion with a dash of Salad Oil' (71), making Bulbus 'a little less bitter to anyone who had tasted a little of hope from his conversation' (72). Later still, we are informed that Staienus has 'seasoned his natural vices with studies in the art of wickedness' (72). The cooking imagery also evokes images of the comedic cook, a frequent bit player in New Comedy characterized by wild braggadocio, a propensity for thievery, and bizarre recipes.[24] More significantly still, the various roles Staienus is called upon to play while carrying out his scheme call to mind the various impersonations practised by *servi callidi* ('clever slaves') in their intrigues.[25] Recruiting Bulbus, Staienus is friendly and conspiratorial, as evidenced by the colloquial *'quid tu?'* with which he starts his pitch. But later when Bulbus asks for his share of the bribe money, Staienus assumes the persona of a pillar of virtue. Eyebrows knitted, he informs Bulbus that Oppianicus has left everyone in the lurch, and declares that he will vote to convict. To emphasize that this is but a pose, Cicero here calls Staienus an impostor (*planus*, 72) known for his mendacious facial expressions. As with the vivid description of Fannius Chaerea in the *Pro Roscio Comoedo*, Cicero relies on comedic characterization to lend credence to a convoluted narrative.

The denouement of the trial is almost an anticlimax. Oppianicus is duly convicted (73–6), and the *popularis* politicians purposely twist the convoluted goings-on behind the *iudicium Iunianum* to their own benefit (77). In the drawn-out musings on the *iudicium Iunianum* that follow, Cicero terms the prosecution's account as a 'fable' (84) and 'hooted off the stage' (86). It is most unlikely that the jurors in the *Cluentiana* were persuaded by Cicero's account, but they were undeniably amused. Even if they had not been convinced that Staienus had acted exactly as Cicero said, Staienus' affinities with the swindling, posturing *servus callidus*, reinforced by the rich comedic stylization – alliteration, sustained metaphor, repetition of words and ideas – portray him as capable of almost anything Cicero might impute to him. Cicero seems not so much concerned to persuade as he is to suspend disbelief for as long as it takes to set forth his audacious explanation. As was the case in *Pro Roscio Comoedo*, Cicero's use of comedy figures heavily in what seems to be an otherwise hopeless case: thus, its efficacy transcends the comparatively narrow boundaries of style. It remains to examine just how, if at all, Cicero's practice is reflected in his mature rhetorical works and the *Institutio Oratoria* of Quintilian.

COMEDY IN ROMAN RHETORIC

The *De Oratore* of 55 BCE was Cicero's attempt to transcend the boundaries of Hellenistic schoolbook rhetoric. He had recently delivered the second of his comedic masterpieces, the *Pro Caelio*; his other speeches of the time, especially *In Pisonem*, show signs of comedic allusions. A decade later, he would borrow heavily from comedy once more in his *Second Philippic*. In reconciling the Hellenistic tradition with his almost three decades of experience, one would expect at least some reference to the possible uses of comedic techniques. His remarks on humour, especially those related to Crassus' *De Lege Servilia*, acknowledge the utility of the farcical aspects of humour that (save for the *narratio in personis* and the discussion of style in *Rhetorica ad Herennium*) were all but ignored in earlier discussions of rhetorical theory. Having discussed examples of Cicero's comedic borrowing, we can now see that he is describing his own practice as well as Crassus' at *De Oratore* 2.241:

> You see how witty this sort of tale is, how elegant and worthy of an orator – whether you have something true to relate that still must be sprinkled with little lies or whether you make it all up. The virtue of this sort of tale is that you demonstrate the facts in such a way that the character (*mores*) of the man you are talking about, his speech (*sermo*), and his entire appearance (*vultus*) are expressed, so that they seem to the hearers to be acted out and happening right then and there.

This acknowledgement of the efficacy of exaggeration and comic invention is followed by an almost predictable injunction against too lifelike an imitation of the farcical characters, which is more appropriate for the most disreputable of genres, the mime. Discussing the more 'technical' topic of *narratio* as statement of facts (2.326–31), he advocates the quality of 'pleasantness' at the expense of the traditional brevity. He offers as illustration two quotations from Terence's *Andria* (51 ff., 117–18), which he lauds for presenting the *mores* ('character'), *sermo* ('way of speaking'), and *vultus et forma et lamentatio* ('face, appearance and mourning') of various characters; that is, the same features emphasized in tales such as Crassus' anecdote. Adding to this implicit endorsement of Terence's expository technique, Cicero assigns the name of *festivitas* ('liveliness') to this new quality he prescribes for the statement of facts; that is, the same quality associated with the *narratio in personis*, the speeches of Caesar Strabo, and the speeches of Crassus Orator. As he had done thirty-odd years earlier in *De Inventione*, Cicero fails to make the connection between comedy and rhetoric explicit, but at least the hints are more abundant. Clarification can be found in the narrowly technical *Partitiones Oratoriae*, which Cicero compiled in the early 40s BCE. In the discussion of *narratio* as statement of facts (31), he prescribes that the ideal *narratio* be plausible, clear, and 'charming' (*suavis*). The factors that contribute to this charm should be familiar (32): 'A statement of facts will have charm (*suavitas*) if it has surprises, suspense, unlooked-for outcomes, an admixture of emotions, dialogues between characters, instances of grief, anger, fear, joy, and desire.' Clearly, this is part of the list of qualities that characterize the *narratio in personis*; *suavitas* ('charm') is just as plainly a synonym for *festivitas* ('liveliness'). As we will see, the passage from *Pro Cluentio* is just the sort of narrative Cicero is talking about. Unless one regards Crassus' anecdote from the *De lege Servilia* as a doublet for Cicero's practice, this is the closest Cicero comes to acknowledging his demonstrated mastery of applying comedic techniques.

Quintilian's praise of Menander in his survey of literature in *Institutio* 10.1.69–71 is heartfelt: his eloquence is such that his works alone would suffice the aspiring orator in his literary studies. By contrast he dismisses Roman New Comedy with the cutting 'in comedy we are weakest of all' (*in comoedia maxime claudicamus*), primarily because of the alleged inferiority of Latin to Greek. For Quintilian, the utility of the study of comedy lies in the familiar places: as an aid to improving one's style, or at best, skill at *ethopoeia*.[26] Over and over he mentions appropriate figures like *prosopopoeia*, *enargeia* and *ethopoeia*, illustrating his remarks with quotations from Cicero that show clear evidence of comedic technique, but always advising extreme caution in its use. Discussing the *narratio* as statement of facts, he mentions at *Institutio* 4.2.52 'a plausible way of relating matters (*ductus rei credibilis*), such as in comedy and mime', fleshed out with the comment that if handled correctly, 'the judge himself will anticipate what you are going to say next'. This is a clear reference to a highly specific set of expectations that can only be based on comedic characters, diction, and plot structures. He recommends against the use of *prosopopoeia* in the statement of facts (4.2.107), but cites the conversation between Staienus and Bulbus (*Staieni Bulbique colloquium*) in *Pro Cluentio* 71–2. Admitting this as a violation of the rule he has just expounded, Quintilian praises it for its 'quickness' and 'plausibility', adding these perceptive remarks (*Inst.* 4.2.107):

> Lest it be thought that Cicero did this without design (quite an incredible supposition in his case), I would point out that in the *Partitiones* he lays it down that the statement of facts should be characterized by passages that will charm and be characterized by unexpected turns, conversations between persons, and appeals to every kind of emotion.

Quintilian obviously recognized comedic borrowing when he saw it in Cicero's work. He also recognized that the declamatory tastes of his own day lent themselves well enough to excess without his encouragement. It would be churlish to fault him for not acknowledging Cicero's comedic borrowing as such. Even the master himself had proven unable to objectify in so many words what went on when

Roscius Amerinus became Eutychus, or Fannius Chaerea played Ballio, or Staienus became a *servus gloriosus* ('braggart slave'). We ourselves have but recently passed beyond the fragmentary evidence, persistent social bias, and hidebound traditions that have kept us from charting the territory between the tribunal and the stage. This chapter, I trust, has made a small but necessary step in the right direction.[27]

NOTES

1 For two Roman formulations of this concept, see Cic. *Opt. Gen.* 1 and Hor. *Ars P.* 73–98.

2 Direct and indirect references to Roman comedy in the works of Cicero have been amply collected and documented in works such as Schaefler 1884; Radin 1911; Zillinger 1912. The *locus classicus* for Cicero's appreciation of Roman drama is still Wright 1931, more recently augmented by Sutton 1984; Fantham 1989b.

3 The connection between playwright and orator has been stated most recently by Gotoff 1993: 290; see also the list of Axer 1989: 299–300. Compare, however, the cautionary remarks of Bers 1994: 179.

4 The most recent study of the antecedents of Roman comedy is Beacham 1992, esp. 1–55. Also worth consulting are Duckworth 1994; Beare 1964.

5 For an overview of the cultural milieu with bibliography, see Gruen 1990: 124–57; 1992: 183–222.

6 See Goldberg 1983: 198–211; Goldberg 1986: 31–60. On the prologue of the *Andria*, see also Leeman 1963: 24–5.

7 Fr. 152 in Daviault 1980 seems to be parodying the traditional rhetorical categories of action (*res*), time (*tempus*) and place (*locus*).

8 Kennedy 1972: 66. On the possibility that Terence may have studied rhetoric, see Goldberg 1986: 70.

9 For an assessment of the influence of comedy on Greek rhetoric, see Harding 1994; Rowe 1966; Rowe 1968.

10 There is a perplexing plethora of names for these two stock characters: *senex* ('old man') is often used as a synonym for *pater* ('father'); the old man/father can also be called *lenis* ('lenient') or *iratus* ('angry').

11 The *narratio in negotiis* ('narrative based on deeds') mentioned at *Inv. Rhet.* 1.27 is also illustrated by a passage from Terence (*An.* 51ff.).

12 I here translate *confecta ex rerum varietate* as 'drawn from a number of factors' and not, as Hubbell 1949: 57 translates it, 'fluctuations of fortune'.

13 See Caplan 1954: 387 n. d, 397 n. c. For an interesting account of the *Rhetorica ad Herennium*'s illustration of 'dialogue', see Sinclair 1993: 576–8. On the influence of the *narratio in personis*, see Calboli 1969: 46–50.

14 For other explanations of this subject, see Axer 1980: 49.

15 Harding 1994: 199–200.

16 Limitations of space preclude even a synopsis of scholarship on the topic.

For Cicero's use of comedy in his post-consular orations include Axer 1980; Geffcken 1973; Dumont 1975. More recent work includes Hughes 1987; Hughes 1992a; Hughes 1992b; Sussman 1994; Sussman (forthcoming).

17 Vasaly 1985; 1993: 157–70.

18 The date of 66 BCE was first advanced by Stroh 1975: 149–56 and supported by Axer 1980: 54–6. Acknowledging difficulties with either date but leaning toward the later one is Craig 1993: 67. I likewise support the later date, arguing that the combination of direct reference and other more subtle techniques Axer has detected in *Pro Roscio Comoedo* have much more in common with the technique I have detected in *Pro Cluentio* than it does with the technique of simple direct reference in *Pro Roscio Amerino*.

19 See Axer 1980; Axer 1989.

20 For the force of *ethos* in Cicero's oratory, see May 1988; for an interesting examination of Ballio's character, see Garton 1972: 169–88.

21 For a thorough discussion of the background, see Kirby 1990b: 5–12.

22 For another view of this passage plus a complete bibliography, see Kirby 1990b: 73–6.

23 Fantham 1972: 113.

24 See Lowe 1985; Gowers 1994: 87–107.

25 For the importance of impersonation and role-playing, see Duckworth 1994: 169; Slater 1985: 160–2.

26 For a discussion of Quintilian's attitude toward the theatre, see Cousin 1975.

27 I am grateful to Lisa Hughes, William Dominik and Lewis Sussman for their assistance. I gratefully acknowledge the assistance of a Southwest Missouri Summer Fellowship in completing this work.

12

Eros and eloquence: modes of amatory persuasion in Ovid's *Ars Amatoria*

Peter Toohey

When eros is unconsummated (whether intentionally or merely through circumstance) one has recourse first to persuasion,[1] then, if that is unsuccessful, to rape.[2] Only in some situations are neither persuasion nor rape useful. The very old must endure their lack of consummation (Ibycus 287 or Anacreon 358).[3] Lovers permanently separated, through death,[4] distance,[5] conclusive rejection,[6] or even physical infirmity (impotence as in Ov. *Am.* 3.7) must also endure. This enforced endurance may lead to a melancholic lovesickness – anorexia and eventual death – of the sort taken for granted in modern literature and in experience.[7] Or it may lead to acts of violence, anger, and crime. This is especially likely if it is a woman who is subject to the frustration.[8]

In this chapter I do not want to talk about the use of rape as a means of remedying frustrated eros, nor about enduring, nor even about the emergence of a melancholic or a violent reaction to the frustration of love. Rather, I would like to look at one of the most fundamental of means by which unfulfilled eros may be treated. This is by persuasion.[9] Pindar, in a very neat formulation, gives us what may be a typical insight into the relationship between eros and persuasion. He has Chiron state that 'secret are keys by which wise Persuasion unlocks the shrines of love' (*Pyth.* 9.39). In this chapter the aim will be to make apparent some of the secrets of this link between eros and persuasion.[10]

First some preliminaries. Most ancient love poetry (and most of what is best of ancient love poetry) was composed on the theme of erotic frustration (see Ov. *Ars Am.* 2.515: 'for lovers there's much pain and little pleasure'). Ann Carson has stressed the link between blocked eros and the literary presentation of self.[11] Blocked eros, she indicates, highlights not just how benighted is the individual, but it highlights the status of the individual. By forcing the lover back onto him or herself it favours introspection and a marked valorizing of the seemingly *personal* speaking voice, the voice that is so easily read as the genuine echo of the author. In such instances the speaking voice of the poem is one of ostensible honesty and usually of extreme intensity.[12]

Erotic poetry, however, can be written with an expectation of amatory success.[13] Such poetry aims to hasten success. It may aim, that is, to persuade. In this form of verse the concept of persona becomes very important. The speaker must project himself (and it is usually a male) in the most efficacious of manners if he is to persuade.[14] The lover must adopt a persuasory mask that will, even deceptively, facilitate his aims. (There is no place in this sort of poetry for genuine introspection or doubt.)

These two responses could perhaps be formulated in the following manner: when amatory frustration expects no release, an intense form of *personal* poetry may emerge and the 'self' may receive great prominence; when the frustration is not necessarily permanent, there is considerable prominence given to a highlighting of what might be described as a persuasory mask or persona.[15]

EROS, PERSUASION, AND OVID'S DIDACTIC ELEGY

My specific interest is erotic persuasion in Roman didactic elegy, in particular erotic persuasion as it is presented in that most persuasory of texts, Ovid's *Ars Amatoria*. The striking feature of amatory persuasion in the *Ars Amatoria* is the distancing produced by its being a didactic poem.[16] Didactic poetry invariably has a speaker (the teacher) and an addressee (the pupil, usually named). This is so for all of Ovid's *Artes Amatoriae* (although the addressee remains unnamed).[17] In most amatory verse the persuasion is directed from the poem's speaker (the lover) to the beloved. In such a case it is enough for the lover (the speaker, the narrator) to make himself or herself (the persona) attractive in a persuasory manner. In didactic poetry persuasion is more complex. The speaker, here the *praeceptor amoris*, is not the lover, but he must still make her or his persona and the erotic theme persuasive to the addressee. The addressee in turn must be taught how to render himself or herself persuasive in an erotic context.[18] Both must exhibit a persuasive persona. If the poet is to be truly persuasive, then he must also create a poem that affirms and demonstrates to the addressee its status as an amatory persuader.

Eros and persuasion, therefore, intersect at three levels: that of the speaker, that of the addressee, and that of the poem itself. Each of these levels may receive characterization (its own ethos or persona). The technique has a parallel in rhetoric. It is that trope that is so well displayed in Lysias – *ethopoeia*.

ONE MODE OF PERSUASION: THE ADDRESSEE AS ORATOR

Persuasion is based upon an exploitation of the female *libido*. Women are subject to extremes of desire (to *furiosa libido*, 'maddened desire', *Ars Am.* 1.281). Their desire, once aroused, knows few bounds. What a male needs to do is to exploit this *libido*.[19] Ovid attempts to demonstrate this at great length in *Ars Amatoria* 1.269–350, then repeats the message within more than one mythological panel (such as that of Ariadne, 1.525–64, or Deidamia and Achilles, 1.681–704). Male passion, being much less strong (1.281–2) but more calculating (1.282), is in a position to exploit these female extremes. It relies above all on 'persuasive speech' (*persuadentia verba*, 1.371; cf. Venus and her *blanda ars*, 'beguiling technique', 1.362). Persuasion, when it functions verbally, seems to operate primarily through 'flattery' (*blanditiae*, 1.439), 'promises' (*pollicita*, 355), and 'entreaties' (*preces*, 440). But this persuasion, not surprisingly, ought to be supplemented by a variety of actions and gestures designed to elicit the favour of the beloved. Such actions are seen as a kind of speech, thus as a kind of eloquence.

It is not surprising that *Ars Amatoria* 1, which aims to instruct on the means by which men may accomplish seduction, is the most helpful in this regard.[20] A male's seduction is accomplished by verbal and material means (by material I mean gestures, dress, persuasory items such as presents, lavish attendance and so forth), by *elocutio* ('speech') and, more or less, *actio* ('gesture') to use the terminology of the handbook.[21]

What better way to characterize the male's mode of seduction than as the art of the orator? Persuasion, after all, requires great powers of eloquence. This is precisely what Ovid would have his seducer become at *Ars Amatoria* 1.459–62:

> Learn the arts of persuasion, I advise you, Roman youth,
> > Not only to look after terrified plaintiffs;
> Like the mob, the severe judge, or the pick of the senate,
> > So will a woman be captured by eloquence.

The mask Ovid would have his seducer don is above all that of the orator, the master of persuasion and of eloquence. Just as the orator can manipulate the emotions of his audience to his own ends by speech (*elocutio*) and gesture (*actio*), so may the lover exploit and manipulate the powerful, but undirected emotions of his female 'audience'.

We ought briefly to look at some of the more prominent examples and representations of these two forms of persuasion within this first book of the *Ars Amatoria*. The notion that eloquence, and indeed speech generally, may become a crucial element within the panoply of skills required by the seducer (always directed towards persuasion) is a dominant theme within this book (the lover's 'pitch' is characterized as a type of *facundia*, 'eloquence', at 1.609). Among the more prominent examples of this theme (see also *Ars Am.* 1.143–6) are the advice to corrupt the beloved's maid with promises and entreaties (1.351ff.), to have the maid use, in her mistress' presence, *persuadentia verba* ('persuasive speech') of the male lover (1.371), and Ovid's observation that letters can bring *blanditias* ('flattery') and *imitata amantum verba* ('words feigning to be those of lovers'), and *preces* ('entreaties', 1.439–40). Dinner parties provide further examples: here one can use a double-meaning language to one's beloved to convey affection (1.569–70), write *blanditiae* ('flattery') in wine on the table (1.571), or allow feigned drunkenness to excuse one's statements (1.598–600). The twin themes of promises and entreaties reappear as Ovid's speaker discusses the usefulness of promises as an aid to seduction (this picks up 1.443–4) at 1.631, and at 1.709–10 where the role of persuasion in first encounters is stressed: *vir verba precantia dicat, excipiat blandas comiter illa preces* ('Let the man utter his pleas; let the woman accept his charming entreaties in a friendly fashion.').[22]

Personal comportment and demeanour, one's gestures and actions, can be just as crucial in the effective application of persuasion as words themselves. It is not enough to speak well, if this is conveyed improperly by one's bodily movement. *Actio*, as this aspect of the lover's persuasiveness may be termed, is a type of a language. And Ovid does sometimes note that gestures speak: thus he states of the silent glance at 1.574 that *saepe tacens vocem verbaque vultus habet* ('often an unspeaking face provides voice and words'). Shortly before, at 1.500, Ovid more tellingly alludes to the lovers' secret language as *loqui notis*, 'speaking in signs' (in this case through eloquent use of the eyebrow; cf. 1.137–8). *Loqui notis* is a designation that aptly characterizes much of the gestural persuasion alluded to in the first book of the *Ars Amatoria*. Following are a few of the more prominent instances of gestural persuasion.[23] Ovid, at 1.487–504, offers advice on how to comport oneself in a persuasive manner when in the street or at the theatre and follows this with instructions on how to dress in such a manner as to make oneself attractive (1.505–24). Comportment and demeanour, as persuasory means, are important at dinner parties (1.525–630). Tears can be persuasive (1.659–62) as can a wan lover's complexion (1.723–38). If these fail, even force can be a persuasive element in courtship (1.673–704; cf. the rape of the Sabines at 1.101–33).[24]

It would be mendacious to press too hard these parallels between what is required of a real-life orator and an Ovidian lover. There are, of course, other prototypes for the lover in this book. This ethos that the lover may adopt can be that of the hunter, the doctor, the farmer, or the actor.[25] Yet, because of the key role played by persuasion, the comparison of the ethos of the male lover and the orator is the one that seems to dominate Ovid's formulation and our understanding of it. We do seem to find that *Ars Amatoria* 1 in particular is organized around two persuasory poles – those of 'speech' (*elocutio*) and 'gesture' (*actio*), which, as may be recalled from texts such as Cicero's *Brutus* and *De Oratore*, were key aspects of the orator's performance.

A SECOND MODE OF AMATORY PERSUASION: POETRY AS PERSUASION

The persona (or voice or ethos) is the key to the lover's persuasive armoury. It hides blemishes and makes the seducer more attractive. Thus he or she becomes more persuasive. This situation is not just applicable to the addressee. As I have stated, if the addressee is to be convinced of the worth of Ovid's persuasion, then both the poem and the narrator must demonstrate an attractiveness and a persuasiveness comparable to that urged upon the addressee. Once again ethos becomes important.

The simplest means by which Ovid 'characterizes' and makes his poem persuasive is by asserting for it this quality. Ovid wants his poetry to be persuasive and he tells this to his addressee. He expresses this very neatly at *Ars Amatoria* 2.11–12:[26]

It's not enough for a girl to come to you because of my poetry;
  If she was snared by my *ars*, she must be held by it.

There is, in the second of these two lines, a noteworthy pun on *ars*. This word can refer, of course, to the 'technique' that Ovid is teaching. But it can as easily refer to the poem he has written, the *Ars* (*Amatoria*). His technique and his poem, therefore, should draw women to his audience (his pupils), 'snare' them, and 'hold' them.[27] How it can manage this is explained more fully at *Ars Amatoria* 3.311–48. In this sequence Ovid is urging his female audience to master the art of song. This is, he suggests, a particularly seductive accomplishment. To demonstrate the claim, he points to the nearly disastrous effects of the Sirens' song on Ulysses (3.311–14) and to the ability to beguile even the non-human of the songs of Orpheus, Amphion, and Arion (3.321–6). The same effects as those procured by these mythical characters can be had over men by women when they will learn a little of the poetry of Callimachus, Philetas, Anacreon, Sappho, Menander, Propertius, Gallus, Tibullus, Varro and Vergil (3.329–38). Almost as an afterthought Ovid adds his own amatory verse (3.339–48) to the list (not just the *Amores* and the *Heroides*, but also this poem, the *Ars Amatoria*). Ovid's poetry, he claims, is capable of beguiling and seducing its listeners.[28]

It is just as well that the narrator is so secure in his knowledge of the persuasive power of his poetry, because great deeds, whether on the battlefield or in the boudoir, require great poetry. That is the very least it can offer its readers. Thus if Ovid is to instil confidence into his audience, then he must convince them of the power of his poetry. This seeming self-confidence leads Ovid to such extravagant vaunts as *Ars Amatoria* 2.1–4:

> Call 'Io Paean' and call it again – 'Io Paean'.
>   The quarry I've pursued has fallen into my nets.
> The happy lover crowns my poems with the victor's wreath,
>   Poems valued more than those of Hesiod or old Homer.

This claim is less extravagant than may seem to be the case on first reading. Ovid's instruction, if it is to persuade, must be good. The poet does no one a favour by feigning modesty. We hear the vaunt again in book 2 when Ovid arrogates for himself surpassing powers as a poet (his readers deserve no less). So at *Ars Amatoria* 2.733–44 he claims a pre-eminence in his ability to instruct in love (cf. 3.812). Just as Podalirius was the greatest of Danaan doctors, as Achilles was the greatest in strength, as Nestor was in counsel, Calchas as a prophet, as Telamonian Ajax was in arms, or Automedon as a charioteer (these are all mythological heroes from Homer's *Iliad*), so is Ovid as an instructor in love. A variation on the vaunt appears at 2.493–8. At this point in the poem the god Apollo appears to Ovid and instructs him to lead his 'disciples' (*discipuli*, 2.498) to his temple. Ovid does not explain to us that he obeyed, but the very existence of this poem is proof enough.

By Ovid's own claim, then, his poetry possesses a beguiling, seductive ethos, one capable of drawing, snaring, holding, and instructing its listeners and their quarry.[29] More still, however, can be said of how Ovid has characterized his poetry. Ovid also wants us to look on his poem as a leisure guide. That matches his conception of the lover's life: this is no angst-ridden Catullan experience, but something enjoyable and worth pursuing for its own sake (it is not just that the poem projects the life of the lover as sensually gratifying and as an ideal means for passing time: Ovid seems to believe that *writing* and *reading* about love represent an ideal pastime). The narrator provides for the *Ars Amatoria* a persona best understood as that of the specialist leisure guide.[30]

This may become clearer still if it is recalled that Ovid is writing a didactic epic. Most of the surviving products of this genre are very serious works. The traditional character of didactic poetry was unsuitable for love. Ovid's themes and approach turn the traditional ethos of the genre on its head. As A. S. Hollis remarks:[31]

> By writing an extended didactic poem on love, with all the proper mannerisms, Ovid achieves a hilarity never captured before. It is not merely a question of pedantry against passion; even the title of the work foretells the tension between love, usually conceived by poets as an overwhelming force which takes the individual by storm, and the precise skill implicit in 'ars'. From here comes the constant ambiguity as to whether Ovid's young men and women are really 'in love', or playing a game according to set rules.[32]

Hollis' insight could be taken one step further. It is not just Ovid's 'young men and women' who may be 'playing a game according to set rules'; it may also be Ovid himself.[33] The game demonstrates the poem's characterization as a leisure guide.

The *raison d'être* for this poem does not reside in instruction.[34] It exists within the poetic texture itself. This may be described as its ludic aspect. What was this? Ovid tells his readers at *Tristia* 2.491ff., where he labels his amatory didactic work as mere play. In this passage (2.471–96) Ovid states that some poets have written poems about dice-playing, others about ball games, swimming, or the hoop; some have written about feasts and entertaining, or on potting. What was the purpose of these poems? Not instruction, it seems. 'Such poems', states Ovid at *Tristia* 2.491, 'are played in the smoky month of December' (*talia luduntur fumoso mense Decembri*). They are, he is saying, parlour games for winter. That they bear scant relationship to life and were understood that way is indicated when Ovid asserts (2.492), 'nobody was ruined by composing them' (*quae damno nulli composuisse fuit*). Just as does Catullus in his poem 16, Ovid insists that there is no necessary relationship between his instruction and 'real life'.[35]

Telling places in which to view the poem's role as a leisure guide are those two passages of the *Ars Amatoria* (2.203–8 and 3.353–80) that actually speak of play and games. In *Ars Amatoria* 2.203–8 Ovid urges the male seducer to ingratiate himself with his lover by deliberately losing at their board game (2.204: 'throw badly and move badly'). It is tempting, given the assertions of *Tristia* 2.491ff., to draw a parallel not just between these games and the game of love on which Ovid is providing instruction but also between these and the poem itself that Ovid is composing. I wonder if this does not become even clearer in the second passage on games – *Ars Amatoria* 3.353–80. This begins with a series of *double entendres* making plain the analogy between love-making and board-play. Ovid also suggests that such games can provide an entrée to a liaison. Then follows a fascinating description of the chaos that overzealous game-play can cause (3.373ff.). Take the game too seriously, lose your temper, Ovid is saying, and this leisure activity ceases to become a game. It becomes a real contest with dire consequences.

It is difficult not to read such passages as commentary on Ovid's intentions in the *Ars Amatoria* and perhaps the mode by which the character of this poem ought to be identified. The *Ars Amatoria* should, like love and like those poems alluded to at *Tristia* 2.471–96, be treated as a game. To enjoy it, one ought to know the moves, be skilled in the rules, but not treat it too seriously. It is play, after all, and not real life. Like all play, its end resides in itself and its importance resides in its capacity to enhance leisure. That is its ethos (and one that matches Ovid's estimation of love). It is that persona that renders it both attractive and persuasive.

A THIRD MODE: AMATORY PERSUASION AND THE NARRATOR

The characterization of the narrator must also be persuasive if the addressee is to be convinced of the value of his advice. Once again persuasiveness is based upon the establishment of an apposite and, in particular, attractive persona.

Ovid had a hard road to hoe. His depiction of eros was so singular. An attack of eros almost invariably in ancient literature is an uncontrollable and often unaccountable thing. It renders one often violent, often suicidal.[36] It is something that one cannot surmount. Ovid seems hardly to be talking about the same emotion. It is easy, given the image within our own culture of the heartless seducer, to forget just how uncommon was Ovid's approach in ancient literature and how novel was his depiction of masculine eros.[37] What is it that actually drives Ovid's seducers? Not traditional eros – that much is clear. A minor venereal itch, it would appear. Its satiation may afford some pleasure, but the question arises inevitably: is the complexity and sheer laboriousness of Ovid's persuasory modes (the sleeping rough, the pallor, the vigilance at dinner parties, the never-ending self-denial required to gain gratification) worth the labour when there existed both marriage and prostitutes?

Ovid glozes over all such difficulties by means of his characterization of the narrator. This comic, shallow voice is that of a cynical, well-born man about town who has unaccountably taken to the academic life and has chosen to become a professor of rhetoric with a speciality in advising those with means on how to seduce without becoming emotionally involved.[38] Ovid's flippant but easily endearing speaker offers a complete tonal inversion of the narrative voice of traditional, serious didactic epic. This speaker exhibits an ethos that is meant primarily to amuse. It is this amusement that establishes a complicit pact of sympathy between reader and speaker.

The characterization of the voice hinges on this amoral, rhetorical narrator's self-conscious humour. This forces a gap between what is said and how it is said. This distancing is, for example, habitual in the ironic deposition of myth and narrative panels. Think of Ariadne abandoned by Theseus and alone on the island of Naxos (1.527–64). Ovid's narrator cannot resist undercutting the pathos (the 'what') with lines (the 'how') such as 1.533–4 (*clamabat flebatque simul, sed utrumque decebat; non facta est lacrimis turpior illa suis*, 'She was wailing and weeping at the same time, but both suited her; she was not made less attractive by her tears.'). Or compare the bizarre presentation of Pasiphae (1.293–326). Our horror at her bestiality is swept away by comic images of her dressing up, using a mirror, and fixing her hair to make herself more attractive to her beloved bull (1.303–8), or becoming jealous of the comeliness of the heifers in her bull's herd (1.311–16). One effect of the humour and irony in these sorts of passages is to redirect attention away from the exemplary message and onto the wit of our didactic interlocutor. Thus is established the persona of the narrator of the *Ars Amatoria*.

But perhaps this technique deserves illustration at greater length. One of the best places to observe the unfolding of the character of the narrator is in the panel on Procris and Cephalus (*Ars Am.* 3.685–746; cf. *Met.* 7.661–865). It is a story of death by misadventure, of death caused by jealousy. Cephalus, always off hunting, used to rest in a glen near Hymettus after hunting. Here he used to call on the breeze (Aura) to refresh him. Procris, his young wife, heard of this. She assumed Aura was another lover and hid, crazed with jealousy, in the bushes in the glen to ascertain the truth of the rumour. When she discovered the real identity of Aura, she rushed from the bushes in relief to embrace her young husband. He shot her dead. He thought that she was game. What does this poignant little story teach Ovid's didactic audience of *puellae* ('young women')? That a woman should not be too quick to believe stories of her lover's unfaithfulness (*Ars Am.* 3.685–6).

The little tale is epyllion-like in its pronounced love-theme, its strong focus on women, its psychological realism, sentimentality, and the use of direct speech. Despite its pathos (and we are meant to be moved), the speaker distances himself from the narrative above all by self-consciousness and humour. This process of distancing forces attention onto how things are said by the narrator rather than onto what he says. Whence the humour? Let us briefly repace the Procris and Cephalus narrative. Three areas deserve examination: situation, voice and language.

The situation can be hyperbolically exaggerated. Consider Procris' melodramatic reaction to the false report of Cephalus' unfaithfulness. She becomes pale, seemingly lovesick (3.701–8; note the deflationary simile of 3.703–6), then is transformed into a frenzied Bacchante. Procris' finding the body traces of Cephalus in the grass (3.721) is another instance of melodramatic exaggeration. Was Procris a tracker? Would grass in such a leafy dell preserve obvious traces from one day to the next? Did Cephalus always lie in the same place, thus depressing the grass permanently? Or the description of Procris' death (3.745–6): Cephalus catches her dying breath with his mouth. This is not unlike the way he solicited the *aura*, or 'breeze'.

The narrator's intrusions create an effect of playful distancing. This can be at times dramatic (so 3.713–14), at times ironic (so *scilicet*, 'plainly', at 3.716). One might also compare the knowing aside at 3.717: *neque enim deprendere velles* ('for you didn't want to catch him'); or the banal, but canny truism of line 720: *et quia mens semper, quod timet, esse putat* ('because the mind always thinks what it fears is true'); or the intrusive, seemingly dramatic insertions of lines 735–6: *quid facis, infelix? non est fera: supprime tela – me miserum, iaculo fixa puella tuo est* ('What are you doing, unhappy one? She's not a wild beast. Control your weapons. Alas, the girl has been pierced by your javelin'). The whole tragedy, it should be stressed, hinges on a play on the word *error*. This is *iucundus* ('pleasant') at 3.729, but hardly so in the final lines of the passage.

Language is easily and deliberately overdone. Consider the clichéd and overrich depiction of the *locus amoenus* with which the passage begins. Or consider the description of Procris as she pales at lines 703–6:

> She grew pale, as pale as the late growing foliage
> after the clusters
> Have been picked from the vine – which the first of
> winter wounds
> As pale as ripe quinces bend the boughs of their
> trees
> And as cornel berries not yet ripe for our eating.

That description is deliberately overdone.

We have lingered over Procris and Cephalus long enough. The point is a fairly obvious one: that the self-consciousness, the irony, and the distancing so evident in the way in which this story is told highlights the voice of the didactic narrator (thus the rhetorical mask adopted by the speaking voice of *Ars Amatoria* is every bit as interesting as the 'reality' – how to seduce – it attempts to convey). The poem intends that we enjoy it for its own sake. It is persuasive precisely in so far as it individuates its attractive narrative persona.

CONCLUSION

The foregoing does not in any way establish a model for the relationship between elegy and persuasion. It may, however, demonstrate a simple characteristic of personal poetry, lyric, elegy or epigram, which aims at amatory persuasion. When persuasion is required, a mask, a persuasory persona, is necessary. What is so singular about the *Ars Amatoria* is that Ovid has taken this implicit notion of ethos or persona to its logical extreme and fixed it at three levels within his didactic poem. This is apparent first when Ovid provides for his didactic addressee the role of the orator, the very essence of persuasory personae. It is also apparent within the poem as a whole: here Ovid asserts an ethos for his poem as an instructive, beguiling medium by stressing the role of his poem as an exemplar of play and leisure, something that matches his conception of love. Finally, the persuasory persona is also apparent in the voice of the didactic narrator. This is achieved particularly through the self-conscious, ironic presentation of his poem's instructional material. One of the most striking aspects of the second and third persuasive levels is that they persistently foreground their medium (the 'how') at the expense of their message (the 'what'). It is as if the poem itself rather than its instructive aim becomes the amatory quarry.[39]

NOTES

1 Persuasion is the first route to follow (*aptius at fuerit temptasse precibus*, *Am.* 2.3.17); see too *Am.* 2.1.22, 23–8, 2.17 and Anio's pleas at 3.6.53ff. Cf. also *Am.* 1.3. (The text for the *Amores* and *Ars Amatoria* is Kenney 1961.) In general see Gross 1985.

2 This pattern is seen most neatly when divine amours are the subject of poetic attention. The god usually indulges in a small amount of persuasion, then at the least signs of resistance rapes the object of his desire. So *Am.* 3.6 (Anio and Ilia, e.g., 81–2; cf. *Met.* 1.490ff. [Apollo and Daphne] and *Ars Am.* 1.703–4); cf. Pind. *Ol.* 1 and the story of Pelops and Poseidon. The tale of Romulus and the Sabine women at *Ars Am.* 1.101–34 offers a human version. (Cf. Fantham 1975. I presume the violence of *Am.* 1.7 is to be seen in this light as may well that of 2.5.45–6. Perhaps the best, albeit most cynical example, is the advocation of the use of force at *Ars Am.* 1.673–722; cf. also Plut. *Eroticus* 751D, 768B.

3 Campbell 1972.

4 Aegialeus, the old fisherman in Xenophon of Ephesus' *Ephesian Tale* 5.1, keeps his dead wife Thelxinoe embalmed in his house. Note Prop. 4.7; Ov. *Am.* 3.9.15–16.

5 Hor. *Carm.* 3.7; Prop. 4.3; Ov. *Am.* 2.16 (cf. 2.11).

6 So Ov. *Am.* 3.11A, 11B, 12, 14 and (seemingly) *Am.* 1.12.

7 See Wack 1990; Toohey 1992. Ovid does not quite depict lovesickness in his elegiac poetry, though he comes close; see *Am.* 1.6, 2.5.2, 2.7.10, 2.9.14, 3.14.37; *Ars Am.* 1.729–36).

8 So Ov. *Ars Am.* 1.283ff., 2.373ff. Vergil's Dido and Apollonius' Medea,

when rejected, present other instances, as do the persuasive exempla with which Gyges is plied in Hor. *Carm.* 3.7.

9 See Gross 1985. In Plato's *Phaedrus* the link between love and persuasion is persistently present; see, e.g., 231ff., 240e; section 263d–e seems to make a link between eros and rhetoric.

10 The extent to which genre influences the representation of these universal human affectivities is something that I cannot adequately touch upon here. Conte 1994: 35–65 is very helpful on this score.

11 Carson 1986; note the review by Walsh 1988.

12 Interesting examples are Catull. 76, Ov. *Am.* 1.3 (where the block forces the poet to introduce himself) and Prop. 4.3.

13 Nowhere more apparent than in the last poem of the second book of the *Amores*. The frustration about which this poem is built resides firmly on the expectation of success.

14 Typical examples of the poet's praise of self may be seen at *Am.* 2.17.27–35, 3.1, 3.12, 3.15.

15 In rhetorical terminology this persuasory mask could be described as instancing *ethopoeia* or *prosopopoeia*; on which see (via the index) Kennedy 1963; 1972. *Ethopoeia* is associated particularly with Lysias. See Suss 1910; Usher 1965. For ancient discussion see Dion. Hal. *Lys.* 8; Arist. *Rh*. 1408a, 1417a.

16 On its status as a didactic poem, see Hollis 1973; Sharrock 1994: 1–20.

17 On the role of the addressee in didactic poetry, see Pöhlmann 1973; Clay *et al.* 1994 and Servius' proem to his commentary on Vergil's *Georgics*. On the addressee in the *Ars Amatoria*, see Miller 1994.

18 It is above all the orator, of course, who requires the skills of persuasion and who must play a dramatic role to succeed. On oratory as performance, see Narducci 1995b: 44ff., 55ff.

19 Hollis 1977: 91 *ad* 281–2.

20 Book 2 (focused less on persuasory verbal skills than it is on suggesting an environment best designed to sustain eros and faithfulness) and book 3 (which, aiming to help women seduce men, concentrates less, alas, on verbal persuasion) are less helpful.

21 Narducci 1995b: 55ff. (on performance) is very useful on this topic. Cic. *De Or.* 3.213–27 discusses delivery (*actio*). Narducci mentions the description of the histrionics of Sulpicius Galba (like the speaker of *Ars Am.* 2, he uses tears) at Cic. *Brut.* 85–96 (cf. also Narducci 1995a: 166ff. *ad* 85–96).

22 It is hardly surprising that Ovid often uses words formed from the root *bland-* in *Ars Amatoria* (see, for example, 1.273, 362, 439, 468, 480, 571, 703, 710). This 'sweetness' should characterize both the effect of the lover's eloquence and its reception.

23 Cf. also the advice on actions designed to encourage the ingratiation of oneself with women at the races in *Ars Am.* 1.135ff.

24 See Richlin 1992c.

25 For the hunter see 1.45ff., 253, 265, etc. and Hollis 1977: 42 *ad* 1.50. The opening sequences of the book, which describe where to meet women, might be compared with those on hunting animals; so Hollis: 'we would expect a work on hunting to start by talking of the beast's lair, as

[Oppian] *Cynegetica* iv.79ff.' At 1.357 we seem to be hearing of a *medicus* ('physician', the narrator of the *Remedia Amoris*), while at 1.399–400 it is of farmers and sailors.

26 Sharrock 1994: 22–3.

27 The pun is repeated at *Ars Am*. 3.42 where Ovid states, *arte perennat amor* ('By means of *ars* love lasts').

28 On this aspect of poetry, see Walsh 1984.

29 On the 'erotics of poetry', see Fitzgerald 1992; Kennedy 1993: 82; Sharrock 1994.

30 The implication of the fascinating argument of Citroni 1989 is to place the *Ars Amatoria* firmly within a strong tradition of leisure-time literature. Cf. also Hollis 1973: 93; Myerowitz 1985.

31 Hollis 1977: xviii.

32 We ought to pause over this notion of the parodic inversion of traditional didactic epic. Didactic epic, as it survives in Graeco-Roman literature, offers detailed technical instruction (not mere admonitions) on topics such as farming, hunting, fishing, astronomy, cosmology, pharmaceuticals, medicine and so forth (see Cox 1969). Didactic epic was, at least in most of the products we have surviving, a fairly serious enterprise. See also Quinn 1979: 120–48. Labate 1984: 121–74 examines the generic and conceptual links between Roman philosophical discourse (Cicero in particular) and Ovid's didactic project.

33 Parker 1992 looks at the *Ars Amatoria* as part of a more literal-minded tradition of instructive manuals.

34 This is something atypical of the poetry of the Alexandrian and post-Alexandrian periods. Instruction provides the excuse for the poem. This is both too straightforward and too time-consuming an assertion for proper demonstration here. Of Nicander (and the same might be said of Aratus) Hopkinson 1988: 143 notes: 'The poem [*Theriaca*] is ostensibly an aid to those suffering from the bites of noxious animals; but the poet's solicitous professions of concern for his 'patients' should fool no one. His real aim is to astonish the reader with a mixture of highly incongruous basic ingredients.' Cf. Hollis 1973: 90.

35 Cf. Hollis 1973: 93. See also Pliny *Ep*. 7.9.9ff.; Mart. 4.49.

36 See Toohey 1992 for some of the effects of love. Hollis 1973: 94 also characterizes elegiac infatuation as violent.

37 Stressed also by Myerowitz 1985: 32. Conte 1994: 43ff., in his discussion of the *Remedia Amoris*, most lucidly distinguishes Ovidian love and elegy from his predecessors.

38 On the persona of the narrator see Watson 1983; Myerowitz 1985: 35. The mask of the narrator can be other – such as that of the *lena* ('madam'); see Hollis 1973: 93; Watson 1982.

39 My particular thanks to Emanuele Narducci. I have also received assistance from Robert Baker, Mario Labate and Ian Worthington. Long-term debts are to Elaine Fantham and Kenneth Quinn.

13

Persuasive history: Roman rhetoric and historiography

Robert W. Cape, Jr

Historia vero testis temporum, lux veritatis, vita memoriae, magistra vitae, nuntia vetustatis, qua voce alia nisi oratoris immortalitati commendatur?

Cic. De Or. 2.36

As for history – the witness of the ages, the light of truth, the life of memory, the teacher of life, the messenger of the past – with what voice other than the orator's can it be entrusted to immortality?

This question, put in the mouth of the great orator Marcus Antonius, has come to represent the Roman – and, to some extent, ancient – attitude toward the relationship between historiography and rhetoric.[1] Until recently, the assumption that history writing requires the rhetorical skills of the orator has been problematic for historians, as it was already to Antonius' interlocutor, Quintus Lutatius Catulus (*De Or.* 2.51). The recent, largely postmodern interest in the rhetorical nature of history shares some of Cicero's assumptions about the relationship between narrative, or narrative style, and historical representation, but ultimately goes beyond Cicero's purpose and scope.[2] On the other hand, Cicero's comments about rhetoric are concerned with the practical function of persuasion through oral speech, which is not the concern of modern historians. Since the topic has become enormously popular among academic historians and literary critics[3] and since they still employ many of the same terms, it is important to recognize Cicero's particular contribution to the history of this relationship and to specify what he meant by subordinating historiography to a practice-based rhetoric.

We have tantalizingly few statements by ancient theorists about the relationship between historiography and rhetoric, so it is easy to take Cicero's comments as representing either an orthodoxy or the idiosyncratic theory of a rhetorician who never wrote history.[4] Both positions are extreme. Cicero realized that some of his views on the relationship between oratory and history were not necessarily shared by others (cf. *Leg.* 1.5). Yet some of those views, such as the didactic function of history, were also held by earlier and later practising historians. Unmistakably Ciceronian are his comments on style, which are pivotal for the direction of Roman historiography. But in order to recognize what is new about Cicero's position it is necessary to understand what is traditional. In addition, we must ask why Cicero made statements about historiography in a rhetorical treatise. It was not obvious that he should have done so (cf. *De Or.* 2.62, 64).

At issue for historians and literary critics alike is a better understanding of how Cicero's comments on historiography in *De Oratore* fit within the larger argument of book 2, where they occur. Recent work by T. P. Wiseman and A. J. Woodman has improved our understanding of Cicero's view of history and specifically his statements about historiography in *De Oratore*.[5] Woodman has rightly stressed that Cicero's statements on the separation of truth from falsehood do not correspond to modern ideas of the same, but to the relative impartiality of the historian toward the treatment of his material.[6] Another way Cicero's view of history differs from modern theory, as Woodman shows, is that Cicero understood the facts of history to be as much a part of the rhetorical superstructure (*exaedificatio*) as their stylistic treatment. Why and how Cicero comes to make the bold claim that historiography should be governed by the rules of rhetoric is an issue treated by Wiseman, who suggests that the appearance of the *rhetores Latini* in the 90s brought to the fore questions of style and the historian's social standing as part of his qualification to write history.[7] More recently, Wiseman has suggested that Cicero distorted his treatment of earlier historians' style, misrepresenting early Roman historiography.[8] Yet, Wiseman's reconstruction of the earlier historians' practice in the use of sources actually supports Cicero's claims about the stylistic levels of their representations. Since Cicero keeps his comments focused on the proper content (*res*) and stylistic treatment (*verba*) of history, not the historian's social status, we need a new explanation for why the relationship between historiography and rhetoric should have been a recent issue in the 90s. To do this, it is necessary not only to re-examine Cicero's statements in *De Oratore* but also to put them in the context of the larger arguments of the book and the whole work.

1

De Oratore is a bold departure from the tradition of treatises on rhetoric that have come down to us. Set as a dialogue between the best orators of the generation prior to Cicero's own, *De Oratore* refuses to define rhetoric narrowly as a complex of prescriptive rules independent of practice.[9] Instead, it offers a picture of the complete orator, a man acquainted with the rules of the rhetoricians, but who is an excellent speaker due to his wider learning and practical experience.[10] Cicero paints this picture by allowing his characters to make a series of statements about major topics and letting them allow for different positions on the same topics. The differences are not always resolved.[11] In this way, the rhetoric that is the subject of *De Oratore* is not a rule-based rhetoric of the Hellenistic handbooks but the lived practice of knowledgeable, eminent men debating issues important to themselves and their friends. Finished in 55 BCE amidst a radical change in traditional government, the scene of the dialogue is set on the eve of a previous political 'revolution' in 91 BCE just before free speech and debate gave way to tyranny and the rule of force at Rome. The words Cicero puts into the mouths of his interlocutors are meant to testify to a time when oratory was valued, public debate was possible (and productive), and the state (to Cicero's way of thinking) was governed in a better fashion (cf. *De Or.* 1.1, 3.8–15). Crassus, the spokesman of Cicero's own views in book 1, praises eloquence as the civilizing force that joins human beings in productive societies and distinguishes mankind from the animals (1.32–3). In book 2 Catulus is made to remark on the suitability of the characters in the dialogue: 'We are all the kind of men who believe that life without these pursuits [debates] is not worth living' (2.20). Yet the socially productive function of the orator does not go unchallenged (1.35–94). Thus the dialogue insists on debate and efforts at persuasion to defend an extended social and cultural function for oratory and the role the eloquent man (*orator*) should play in Roman society (cf. 1.30–4).

Book 2 of *De Oratore* is dominated by the figure of Marcus Antonius, who represents Cicero's ideas in this book much as Crassus does in the others. Antonius' main argument is that practical experience is more important to the orator than learning the so-called 'rules' (2.77–92). To some extent this is an old-fashioned, particularly Roman, view. Cicero is at pains to point out, however, that Antonius was not devoid of the learning he affects to despise (2.1–5, 59–61).[12]

Furthermore, while Cicero rejects the narrow and technical *doctrina* and *praecepta* offered by Greek rhetorical teaching (2.28–30), he still believes it possible to give rules, but rules based on observation of practice rather than from abstract theory (2.32–3). Within this argument, and supported by it, he introduces a third kind of oratory, not usually treated in the handbooks, and one which is so straightforward that it needs no rules: demonstrative or epideictic oratory. Through this third kind (*tertium genus*), he is able to maintain a broader view of the function of the orator and support his claim that the ideal orator does not rely on the rules of rhetoric in the narrow sense.

Antonius' statements on historiography appear in the first part of his speech (*De Or.* 2.36, 51–64). Prior to his first comment, he outlines his plan for the discussion (2.33):

> Now I propose the following, about which I have persuaded myself, that although it [rhetoric] is not an art (*ars*), there is nothing more illustrious (*praeclarius*) than the perfect orator; for, to pass over the practice of speaking (*usum dicendi*), which rules in every peaceful and free state, there is such delight (*tanta oblectatio*) in the very skill of speaking (*in ipsa facultate dicendi*) that nothing more pleasant (*iucundius*) can be perceived by the ears and minds of men.

The formulation of this statement indicates Antonius' method of argument in his speech: the practice of speaking and the function of the speaker can be assumed; the point to be proved concerns the illustrious nature, delight in, and pleasantness of the orator and his speech. In particular, Antonius is concerned with *facultas dicendi*, which produces the proper effect of oratory. He is concerned with style.

In his first comment on historiography, Antonius links oratory and history explicitly in terms of both style and function (*De Or.* 2.35–6):

> Nor is there anything that needs to be said with elegance and severity that is not the province of the orator. It is his task when giving advice on the most important matters to give his opinion with authority; it is his task both to rouse a faint-hearted populace and to temper the unbridled. With the same faculty are the crimes of men called to punishment and the integrity of others preserved. Who can exhort men to bravery more

215

brilliantly (*ardentius*)? Who can turn them back from vice more sharply (*acrius*)? Who can castigate the wicked more harshly (*asperius*)? Who can praise the good more elegantly (*ornatius*)? Who can break up unlawful desire more vehemently (*vehementius*) when making an accusation? Who can soften grief more tenderly when he consoles? And as for history – the witness of the ages, the light of truth, the life of memory, the teacher of life, the messenger of the past – with what voice other than the orator's can it be entrusted to immortality?

The functions of oratory are again assumed: to exhort men to bravery, turn them back from vice, castigate the wicked, praise the good, and so forth. These are the special functions of epideictic (*obiurgatio*, 'rebuke'; *cohortatio*, 'exhortation'; *consolatio*, 'consolation', 2.50). Antonius' main point comes in the addition of the adverbs *ardentius*, *acrius*, *asperius*, *ornatius*, and *vehementius*. An appropriate style renders speech more effective at carrying out its function. The statement about history becomes the final, most forceful example of this. The factual and didactic nature of history is assumed: witness, light, life, teacher, messenger; what is new is the addition of the orator's voice, a suitable style, to enable history to perform its function most effectively.

2

As part of his project to extend the social function of oratory and the orator by painting a new picture of the orator who is not limited to the narrowly defined functions assigned him in the rhetorical handbooks, Cicero has Antonius argue the inclusion of the *tertium genus*, demonstrative or epideictic oratory, which is customarily didactic and concerned with moral exhortation (*De Or.* 2.41–73). This type of oratory, he claims, has been left out of the rhetorical handbooks, although it had been discussed by Aristotle (2.43). Antonius is not interested in treating the material of epideictic oratory, for it does not need rules, but it is precisely because it does not require the rules of rhetoric that he feels he must discuss it: he does not want its function to be excluded from the proper sphere of the orator (2.47–8, 68–70, 348). His concern is so great that he returns to the topic after the main discussion of the book, reminding his audience of the importance of this kind of oratory even though it does not require the elaborate rules traditionally given for the other genres (2.341–9). It is in the first part of his discussion that he links demonstrative oratory closely with historiography, for it helps him make his argument: history, too, is a clear case where rules are not required ('For who doesn't know that the first rule of history is not to dare to say anything false?', 2.62). Moreover, by using history to help him make his point with epideictic oratory, he can draw on the accepted Roman view that history serves an important social and cultural function.

That Romans intended their history to serve an overt didactic and moralistic purpose is well recognized as a distinctive feature of Roman historiography.[13] Although we cannot be sure, there was most likely a didactic, nationalistic, or 'pragmatic' purpose to the earliest histories of Fabius Pictor and Cincius Alimentus.[14] There was certainly a statement about the 'good of history' in the first Latin history by Cato in his *Origines*[15] (cf. fr. 3, *historiae bonum*).[16] Another fragment of Cato's *Origines* supports the idea that history is important and is an honourable occupation for an illustrious man in his free time (fr. 2). If the story told by Plutarch that Cato wrote his histories for the education of his son is true, then it would provide additional support for the view that the *Origines* were didactic – perhaps hortatory – in character.[17] Moreover, the fact that Cato chose to write in Latin rather than Greek may indicate a didactic or nationalistic purpose.[18]

Roman historians after Cato regularly claimed that their history was more than the accurate recording of events: it was meant to accomplish something, to be practical. The Gracchan historian Sempronius Asellio stated that it was not enough simply to list deeds and events (fr. 1):

> But there is this one difference between those who wanted to leave annals and those who tried to write Roman history (*res gestas a Romanis*). Annals make known only what was done and in which year it was done, just as if someone were writing a diary, which the Greeks call *ephemeris*. I think that for us it is not enough to say what was done, but also to show for what purpose and for which reason things were done.

This must have been similar to what Cato said in the *Origines* when he remarked that he would avoid the trivial events he found in the yearly pontiff's records (fr. 77). Asellio was explicit (fr. 2):

For in no way can annals move men to be more eager to defend their country or be slower to do wrong. To write when a war was begun and by which consul, who entered the city in triumph after the war and what happened in that war, is to tell stories to children, not to write history.

Cicero's Marcus Antonius would agree: history should exhort the young to follow the *mos maiorum* and stir up feelings of national pride. What is new in Antonius' account is the understanding that history – just as oratory – requires a style suitable to its function.

3

The problem with the early historians, according to Antonius, is that they did not use any stylistic ornaments, but presented material dryly – like the pontiff's accounts – and thought the highest praise of style was for brevity (*De Or.* 2.51–3). Wiseman has recently criticized Cicero's account of early Roman historiography, accusing Cicero of making the histories out to be too much like the pontiff's accounts.[19] He constructs an alternate theory of the origins of historiography at Rome, suggesting a more lively, dramatic, sympotic tradition than Cicero indicates. While Cicero's account of the development of early Roman historiography is clearly simplified, the main thrust of his criticism is not of the *materia* or the sources used, but of their treatment. He makes Antonius object to historians reporting *only* (*solum*) the 'accounts of the times, people, places and things that were done "without any ornament"' (*sine ullis ornamentis*, 2.53). Antonius argues against Catulus, representing the traditional Roman view, who thinks the Greek historians need to know about the persuasive use of language, not the Romans, for whom it is enough if the historian is not a liar (2.51). For Cicero, history should be dramatic and entertaining, relating the vicissitudes of fortune and moving the audience to an emotional response (*Fam.* 5.12.4–6). History should, in fact, capture the power of those dramatic institutions and oral traditions that Wiseman suggests were what actually preserved information about Rome's early past. In Cicero's view, the early historians may have failed to include the proper *materia* for a didactic history but, what is worse, they failed to convey the power and force of historical events through their style.

4

Antonius assumes a similarity between the functions of history and epideictic oratory, yet it seems that the stylistic connection between historiography and rhetoric had not been made before. 'Don't you see', he asks (*De Or.* 2.62; cf. 64),

> how great a task (*munus*) history is for an orator? In terms of fluency of discourse (*flumine orationis*) and variety (*varietate*) it is probably his greatest task (*maximum*), yet I can't find a separate treatment of the subject anywhere in the rules of rhetoric (and they're easily available for inspection).[20]

That the treatment of history is probably the greatest task for the orator is represented as an obvious idea. It may have been obvious to Romans, but it was not part of the rhetorical handbook tradition, which was a product of Greek schools (cf. 1.22–3). This statement follows an interlude where Antonius demonstrates a thorough acquaintance with Greek ideas while affecting the position of an unlettered Roman who cannot follow the complexities of Greek thought (2.59–61; cf. 77). When Antonius insists that the rules of history are perfectly clear to everyone but are not treated in the handbooks, there are traces of a game of cultural one-upmanship: Roman practical wisdom is preferred over abstract Greek theory.[21]

Wiseman has pointed out that Antonius' problem seems to be a new concern in the 90s BCE.[22] He suggests plausibly that it may have been prompted by the recent activities of the *rhetores Latini*, who were now plying their rhetorical wares in Latin to train young men how to speak in court. But he also suggests that the reason the problem of proper rhetorical treatment of history has not been solved is because these *rhetores* are not of the proper social standing:

> Literary elaboration such as [Antonius] wanted applied to history was, as he points out in passing, a very recent arrival in Rome. What he does not point out – for it would spoil Cicero's argument to have him do so – is that the men who practised it, the self–styled 'Latin rhetors', were not senators and public men but professional teachers, who had had their schools closed by the censors of the previous year as an undesirable innovation.[23]

The social distinction is tempting, but it is not, as Wiseman notes, in Cicero.[24] Nor has his candidate for the first non-senatorial historian remained attractive.[25] The reason why Latin history has not been written as it should is a stylistic one, and Antonius gives it directly after the words quoted above (*De Or.* 2.62–4):

> Everyone of course knows that the first law of historiography is not daring to say anything false, and the second is not refraining from saying anything true. . . . (63) These foundations (*fundamenta*) are of course recognized by everyone, but the actual superstructure (*exaedificatio*) consists of content and style (*in rebus et verbis*). It is the nature of content (*rerum ratio*), on the one hand, that you require a chronological order of events and topographical descriptions. . . . (64) The nature of style and type of discourse (*verborum autem ratio*), on the other hand, require amplitude and mobility (*genus orationis fusum atque tractum*), with a smooth and regular fluency (*cum lenitate quadam aequabili profluens*) and without any of the roughness and prickliness associated with the law-courts (*sine hac iudiciali asperitate et sine sententiarum forensium aculeis*).[26]

Woodman stresses the rhetorical nature of both *res* and *verba* in the *exaedificatio*, making both the material and the style a part of the orator's process of *inventio*.[27] In the full version of Antonius' statement, it is casually implied that the earlier historians failed to treat some unspecified aspects of the *res* in a properly rhetorical way (2.63). That is, what they included and/or omitted was inconsistent with what one would have thought necessary to include/omit from a persuasive speech. From the way Cicero makes him express the *verba* requirements, however, it is clear that Antonius is reacting to a particular stylistic deficiency in the historical accounts. The specific prohibition *sine hac iudiciali asperitate et sine sententiarum forensium aculeis* suggests that some had written in what might be called a judicial style, which Antonius declares inappropriate. If the rhetorical material that was needed to write history properly was only recently imported to Rome (*modo enim huc ista sunt importata*, 2.53) and was done so by the *rhetores Latini*, as Wiseman suggests, then the reason that they could not produce history was because they used the rhetorical techniques they taught, which were aimed at producing speeches for the law-courts (2.55):

> 'It is hardly surprising', said Antonius, 'if this material has not yet been illustrated in our language, for no one of our people devoted himself to eloquence unless he could shine in court

cases and in the forum (*in causis atque in foro*). The most eloquent of the Greeks, however, removed from judicial cases (*remoti a causis forensibus*), applied themselves first to other honourable matters and then especially to writing history.'

Antonius' complaint is specific: history provides the greatest task for the orator but those who would apply the rules of rhetoric are applying the wrong rules, since history requires not the 'rough' and 'prickly' style associated with the courts, which is what students learn, but 'amplitude and mobility, with a smooth and regular fluency', which they are not learning. It is not enough that the writers have participated in public life or that they know the rules of rhetoric: they need to avail themselves of an appropriate style of rhetoric, one which the Greek teachers are not teaching. The proper style for history will be that third genre (*tertium genus*), epideictic rhetoric, which, in its Roman manifestations, corresponds to nothing in the Greek handbooks.[28] Thus historiography requires a broader view and the varied style of rhetoric for which Cicero makes Antonius argue throughout book 2.[29]

If we need a single target for Antonius' remarks about the failure of courtroom rhetoricians to write history, another candidate might be one of the *rhetores Latini* we know was active at the time of the censorial edict, Lucius Plotius Gallus.[30] Plotius most certainly trained young men to speak in the courts and later supposedly wrote a speech for the prosecutor in a case against Marcus Caelius Rufus. His style is derided as *inflatum ac levem et sordidum* ('bombastic, trifling and vulgar') by Caelius, but that is to be expected. It must have been harsh enough to make it suitable for a prosecution. Yet it must have had some good qualities to prompt Marius to invite Plotius to celebrate his *res gestas* (Cic. *Arch.* 20). It is doubtful that Plotius actually wrote a history of Marius' campaigns, but the possibility of his doing so in the late 90s would suit Antonius' remarks and adds an element of realism to the discussion. Moreover, Plotius' connections with Marius in the late 90s and early 80s would probably have estranged him from Antonius.

5

Whether or not Cicero meant Antonius to attack individual Latin rhetoricians, he does have him claim that one recent historian has nearly succeeded in writing history with the appropriate attention to style. Lucius Coelius Antipater is said to have 'added the more weighty sound of the orator's voice to history' (*addidit maiorem historiae sonum vocis, De Or.* 2.54).[31] Coelius was trained in rhetoric and taught Crassus (*Brut.* 102). He was the first Roman to write a historical monograph, rather than a general history, and seems to have been the first to treat the material of his history in a rhetorical manner, by embellishing it or even inventing it. He included dreams and prodigies, and occasionally exaggerated events for dramatic effect. He was also the first historian to craft speeches for his historical figures, both Romans and foreigners. In this aspect of historiography he seems to have been relatively successful, providing the proper *inventio* to the *res* of history, for Catulus makes his famous statement about the other historians by comparing them to Coelius: 'The rest were not embellishers of their materials, but only narrators of events' (*ceteri non exornatores rerum, sed tantum modo narratores fuerunt, De Or.* 2.54).

Yet Coelius failed to write the kind of history Antonius wants because of his style, and because he does not have the sensibilities of an orator, as Catulus continues (2.54):

He neither adorned his history with a variety of colours (*varietate colorum*)[32] nor did he thoroughly polish (*perpolivit*) his work through the arrangement of his words (*verborum conlocatione*) and a smooth and uniform movement of his discourse (*tractu orationis leni et aequabili*); but like a man neither learned nor very good at speaking (*neque maxime aptus ad dicendum*), he hacked away to the best of his ability.

In this passage Catulus indicates the components of the proper historical style, which agree with Antonius' requirements considered above (2.62–4). Particularly noteworthy is the parallel structure of the statements: both specify the same stylistic qualities, *varietas* ('variety'), *tractus* ('movement'), *lenitas* ('smoothness') and *aequabilitas* ('uniformity') in connection with *oratio*, before adding a comment on the historian's actual oratorical practice. Antonius forbids a judicial style (*sine hac iudiciali asperitate et sine sententiarum forensium aculeis*, 2.64), and Catulus says Coelius was not at all adept at public speaking (*neque maxime aptus ad dicendum*, 2.54).[33]

It is clear that the historian should control the moving style of the experienced orator. One is left to imagine when the historian would employ this style, since it would not be appropriate for all circumstances. Orations occurring in the historical narrative are a likely place. With the emphasis on *varietas* it seems possible for the speeches to be different in style from the rest of the narrative. But the equal emphasis on *lenitas* and *aequabilitas* suggests that the various styles be joined together smoothly. Since one of Coelius Antipater's most noteworthy innovations was the addition of fictitious speeches, it may be the style of these speeches in relation to the narrative that underlie the criticisms of Antonius and Catulus. Due to his lack of *varietas*, Coelius probably did not vary the style of speeches from that of the main narrative, erring on the side of being overblown, rather than with the other historians, on the side of *brevitas*.[34]

Coelius may have been the first to invent speeches for his characters, but the problem of abrupt style changes between speeches and narrative extended back to the first history written in Latin. Cato had included in the *Origines* the texts, or parts of texts, of at least two speeches he had actually delivered.[35] Earlier historians had included 'speeches' of a sort, short expressions by individuals, but those accounts were either in Greek, as Fabius Pictor's *Annales*, or, when in Latin, in verse, such as Ennius' *Annales* and Naevius' *Bellum Punicum*. Cato's decision to write his *Origines* in Latin and to include actual speech texts fused for the first time the close connection between the *verba* and *res* of the orator and the historian writing in Latin that would become Antonius' problem half a century later.[36]

Cato viewed his speeches as the *materia* or *res* of history. By including them, he was able to include *monumenta* of Rome's domestic history to complement the military *monumenta* traditionally associated with *res gestae*. Thus, his history was truly an account of *res domi militiaeque*, wherein oratory could document events at Rome. But when he included these speeches he evidently created a disparity with the celebrated *brevitas* of his narration. Analyses of the longer fragments of the Rhodian speech (fr. 95) and the narration of the military bravery of Caedicius (fr. 83) reveal significant differences in style between the speeches and the military narrative.[37] We do not have any of the transition passages to help us discern how Cato joined the two styles, but the fact of the differences must have been noticeable.

6

The discrepancy between the stylistic levels of orations and narrative that underlie the criticisms of the earlier historians by Antonius and Catulus was probably first noticed by the more refined orators of the 90s BCE, as Wiseman suggests. And the problems Antonius has with historiography are primarily concerned with style, not with the *res* of history. Orations were an integral part of that *res*, and the 90s witnessed the impressive power of political oratory to effect change in the state.[38] Thus a stylistic connection between historiography and oratory seems natural, given that they share the same purpose. The connection also serves Antonius' argument that the ideal orator must transcend the narrow rules of the rhetorical handbooks if he is to accomplish his proper role in society. That role is similar to, though broader than, the historian's. Yet historiography is not treated in the handbooks.

If Cicero insists that the orator is best qualified to write history, it is because of the necessary similarity of function, which requires similarity of style (cf. *De Or.* 3.23–4). The style is thus determined by the style best suited to arousing people to action. In Cicero's day, and to his way of thinking, it was a full style, powerful and vivid (cf. *Brut.* 279, 322ff.). It possessed all the vigour of oral speech, dramatically presented.

One historian who followed Cicero's advice was Livy.[39] Quintilian thought words insufficient to praise the eloquence of his speeches, the suitability of his style in general, and his superb ability to stir his reader's emotions: 'No historian has ever accomplished it better' (*Inst.* 10.1.101). But Livy looked longingly to the past, trying to recover the *virtus* of a lost age, perhaps even the power of a fuller, oratorical style. We can appreciate Livy's artistry in his surviving books, which relate Roman history during a period when oratory was still important. It would be interesting to know how he treated speeches in the part of his history that covered the Augustan years, when free speech was no longer truly possible in the way that it had been during Cicero's day and when Roman politics were negotiated not by speeches but by the nod of one man. Later, the emperor Domitian put to death the senator Mettius Pompusianus for, among other things, carrying around a collection of speeches culled from Livy (Suet. *Dom.* 10.3).

Public speech lost its power to effect change at Rome shortly after Cicero wrote *De Oratore*, and it ultimately died with him.[40] The reason Cicero's stylistic advice was not followed by later historians such as Sallust and Tacitus lies partially in this changed environment. The written word, rather than the orally delivered speech, accomplished more. And style necessarily changed to suit the new medium.

Yet, although Sallust and Tacitus adopt different styles on the whole, they still maintain *mutatis mutandis* the aspects of *varietas, lenitas, aequabilitas*, and *tractus* that Antonius and Catulus advocated in *De Oratore*. Thus the relationship between historiography and rhetoric remained the same as Cicero suggested it should; what changed was the function of oratory and the orator at Rome.[41]

NOTES

1 Characteristic is Wiseman 1986. The bibliography on the topic is enormous and cannot be adequately covered here. For a general account see Mellor 1988. Wiseman 1979; 1987; 1994 contain his many articles on the subject. See also Leeman 1963; Woodman 1988.

2 For instance, although Cicero questions the ability of certain styles of writing to convey their material correctly, he does not consider whether narrative is capable of representing action or not. Nor does he indicate that all human discourse is symbolic and necessarily rhetorical. Here, again, the bibliography is enormous. Good introductions are White 1987 and, most recently, Carpenter 1995.

3 The topic is 'in danger of becoming one of the most hackneyed themes of current writing', according to Cameron 1989: 1.

4 Evidence can be found in the works cited above, n. 1.

5 Woodman 1988, in particular, has shown how Cicero's remarks about history in his different works, despite some apparent discrepancies, yield a consistent view of history. For this reason, I shall focus on *De Oratore*, which is Cicero's most influential statement on the subject, and which, in the words of Woodman 1988: 75, 'has been consistently and fundamentally misunderstood'.

6 Woodman 1988: 70–116.

7 Wiseman 1981.

8 Wiseman 1994: 4.

9 This is Cicero's argument *passim* (e.g., 1.13–23, 2.77–92, 3.22–4) and clearly his intent (*Fam.* 1.9.23).

10 See the passages cited above, n. 9; Michel 1960: 40ff.

11 Cf. Leeman 1975: 149.

12 For a general treatment of this cultural phenomenon, see Gruen 1992: 223–71.

13 As Leeman 1963: 67 says, for the Romans 'this idea formed the *raison d'être* of historiography and determined its pattern'.

14 Still useful is Gelzer 1964: 51–110. See also Leeman 1963: 72–6; Badian 1966.

15 For general discussions of Cato's *Origines*, see Astin 1978: 211–39; Gruen 1992: 52–83.

16 All fragments of the *Origines* and of other early historians in this chapter are cited according to Peter 1914. The more recent edition of Cato's fragments by Chassignet 1986 includes a discussion of some of the

problems mentioned below and provides references to the most important secondary literature (pp. vii–xxi), but adds nothing new.

17 I agree with Badian 1966: 9 n. 44 that *istorias* at Plut. *Cat. Mai.* 20.7 refers to the *Origines* and do not see it, as Peter 1914: cxxix–cxxx suggests, as evidence for another work entitled *Praecepta*. Astin 1978: 182–3 thinks it refers to a book Cato did not intend to publish. Scholars seem about evenly divided on this issue, with most of those who are concerned primarily with Cato holding that *istorias* refers to something else, and those whose primary interest is Plutarch seeing agreement with Plutarch's parallel use of *istorias* at 25.1, where it clearly refers to the *Origines*. At issue is a discrepancy about when Cato was writing the work, not his purpose in doing so.

18 Cf. Gruen 1992: 82.

19 Wiseman 1994: 4.

20 The translation is by Woodman 1988: 80. He gives an important discussion of the topic on pp. 70–116.

21 Cf. Cicero's characterization of Antonius at *De Or.* 2.4. See also Gruen 1992: 223–71.

22 Wiseman 1981; see also Wiseman 1994: 4.

23 Wiseman 1981: 380.

24 We may be too much influenced by the 'Senator as historian' idea promulgated by Syme, as Cornell 1986: 79 argues.

25 Wiseman's candidate is Lucius Volticius Plotus, due to his status as a freedman (Suet. *Rhet.* 3). The information on this man has been discussed recently by Kaster 1995: 297–304, who restores the rhetorician's name to M'. Otacilius Pitholaus and provides rather more evidence for his being active in the late 50s and 40s than in the 90s.

26 Translated by Woodman 1988: 80 with one alteration: *lenitate* as 'smooth' rather than 'slow'.

27 Woodman 1988: 83–95.

28 Antonius' words do not fully support the assertions of Woodman 1988: 95 that he 'sees historiography in terms of *judicial* oratory'. In fact, they are in line with Cicero's other statements on the closeness of history and epideictic rhetoric (e.g., *Orat.* 67), to which Woodman 1988: 95–8 feels a need to reconcile the *De Oratore* passages. It should also be noted that Antonius' pronouncements on history occur in a section where he is trying to define a *tertium genus* of oratory in addition to the *duo prima genera* that the Greeks describe (*De Or.* 2.41ff.). Antonius contends that some of the types of speeches/writings falling under this *tertium genus* do have rules, history being one of those types, but Catulus wants the whole deliberative genre to be one which does not require rules, which is why he says the Greeks need great orators (*summi*) but for the Romans it is enough if the writer is not a liar (*satis est non esse mendacem*, *Orat.* 2.51).

29 This interpretation differs from that offered by Woodman 1988: 95–8, but resolves a major problem which troubles his account: how can Cicero say historiography is connected with both demonstrative (epideictic) and judicial oratory? Woodman interprets Antonius' discussion of historical

narratio too narrowly as referring to *narratio* in judicial oratory, 'of which the *narratio* was an integral part', because the rules the handbooks give for *narratio* concern judicial speech. Woodman is then at pains to reconcile this view with the unanimous testimony of the ancient sources that connect historiography with epideictic. In *De Oratore*, however, Antonius explicitly argues against using the judicial style the handbooks teach. Cicero makes the same argument at *Orator* 37–42.

30 For a thorough discussion see Kaster 1995: 291–7.

31 Discussion and sources in Peter 1914: ccxi–ccxxxvii, 158–77; see especially pp. ccxvii ff. and frr. 5, 6, 16, 26, 47, 58, with his notes. Cf. Woodman 1988: 78, 103 n. 25. Summaries are in Leeman 1963: 74–6; Badian 1966: 15–17.

32 See Woodman 1988: 103 n. 26.

33 I have taken the passages out of order in this paragraph, but in proper sequence the argument runs as follows: the early historians fail because they do not treat their material and expressions as an orator does (*De Or.* 2.51–3); Coelius does better than the others in his treatment of material but not in terms of style (54); most people consider style narrowly as what is taught by rhetoricians, namely judicial style (55); but the best Greek historians were not courtroom speakers (55–8); interlude (59–61); history is an extremely important task for the orator, requiring proper treatment of material and expression, and the proper expression has *varietas, lenitas, aequabilitas*, etc., which is not that of the courtroom (62–4).

34 For Coelius' style being overblown, see *Leg.* 1.7. In *De Or.* 2.54 Coelius' *maiorem ... sonum vocis* and the fact that 'he did not polish' (*neque ... perpolivit*) his work may point in the same direction. It is also indicated by comparing fr. 86 of Cato's *Origines* with fr. 25 of Coelius' work, as Aulus Gellius does (*NA* 10.24.6–7).

35 Why Cato included the texts of *his own* speeches – a unique practice – is a vexed issue. For one answer see Astin 1978: 233–6. Given the present state of the fragments and evidence for the *Origines*, we cannot determine whether he included actual speeches by other men (as they wrote them out or as he remembered them). My own opinion is that Cato considered speeches actually given to be the only appropriate speeches to use when illustrating Roman domestic history, and he had his speeches at hand or could reconstruct them with some degree of confidence (cf., e.g., the opening fragment from his speech *De Sumptu Suo* (Malcovati 1975: 70–1 no. 173).

36 The problem is also discussed by Crassus in *De Or.* 3.19–24.

37 There are good analyses in Leeman 1963: 44–9, 70–1; Goldberg 1986: 40–6, 174–5. The stylistic level of the speeches is considered fairly high for early Latin prose and is thought to be influenced by Greek rhetorical theory (as the remarks in Gell. *NA* 6.3 about fr. 83 suggest); see Kennedy 1972: 45–60; Calboli 1978: 225–43. It must be admitted that the fragments are all relatively brief and that the 'hard' evidence for Greek influence is meager; see Albrecht 1995: 24–50.

38 See Millar 1986.

39 Leeman 1963: 179–97; cf. Walsh 1962: 219–44.

ROBERT W. CAPE, JR

40 So said the generation of declaimers that followed Cicero (Sen. *Suas.* 6.1–27, esp. 26–7).
41 I am very grateful to Sander Goldberg, James May, and William Dominik for detailed comments on an earlier version of this chapter. I wish to thank the Deutscher Akademischer Austauschdienst and the Sid Richardson Foundation for funding the research for this chapter.

228

14

Substructural elements of architectonic rhetoric and philosophical thought in Fronto's *Epistles*

Michele Valerie Ronnick

GREEK BACKGROUND

Much ink has been spent discussing the so-called 'battle' between philosophy and rhetoric, as articulated in the Graeco-Roman period and as interpreted later on in the western Middle Ages, in the Renaissance and in modern times. Underlying the particular questions argued in each of these time periods has been a fundamental struggle to gain power and dominance. In the words of Stephen Halliwell, 'at stake in the emergence and elaboration of these concepts' is 'the status of intellectual authority and cultural influence – an authority that would give the practitioners and teachers of certain activities a pre-eminent claim to wisdom and expertise (*sophia*), and a corresponding right to present themselves as possessors of politically, socially and educationally valuable knowledge'.[1]

The most influential debates about rhetoric have been based upon the thought of Plato, Aristotle and Cicero, each of whom established particular parameters and special terminology on which later discussion has depended. Despite their differences in thought, their conceptual constructs concerning rhetoric fall into two broad types. When rhetoric is concerned with an 'act of enumeration on a specific occasion', used primarily 'in civic life', and is 'primarily oral', it is classed as 'primary'.[2] Once those words leave the mouth and are inscribed with a pen in a text, painted with a brush on to a surface, or chiselled out of a stone, the focus of that process is called 'secondary rhetoric'. This type of rhetoric concerns 'the apparatus of rhetorical techniques clustering around discourse or art forms when those techniques are not being used for their primary oral purpose'.[3]

As a young culture grows into its maturity, 'it has been a persistent characteristic of classical rhetoric in almost every phase of its ancient and modern history to move from primary into secondary forms'.[4] This dynamic, termed the '*letteraturizzazione* of rhetoric' by George Kennedy, manifests itself through a 'shift in focus from persuasion to narration, from civic to personal contexts and from discourse to literature including poetry'.[5] The rate of speed with which the '*letteraturizzazione* of rhetoric' develops in a society depends upon the 'opportunities or lack of opportunities, open to primary rhetoric' and the 'recurring tendency to teach it by rote to young children rather than make it a more intellectually demanding advanced discipline'.[6]

Thus, as an oral culture like that of early Greece and Rome changes over into a literate society, theoretical systems articulate the principles of that culture's primary and secondary rhetorics. In the Greek world this phenomenon began with Homer and moved forward into the fifth century BCE when systematic approaches to support the formal study of rhetoric were devised by men like Corax of Syracuse and his pupil Tisias, who were the first serious students of rhetoric. In the same century formal codification of such knowledge began to be set forth in handbooks.

Accompanying the development of the systematic presentation of rhetorical principles in handbooks was the establishment of schools by professional sophists. Their ability to argue both sides of an issue and to instruct others in their methods was perceived by some as a dangerous form of immorality and irreverence. In response various philosophical sects, who were suspicious of the sophists' intentions and perhaps envious, developed their own methods and styles of exposition to pursue and state formally their perceptions supporting philosophical knowledge and reviling rhetorical casuistry and ethical relativism.

Foremost among these expository devices, which include the diatribe used by the Cynics and the epistle used by the Epicureans, was the Platonic dialogue. Among its most influential products was the *Gorgias*. In this 'brilliant and unscrupulous performance', in which Socrates declared open season on the sophists, Plato does not 'work by an open-minded evaluation of the whole art, allowing both good and bad sides to appear, but rams home a series of dichotomies, or excluding categories, in which rhetoric is dismissed by analogy'.[7] The result is a 'rhetoric, if it is rhetoric, of a highly dubious sort, manoeuvring categories and analogies by sleight of hand to effect an arbitrary identification of rhetoric with ignoble and disreputable arts and seeking to arouse in the listener or reader emotions of disgust and contempt'.[8]

To the biased and overtly antagonistic stance assumed by Plato toward the sophists in the *Gorgias* must be credited the establishment of an enduring paradigm in the discussion of rhetoric and philosophy. This is the dynamic of a bilateral rivalry, based upon what Brian Vickers calls 'territorial rights'.[9] Once rhetoric was equated with sophistry, therein began as well the long-lived and contagious hand-wringing over the 'pathology of rhetoric', a phrase coined by T. S. Eliot to discuss Elizabethan literature.[10]

ROMAN REACTION

The reception in Rome of these ideas about rhetoric and philosophy and their presentation in written and oral communications was mixed. A Roman such as Scipio Aemilianus, a pronounced philhellene, readily absorbed the concepts. Another like the elder Cato, considered by some to have been the first Roman orator, craftily hid the extent of his familiarity with Greek learning during Rome's early national period under a cloak of xenophobia. The result was not without its own element of irony. By an act of intellectual imperialism, so to speak, Cato quietly brought technical devices from Greek into Roman discourse, just one such example being *praeteritio*, which is found in his speech *On His Own Expenses*. However, while rhetorical training based on Greek learning became part and parcel of Roman schooling, the serious pursuit of Greek philosophical studies was never accepted as an end in itself.

The Roman attitude is epitomized by the events of 155 BCE when Carneades the Academic, Critolaus the Peripatetic, and Diogenes the Stoic came to Rome from Athens as ambassadors. Carneades' speeches, which were argued on consecutive days, the first in support of justice and the second against it, threw certain Romans into a frenzy of angry concern.[11] The elder Cato suggested that the visitors be expelled, but they were not. Nevertheless, however long the actual stay of the philosophers was in Rome, the philosophers' speeches raised serious questions about the relationship between technical skill and verbal expression versus concepts of truth and content, which remained in Roman minds long after the trio left the city. Thereafter the acceptable mixture of rhetorical skill, philosophical endeavour and Janus-faced duplicity remained forever a variable and volatile subject in Rome.

Roman culture, however, did encourage the members of its well-born classes to study philosophy in order to gain a veneer of cultivation. Cicero endeavoured to effect a compromise between philosophy and rhetoric by requiring the would-be orator to include the study of both disciplines along with a broad range of other subjects. 'A knowledge of very many things', Cicero declared, 'must be grasped, without which oratory is but an empty and laughable whirlwind of verbiage' (*De Or.* 1.17).

A good portion of his program to harmonize philosophy and rhetoric was laid out in the first book of the *De Oratore*, in which he discussed 'that separation – absurd, harmful and regrettable as it is, between the tongue and the heart, whereby one group of people teaches us to be wise, another to be eloquent' (*De Or.* 3.61). He saw the 'ideal speaker' (*orator perfectus*) as one whose knowledge was universal. Cicero's fully formed orator would be conversant with legal, historical, political and literary knowledge, but above all he would have a knowledge of philosophy (*Brut.* 118). Furthermore, the orator's knowledge would be so smoothly and thoroughly integrated that it would not matter whether he were identified as a 'wise speaker' (*orator sapiens*) or as an 'eloquent philosopher' (*philosophus eloquens*), for the two phrases would be synonymous (*De Or.* 3.142).

In Cicero's eyes, 'the harmonizing of rhetoric and philosophy was a humanistic ideal consistent with a free society in a non-violent constitutional republic'.[12] He felt that 'in his own decadent time, rhetoricians [had] become shysters and philosophers ivory-tower recluses, while the unworthy [filled up] the vacuum'.[13] Behind Cicero's program lay the moral imperatives of the elder Cato, who believed that the orator must be 'a good man skilled in speaking' (*vir bonus, dicendi peritus*, Cato *Libri ad M. Filium*).[14] For Cicero was well aware of what could happen if the tools of a persuasive rhetorical technique came into the possession and use of a morally corrupt person. He declared (*De Or.* 3.55, 57) that

> if we hand over the art of speaking [to men without virtue], we will not have made them into speakers, but we will have given certain arms to madmen. . . . Years ago the very same course of study seems to have been a good teacher of correct behaviour and proper speaking; the educators were not separated by specialty, but rather the teachers of living and of speaking were one and the same, as in the case of Homer's

Phoenix, who said that he was appointed the companion of Achilles in war by Achilles' father Peleus so that he might make him into a speaker of words and a doer of deeds.

Thus Cicero's words provide a glimpse of primary rhetoric in its infancy.

During the empire the practice and teaching of rhetoric was divorced from philosophy and aspects of professionalism emerged at the time that testify to the increasing levels of specialization of knowledge. The establishment of the first chairs of Latin and Greek in Rome under the emperor Vespasian clearly heralded the advent of the learned expert who, like the Athenian sophist, was a confirmed careerist but who, unlike the sophist, was directly tied to the government.

Quintilian was the first person to hold the chair of rhetoric in Rome. Compelled by attendant circumstances or his own convictions, he abandoned Cicero's stance in day-to-day behaviour and assumed a posture of territorial antagonism like that presented in the *Gorgias*, but one that was reversed in favour of rhetoric. Quintilian claimed the higher moral ground for rhetoric and averred that the 'rules of upright and honourable living' did not solely belong to philosophy. Sounding very much like Seneca the younger on the subject of ersatz philosophers, Quintilian declared that orators must eschew those who make 'noticeable professions . . . of being philosophers' and 'who feign moral superiority, while living a life of wantonness at home' (*Inst.* 9.1.33). They must instead embrace the study of moral philosophy and look to the actual experiences of life (*Inst.* 12.2.6–9, 15–20). But his actual posture was like that maintained by Isocrates, who manifested 'a fugitive and cloister'd vertue, unexercised & unbreath'd', as Milton expressed it in the *Areopagitica*. For Quintilian's professional career was closely allied to the imperial government. Like Fronto, he was appointed imperial tutor.

The argument between philosophy and rhetoric at this point was clearly marked on both sides by self-righteousness and a sense of holding a monopoly on the truth. Rhetoric under those conditions was accused of being merely 'a verbal art of persuasion' narrowly focused on techniques of argument.[15] Bereft of a wider context, this view of rhetoric exacerbated the division between words and things and between ideas and expression. In such circumstances philosophy became narrowly focused upon questions of epistemology and upon the formulation of rules for behaving ethically. As Richard Rorty says, 'in the mainstream of Western philosophical tradition, this paradigm [of human activity] has been knowing – possessing justified true beliefs, or, better yet, beliefs so intrinsically pervasive as to make justification unnecessary'.[16] By the second century CE in the Roman empire, evidence that this was happening can be seen as experts on subjects like geography, medicine, authors of textbooks of rhetoric and juridical learning, such as Ptolemy, Celsus, Hermogenes and Gaius, respectively, organized the presentation of their learning according to their own estimation of the truth.

In every instance, the 'arbitrary separation of philosophy from rhetoric, the divorce so to speak of rhetoric from philosophy, and of expression from content, prevents the intellectual synthesis essential to resolving the persistent problems of being, thinking and acting'.[17] If this division is enforced, neither rhetoric nor philosophy has importance to daily life. During the Roman republic the problematic separation of the arts of knowing from the arts of expression led Cicero to attempt to rejoin wisdom and eloquence in a civic philosophy based on Roman law.[18] Cicero could do this because rhetoric, having no absolute subject matter, can only be understood in the context of method and result in actual language. Rhetorical theory is intimately wedded to practice and each ultimately depends upon the other. In short, although oratory and rhetoric are distinct genres in terms of form and content, to borrow Ian Worthington's comment, 'oratory is rhetoric in action'.[19] Cicero, in his effort to create a civic philosophy for Rome, had turned the rhetoric of his day into what modern scholars call 'an architectonic art', one that 'laid down the structure of a program of education and culture designed to reunite eloquence and wisdom in action'.[20]

For architectonic rhetoric has its *telos* in action. It goes beyond being a means of expression alone to become a principle of organization that structures thinking about any subject matter. Actions, situations and organizations lead to the creation of new terminologies; however, 'words themselves do not determine actions; they bridge the gap between experience and the novel'.[21] Thus the act of naming a thing or event that had gone unnoticed or had not existed until that moment becomes empowered as a component in subsequent forms of human communication. Productive architectonic rhetoric is in fact a 'universal art, an art of producing things and arts, and not merely one of producing words and arguments'.[22] *Logos* ('speech') is linked with *technê* ('skill'), emotion with cognition, and knowledge with expression. In this way architectonic rhetoric becomes a 'managing skill that creates commonplaces for systematic action out of the data, facts and consequences of actual cases, and rises above the immediate requirements of persuasion'.[23]

During the early empire, this idea was present in theory but not in practice. While Quintilian could state in his *Institutio Oratoria* that theory should not be separated from practice, the activities of the Roman educational system show us that the actual situation was otherwise. Affected by the principles of *letteraturizzazione* as it moves into its phase of secondary rhetoric, the formal study of oratory for the first time in Roman history drew back from reality and techniques of on-hands training into the realm of pretence and artificiality in which deliberative (*suasoriae*) and forensic (*controversiae*) speeches focused upon fantastic scenarios.[24]

Although the diremption between rhetoric and philosophy remained a constant motif in the thought of Graeco-Roman civilization, the written sources suggest that at times a fragile synthesis was achieved. This happened whenever architectonic rhetoric found a voice that could contribute to the formation of culture by informing the shape of all knowledge and communicating it – one of the most important, but often overlooked, products of rhetoric. We know that Plato was aware of this phenomenon. In the *Gorgias* Socrates tells Callicles that 'there is another sort of rhetoric; this other type is a beautiful kind that tries to make souls of citizens as good as they can be and tries to state what is best whether it is more or less pleasing to the audience' (503A–B); however, he quickly turns the direction of the conversation around and cries out, 'But this is a rhetoric that you have never seen!' In Rome Cicero described the heights to which such a rhetoric could ascend as the time when one discovered 'that there is a marvellous agreement and harmony of all learning' (*De Or.* 3.21). The effort to keep this idea alive is no doubt one of Cicero's lasting achievements. This is also the case with Fronto, whose private epistles at certain points brought architectonic rhetoric together with philosophy and thereby fulfilled in part his obligation as Roman citizen and as tutor to his imperial charges Marcus Aurelius and Lucius Verus to pass on vital elements of Roman culture.

EVIDENCE IN FRONTO

Marcus Cornelius Fronto lived during the period when the literature that we now call the second sophistic was written. It was an era in which Greek-speaking orators especially showcased themselves by delivering elaborate speeches. Some were confirmed practitioners of Atticism and strove to revive interest in and use of the pure language of Xenophon, Plato and Demosthenes. Aelius Aristides rose up in support of rhetoric and oratory with a speech such as *To Plato: In Defense of Oratory*. Sounding as if he were a combination of Plato and the elder Cato, Aristides defined the best speaker as 'the one who is the best sort of man' (146D). He also stated flatly that Plato's accusations and complaints were actually lodged against flattery and slander, not oratory (150D–152D).

In the face of the sophists' achievements and wide-spread reputation in Greek letters, Fronto gained fame as the greatest Latin orator of his time (Dio Cass. 69.18). Fronto was, as his recent biographer Edward Champlin says, 'without a doubt one of the great figures of his century'.[25] Fronto, Champlin informs us

> was indisputably the guiding genius of Latin letters through three reigns, and was perceived in later times as a second Cicero. He was recognized as the leading advocate of his day. He was an intimate and counsellor of the imperial family for over thirty years, and the teacher and mentor of two emperors.[26]

Fronto's renown grew even greater after his death. Michael Grant provides us with this recent summary of Fronto's posthumous fame:[27]

> People echoed the view of those who lived in his time that he was the Cicero of his epoch, or at least not very far short of him: 'the alternative glory of Roman eloquence', as Eumenius still described him in the fifth Latin *Panegyric*, in 297 CE. About a century later Macrobius declared Fronto the master of the plain, precise, down-to-earth kind of oratory, in contrast with the copious kind, in which Cicero had been supreme. Saint Jerome (*c.* 348–420), writing of the special qualities of various authors, indicates 'serious dignity' as the particular characteristic of Fronto. A little later Claudius Mamertus, likewise discoursing on the typical features of writers, singles out Fronto for splendour (*pompa*). Sidonius Apollinaris saw in him *gravitas*.

The last mention made of Fronto occurred during the twelfth century. It is found in the works of John of Salisbury, who quoted with a sense of affirmation 'an obscure remark' of Fronto's 'concerning Seneca', an author for whom 'Fronto as we know him, has no word of praise'.[28]

Despite this reputation, no extended portion of his work was available for scholars to examine until the early nineteenth century when two codices in palimpsest were found.[29] At this point the esteem with which Fronto had been held for fifteen hundred years or so vanished. Eager readers, each harbouring impossible hopes in regard to the contents of the letters, were sorely disappointed with what they read in the first printed texts established by Angelo Mai and published in 1815 and 1823. As Champlin notes, 'with the weighty exception of Leopardi, whose enthusiastic *Discorso* on Fronto's life and works is still worth reading, a uniformly negative attitude to his personality has grown up since the publication of his letters'.[30] Distaste for Fronto still remains. M. Dorothy Brock's work on Fronto published early this century has an array of statements by various scholars ranging from acerbic to blistering about Fronto's character and writing.[31] The sentiments expressed therein have been restated in various forms since then.

Despite these efforts to revile Fronto, two points Champlin has made about him remain true: first, 'much of the material remains unexploited';[32] second, 'to read the letters of Fronto without the closest consideration, to dismiss them as fatuous, is to dismiss evidence'.[33] Certain scholars, for example, have declared that Fronto hated philosophy.[34] Yet they do not then explain how he tolerated the company of his many friends and colleagues who were most interested in philosophy, nor for that matter how he was able to admire Cicero, who steeped himself in philosophical studies. Fronto's circle of friends, however, 'reveals no fixed battlelines, for students of philosophy were numerous among his friends and they were often students of rhetoric as well; thus Fronto might have spoken just as casually as did his follower Aulus Gellius (19.5.1) of "my contemporaries and intimates, followers of rhetoric or philosophy"'.[35]

A recent study by Pierre Grimal goes even further in its findings about Fronto's relationship with philosophy and maintains that Fronto was in fact thoroughly imbued with Platonism.[36] What Fronto clearly and indisputably did not like was an unhealthy imbalance. The idea of an emperor who was without eloquence and who imitated or seemed to imitate the affected behaviours of the more flamboyant Cyno–Stoic philosophers was abhorrent to him (*Ad M. Caes.* 4.12; *De Feriis Alsiensibus* 3; *Ad Verum (?) Imp.* 1.1;

Ad Antoninum Imp. 1.2; *Ad Antoninum De Eloquentia* 1).

Furthermore, Fronto saw Latin give way to Greek 'in his century as a vehicle of philosophical inquiry'.[37] Rome, however, was the centre of the empire and the bastion of all that was best in Roman culture. Fronto's effort to maintain the position of Latin as a vehicle of communication and to encourage others to believe that the best form of discourse was the one that not only pleased the audience but also was appropriately adorned was an important socio-political and cultural stance with national and racial overtones.

Roman civic life had been built upon communication skills. An orator's achievement reflected well upon the orator and his nation. 'Although the general effect of Fronto's teachings is quite unknown', the epistles show that this attitude formed part of Fronto's conscious-ness.[38] Like Cicero and the elder Cato, Fronto was determined to encourage the pursuit of the highest levels of eloquence in the highest levels of government. The correspondence shows us that Fronto continually reminded Marcus Aurelius and Lucius Verus of the importance of skilled communication. Clear thinking, clear speaking and clear writing meant strong leadership and good government.

Much of this attitude can be easily espied in the straightforward declarative portions of the letters, but Fronto used other techniques to deliver his message. If this were not the case, scholars would not be so divided over questions concerning what value Fronto had placed on the correspondence and whether he had conceived a plan for publication or not. Theodor Mommsen felt in 1874 that Fronto arranged and published the letters himself.[39] D. A. Russell stated in 1990 that 'one can hardly believe ... that their letters were not meant to be published'.[40] Champlin, however, in 1980 argued that 'there is no hint that Fronto himself ever contemplated any collection of his correspondence'.[41] In 1987 F. R. D. Goodyear averred that 'these letters were probably never meant for publication or published by Fronto'.[42] We must attribute the generation of these disparate conclusions to the elusive combination of public and private rhetoric inherent in the entire correspondence along with strong scholarly bias against Fronto. With the exception of Champlin, common scholarly sentiment holds that the social status of the correspondents was in itself enough to justify publication. On the other hand, the letters have been deemed so inferior that surely Fronto himself must have wanted but failed to block their promulgation. With these ideas in mind, let us examine two particular letters.

Epistulae Graecae 1, dated to 143, is an ornate letter of apology written in Greek to Domitia Lucilla, the mother of Marcus Aurelius.[43] Fronto expresses regret over his unresponsiveness to her. In the first section, he tells her that he has what we would call a 'one-track mind'. Once he is involved in a project, he cannot stop and attend to other things. In an effort to win her over, Fronto offers three similes. He writes (*Epist. Gracecae*: 1)

> I am [like] the creature the Romans call a hyena whose neck can be stretched straight ahead in a forward direction, but cannot be bent to either side. So when I am creating anything with more than usual care, I am in a way immovable, and having abandoned all else, I focus on that alone like the hyena neither turning to the right hand nor to the left.... I am [like] the snakes known to us as 'the darters' who in a similar fashion extend themselves straight forward but never move side-ways.... I am [also similar to] spears and arrows when they travel straight ahead untouched by the wind, unhindered by the hand of Athena or Apollo, as were the arrows of Teucer or of the suitors.

After stating that he could extend this series of similes by adding a fourth simile based on the concept of a straight line and a fifth one based upon the wind, Fronto tells Domitia Lucilla that he was deeply involved in work on an encomium for the emperor. He then expresses the hope that she does not find his Greek too barbarous, for he is after all 'a Libyan of the Libyans'. He closes the letter by saying that he will end this 'writing of nothing but similes'.

On the surface the letter looks like a piece of self-serving bombast. Perhaps it is, but there is a degree of artistry here. For through his choice of similes Fronto has taken care to inform Domitia Lucilla of his African origin and his considerable learning. Like Fronto, the hyena and the darter snake come from Africa (Luc. 9.720; Pliny *HN* 8.108.46). The image of the straight line in the first section is worked back into the letter in the fifth section where Fronto asks, 'It remains for me to inquire in the manner of the geometers – what?' Likewise the final simile concerning the wind is worked into the closing lines of the apology by means of an image of air in motion over land or vocal chords. Fronto is like the Scythian nomad Anachasis. Both can 'browse in fresh pastures' and 'bleat'. Fronto playfully but purpose-fully brings together the movements of nomads, the production of barbarous speech and the airborne sounds of bleating animals, then quickly breaks off the 'bleat' of his letter.

At another point in the correspondence (*Ad M. Caes.* 3.8), Fronto has asked Marcus Aurelius to work out ten similes as a propaedeutic exercise. Marcus tells Fronto he is stymied by the ninth problem, which concerns an inland lake located on the island of Aenaria in which is found another island. About this assignment Russell has commented:[44]

> The exercise seems to be to find an application for the image and this means drawing out all the implications of the object suggested for description. Marcus is puzzled about one of the ten topics on which he has been working. It is that of the lake on the island of Aenaria, which has an island itself on it. Fronto explains how this could be used in Marcus' address of thanks to his father, probably for the title of 'Caesar' bestowed on him in 139 (so Haines, but not Champlin, who dates the letter later). Antoninus is like the main island, Aenaria, because he protects his young successor, who corresponds to the sheltered island in the inland lake. The point of the analogy is an accident ... of the subject, the similarity between the safety and pleasure of the inner island and that of the cherished young prince.

Russell, preoccupied with the problem of dating the letter, has completely missed the point in regard to the purpose of the exercise. Before Fronto provides some carefully written lines of technical advice to Marcus in the body of the letter, he drops an important hint. In the first line of the letter he says (*Ad M. Caes.* 3.8),

> As to the simile, which you say you are puzzled about and about which you summon me as your ally and assistant in the hunt for a clue, you will not be cross, will you, if I seek the clue to that concept in your heart and in your father's heart (*in tui patris sinu*)?

Fronto underscores the hint by bringing the letter to an end with an exhortation to Marcus to do his own work. Using the imagery and vocabulary of travel, Fronto says significantly, 'Now it remains for you by the footpaths and roads I have shown you above to discover how you may most conveniently come to your own Aenaria.' Here, by bringing up Marcus' father for whom the similes were being written, the master is trying to focus his pupil's attention on practising the rhetorical arts of discovery and invention. Marcus should discover that the connection between Aenaria and Marcus lies not only in the geographical imagery of the shelter and protection of an inland lake but more specifically in the devotion between a father and a son. Aenaria, in fact, gained its name for having given anchorage to Aeneas' travel-weary fleet. Thus the simile in an expanded form would include some comparison of the protection Aenaria gave Aeneas with the tender care that Aeneas, upon reaching his maturity, gave his aged father Anchises. The analogy should then be carried over to the loving relationship between Marcus and his own father. The noun *sinus* used in the important opening sentence has meanings ranging from 'heart' and 'asylum' to 'gulf' and 'bay' and could have held a place in expanding the simile to its fullest form. Fronto's talented pupil also could have worked out a fine alliterative sequence using the names Aeneas, Aenaria, Aurelius, Antoninus, and Anchises.

Fronto communicates with his readers in other ways. In some cases for his imperial pupils, he merely reworks received ideas. At the beginning of an epistle dated to 139 (*Ad M. Caes.* 4.3), for example, Fronto discusses the nature of real learning as distinct from superficial knowledge using the examples of eloquence and philosophy. He tells Marcus that in some disciplines such as philosophy a small bit of knowledge is a dangerous thing. In those fields knavish poseurs can exist for a time, but in the field of eloquence there is no room for any level of pretence – either one is skilful or one is not.

This idea was treated in part by Quintilian in the final book of his *Institutio Oratoria*. Here Quintilian succinctly summed up the situation by saying that 'philosophy can in fact be feigned, eloquence cannot' (*philosophia enim simulari potest, eloquentia non potest, Inst.* 12. 321). On the surface this parallel seems rather banal, for Fronto was certainly acquainted with Quintilian's life and work. However, because 'Fronto never mentions Quintilian by name in the extant letters', but nevertheless reminds the reader of Quintilian in regard to his 'attitude toward government' and his 'written reaction to the death of his grandson' (*De Nepote Amisso* 2), we must therefore conclude that this similarity of thought is not accidental.[45] The subtexts to Fronto's words show us that he not only accepted Quintilian's viewpoint on these particular items but also has silently subsumed them into his own written discourse.

The didactic function of this allusive technique is twofold. Fronto wants first to convey an important idea, and good ideas are common property. His second motive is to allow the reader, Marcus Aurelius in this case, to discern the range of his learning. Over time, as Marcus becomes more familiar with Latin literature, he might well be able to link the concatenation of the ideas found in his master's thought with those in the works of other writers.

Fronto also ornaments his letters with notable words and phrases taken from other authors for which he provides no attribution. Using their 'buzz words', as it were, he could display his learning and delight his cultured audience, who would find pleasure in recognizing familiar expressions embedded within his text. In a letter to Marcus, for example, concerning eloquence, dated to 139, Fronto borrows the phrase *fons et caput* ('fountainhead') from Cicero's famous description of the status of Socrates among the philosophers (*De Or.* 1.42) to describe Cicero's own position among the orators. Fronto writes that Cicero 'is esteemed as the head and fountain of Roman eloquence' (*Ad M. Caes.* 4.3).

Marcus himself is not unresponsive. He readily adopts his master's style on occasion by using some unusual words whose origin would have been familiar to Fronto. In *Ad Marcum Caesarem* 4.6, Marcus tells Fronto that he dined with his family in an 'olive press-room' (*torcularium*) in the countryside. In Latin this noun is found most frequently in the elder Cato; Columella's usage is second. By selecting that special word, Marcus is telling his teacher that he has not only been studying Cato, one of Fronto's favourite writers, but also has been following his teaching by practising a virtuous, agrarian lifestyle.[46]

Of greater significance is Fronto's metaphorical language, which he terms *eikones* (*Ad M. Caes.* 4.12) and *imagines* (3.8). It is through the metaphors and the commonplaces that derive from them that we see what meaning a culture has made out of the myriad details of its own day-to-day existence. As Elaine Fantham has noted, 'no aspect of language is quicker to offend against taste than metaphor'.[47] For metaphor reveals the tastes of a society. If Fronto were as pernicious an influence as his critics would have us believe, the effects of his bad style should be apparent here, but they are not. There is instead a marked adherence to tradition in general along with a particularly strong preference for the metaphorical language of Cicero. The agricultural and vegetal themes from the works of the elder Cato are also present. They form a noticeable part of Marcus' letters and he seems to have enjoyed his efforts to describe and elaborate them (*Ad. M. Caes.* 2.5, 6, 12; 4.2, 4, 6).

A number of Ciceronian metaphors concerning words and speech appear in Fronto. Among them are example dealing with rivers, garments, ships and soldiers. For the sake of example, let us examine the last two categories. In a letter dated to 162 (*Ad Antoninum Imp.* 1.2), Fronto likens Marcus to a well-equipped ship that sails in quest of eloquence. 'Although you have not always set every sail in pursuit of eloquence, you have yet stayed on course using oars and topsails. As necessity forces you to unfurl the main sails, you are out-distancing with ease all other students of eloquence like cutters and yachts.' In the use of this image, the 'voyage of a speech', as Fantham has aptly put it, Cicero took a negative course in his most striking application of it.[48] At *Pro Caelio* 51, Cicero feels as if his speech is faltering like a foundering ship and declares that it 'seems to have already sunk and been carried away from the shallows on to the rocks'.

Good examples of the second image are found in two lengthier letters written by Fronto sometime during 162–3. One is addressed to Marcus (*De Eloquentia* 1) and one to Verus (*Ad Verum Imp.*). Both describe the accomplished orator as one who is armed with words – figurative language that did not originate with Fronto but seems to have been popular in Fronto's group. His contemporary Aulus Gellius, for example, employed the image in his essay on Cato's speech *For the Rhodians*, noting that Cato had called upon 'all the armaments and auxiliaries of rhetorical studies' (*NA* 6.3.52).

Fronto's thought is similar in both letters. The final section of the latter (*Ad Verum Imp.* 20) breaks off with ideas found in the beginning of the former (*De Eloquentia* 1). In the opening section of *De Eloquentia*, Fronto tells Marcus to sort and station his words like soldiers, and in a lacunate portion of the fourth section, he carries the metaphor forward, mentioning 'fortresses and assembly places of words'.

A quote from an unknown speech by the elder Cato takes up most of the last section of *Ad Verum Imperatorem*. There Cato's assessment of the abilities of his various troops recalls the language of *De Eloquentia*. About two-thirds into the letter, Fronto asks Marcus if 'the gods will permit the comitium, rostra, and tribunals that once rang out with the speeches of Cato and Gracchus and Cicero to fall silent in his age'. He then tells Marcus to 'equip himself with speech that is worthy of the thoughts he takes from philosophy' and to 'summon eloquence, the comrade of philosophy' (18).

Fronto, however, keeps Marcus in mind as he addresses Verus. By way of apostrophe in section 3, we learn Marcus' view of Verus' recent achievements as a soldier–statesman in Syria. Marcus tells himself that he 'has what he has asked for in every prayer – a brave brother, a good man skilled in speaking (*vir bonus, dicendi peritus*)'. Later Fronto declares hyperbolically that emperors before the Antonines 'were no more able to speak about their military accomplishments than their helmets' (12). 'Verus,' Fronto writes, 'you have used eloquence as your mistress in the art of war' (18); in the final section (20), Fronto cries out, 'Hasn't Cato, as great a general as orator (*orator idem imperator summus*), been your teacher?'

In these examples from Fronto's letters, his opinions concerning rhetoric and philosophy find an important and summary juncture. Avoiding the limitations of 'verbal rhetoric that produces arguments', Fronto has attained to the level of 'architectonic rhetoric that produces attitudes'.[49] To his students he declares that like Cato one can marshal words as one marshals soldiers. With the image of the *orator/imperator* ('orator/general'), Fronto has created his own *Kulturträger* and along with it a template of systematic action and winning behavior for his imperial pupils. In it *vita activa* and *vita contemplativa* are united. *Logos* ('speech') becomes *technê* ('skill'). The medium becomes the message and the man of action and the man of words become one. If we concede anything to the theory of *elocutio novella*, we must find its 'novelty' here in Fronto's overarching effort to achieve a form of cultural continuity. By restructuring certain elemental ideas about philosophy and rhetoric recurring from the time of the elder Cato, Fronto has worked to construct soldier–statesmen for his own era.

NOTES

 1 Halliwell 1994: 223.
 2 Kennedy 1987: 4.
 3 Kennedy 1987: 5.
 4 Kennedy 1987: 5.
 5 Kennedy 1987: 5.
 6 Kennedy 1987: 5.
 7 Vickers 1982: 250.
 8 Vickers 1982: 250–1.
 9 Vickers 1982: 251.
10 Eliot 1930: 30.
11 Kennedy 1972: 54.
12 MacKendrick 1989: 16.
13 MacKendrick 1989: 14.
14 Jordan 1860: 80 no. 1.
15 Backman 1987: vii–viii.

16 Rorty 1980: 366.
17 Backman 1987: xi.
18 McKeon 1987: 7.
19 Worthington 1994a: viii.
20 McKeon 1987: 7.
21 Backman 1987: xxii–xxiii.
22 McKeon 1987: 12–13.
23 Backman 1987: xxviii.
24 See also Winterbottom 1982: 59–69, who argues that the declamation schools of the early empire had good results in training students and that the unreality of the topics helped to develop skills in invention.
25 Champlin 1980: 2.
26 Champlin 1980: 2.
27 Grant 1994: 84–5.
28 See, e.g., Haines 1920: 1.xviii; Henderson 1955: 256–67.
29 Haines 1920: 1.xi–xvi, xliii–li; Reynolds 1983b.
30 Champlin 1980: 2.
31 Brock 1911: 1–7, 159–160.
32 Champlin 1980: 29.
33 Champlin 1980: 2.
34 Haines 1920: 1.xxxiv; Grant 1994: 86.
35 Champlin 1980: 57.
36 Grimal 1992: 255.
37 Champlin 1980: 57.
38 Champlin 1980: 57.
39 Mommsen 1874: 198–217.
40 Russell 1990: 13.
41 Champlin 1980: 3.
42 Goodyear 1987: 676–7.
43 Reference to the works of Fronto are to the edition of Haines 1920. All translations are my own.
44 Russell 1990: 16.
45 Kennedy 1972: 594.
46 See Pepe 1958: 12–25. Another example of this is Marcus' use of the noun *conciliatrix* ('conciliator', *Ad M. Caes.* 4.6), which is found in Plautus and Lucilius but used most frequently by Cicero.
47 Fantham 1972: 181.
48 Fantham 1972: 219.
49 McKeon 1987: 24.

Bibliography

Adler, A. (ed.) (1928–38) *Suidae Lexicon*. Leipzig.

Ahl, F. M. (1986) 'The *Thebaid*: A Reconsideration', *Aufstieg und Niedergang der römischen Welt* 2.32.5: 2803–912.

Alberte, A. (1993) '*Dialogus de Oratoribus* Versus *Institutio Oratoria*', *Minerva* 7: 255–67.

Albrecht, M. von (1995) *Meister römischer Prosa*. 3rd edn. Tübingen.

Alexander, M. C. (1985) '*Praemia* in the *Quaestiones* of the Late Republic', *Classical Philology* 80: 20–32.

Alexander, W. H. (1934–5) 'The Professor's Deadly Vengeance', *The University of Toronto Quarterly* 4: 239–58.

Anderson, W. S. (1982) *Essays on Roman Satire*. Princeton.

Ardener, S. (ed.) (1993) *Women and Space: Ground Rules and Social Maps*. Oxford.

Astin, A. (1978) *Cato the Censor*. Oxford.

Atherton, C. (1988) 'Hand over Fist: The Failure of Stoic Rhetoric', *Classical Quarterly* 38: 392–427.

Austin, R. G. (1948) *Quintiliani Institutionis Oratoriae Liber XII*. Oxford.

Axer, J. (1980) *The Style and the Composition of Cicero's Speech 'Pro Q. Roscio Comoedo'*. Warsaw.

—— (1989) 'Tribunal–Stage–Arena: Modelling of the Communication Situation in M. Tullius Cicero's Judicial Speeches', *Rhetorica* 7: 299–311.

Backman, M. (ed.) (1987) *Rhetoric: Essays in Invention and Discovery*. Woodbridge.

Badian, E. (1966) 'The Early Historians', in Dorey 1966: 1–38.

Balsdon, J. P. V. D. (1979) *Romans and Aliens*. Chapel Hill.

Barnes, T. D. (1986) 'The Significance of Tacitus' *Dialogus de Oratoribus*', *Harvard Studies in Classical Philology* 90: 225–44.

Bartsch, S. (1994) *Actors in the Audience: Theatricality and Doublespeak from Nero to Hadrian*. Cambridge, Mass.

Barwick, K. (1954) 'Der *Dialogus de Oratoribus* des Tacitus: Motiv und Zeit seiner Entstehung', *Sitzungsberichte der Sächsische Akademie der Wissenschaften, Leipzig. Philologisch-Historische Klasse* 101.4.

Bauman, R. A. (1983) *Lawyers in Roman Republican Politics. A Study of the Roman Jurists in Their Political Setting: 316–82 BC*. Munich.

246

—— (1985) *Lawyers in Roman Transitional Politics: A Study of the Roman Jurists in Their Political Setting in the Late Republic and Triumvirate.* Munich.

—— (1989) *Lawyers and Politics in the Early Roman Empire: A Study of Relations Between the Roman Jurists and the Emperors from Augustus to Hadrian.* Munich.

Beacham, R. C. (1992) *The Roman Theater and Its Audience.* Cambridge, Mass.

Beard, M. (1980) 'The Sexual Status of Vestal Virgins', *Journal of Roman Studies* 70: 12–27.

Beard, M. and Crawford, M. (1985) *Rome in the Late Republic.* Ithaca, NY.

Beard, M. *et al.* (1991) *Literacy in the Roman World.* Ann Arbor.

Beare, W. (1964) *The Roman Stage: A Short History of Latin Drama in the Time of the Republic.* 3rd edn. London.

Bers, V. (1994) 'Rhetoric and Tragedy', in Worthington 1994a: 176–95.

Betts, J. H., Hooker, T. J. and Green, J. R. (eds) (1986) *Studies in Honour of T. B. L. Webster.* Bristol.

Bing, P. (1988) *The Well-Read Muse: Present and Past in Callimachus and the Hellenistic Poets.* Göttingen.

Binns, J. W. (ed.) (1973) *Ovid.* London.

Bloom, H. (1994) *The Western Canon: The Books and Schools of the Ages.* New York.

Bloomer, M. (1995) 'Schooling in Persona'. Paper presented at a conference on 'Creating Roman Identity: Subjectivity and Self-Fashioning in Latin Literature' held on 9 September 1995 at the University of California, Berkeley.

—— (forthcoming) 'Whose Speech? Whose History? A Preface to the History of Declamation', in Habinek and Schiesaro (forthcoming).

Bonner, S. F. (1939) *The Literary Treatises of Dionysius of Halicarnassus.* Cambridge.

—— (1949) *Roman Declamation in the Late Republic and Early Empire.* Liverpool.

—— (1968) 'Roman Oratory', in Platnauer 1968: 416–64.

—— (1977) *Education in Ancient Rome.* Berkeley.

Booth, W. C. (1961) *The Rhetoric of Fiction.* Chicago.

—— (1974a) *A Rhetoric of Irony.* Chicago.

—— (1974b) *Modern Dogma and the Rhetoric of Assent.* South Bend.

Bowra, M. (1945) *From Virgil to Milton.* London.

Boyle, A. J. (ed.) (1995) *Roman Literature and Ideology: Ramus Essays for J. P. Sullivan.* Bendigo.

Braden, G. (1985) *Renaissance Tragedy and the Senecan Tradition.* New Haven.

Brandes, S. (1981) 'Like Wounded Stags: Male Sexual Ideology in an Andalusian Town', in Ortner and Whitehead 1981: 216–39.

Braund, S. H. (ed.) (1989a) *Satire and Society in Ancient Rome.* Exeter.

—— (1989b) 'City and Country in Roman Satire', in Braund 1989a: 23–47.

—— (1992) 'Juvenal: Misogynist or Misogamist?', *Journal of Roman Studies* 82: 71–86.

Braund, S. M. (1996) *Juvenal: Satires Book I.* Cambridge.

—— (forthcoming) 'A Passion Unconsoled? Grief and Anger in Juvenal, Satire 13', in Braund and Gill (1997).

Braund, S. M. and Gill, C. (eds) (1997) *The Passions in Roman Thought and Literature*. Cambridge.

Bretone, M. (1992) *Storia del diritto romano*. Bari.

Brink, C. O. (1989) 'Quintilian's *De Causis Corruptae Eloquentiae* and Tacitus' *Dialogus de Oratoribus*', *Classical Quarterly* 39: 472–503.

Brock, M. D. (1911) *Studies in Fronto and His Age*. Cambridge.

Brugnoli, G. (1959) 'Quintiliano, Seneca e il *De Causis Corruptae Eloquentiae*', *Orpheus* 6: 29–41.

Brzoska, J. (1883) *De Canone Decem Oratorum Atticorum Quaestiones*. Diss. Breslau.

Butler, J. (1990) *Gender Trouble: Feminism and the Subversion of Identity*. New York.

Buxton, R. G. A. (1982) *Persuasion in Greek Tragedy: A Study of Peitho*. Cambridge.

Cairns, F. (1972) *Generic Composition in Greek and Roman Poetry*. Edinburgh.

Calboli, G. (ed.) (1969) *Cornifici Rhetorica ad Herennium*. Bologna.

—— (1972) 'L'oratore M. Antonio e la *Rhetorica ad Herennium*', *Giornale Italiano di Filologia* 3 (1972): 120–77.

—— (ed.) (1978) *M. Porci Catonis Oratio pro Rhodiensibus, Catone, l'Oriente Greco e gli Imprenditori Romani: Introduzione, Edizione Critica dei Frammenti, Traduzione e Commento*. Bologna.

—— (1982) 'La retorica preciceroniana e la politica a Roma', in Reverdin and Grange 1982: 41–108.

—— (1993) 'Zur Textüberlieferung der *Rhetorica ad C. Herennium*', in Montefusco 1993: 1–18.

Cameron, A. (ed.) (1989) *History as Text: The Writing of Ancient History*. London.

Campbell, D. A. (1972) *Greek Lyric Poetry: A Selection of Early Greek Lyric, Elegiac and Iambic Poetry*. London.

Canter, H. V. (1925) *The Rhetorical Elements in the Tragedies of Seneca*. Urbana.

Caplan, H. (ed. and tr.) (1954) *[Cicero] Ad C. Herennium De Ratione Dicendi (Rhetorica ad Herennium)*. London.

Carpenter, R. (1995) *History as Rhetoric: Style, Narrative, and Persuasion*. Columbia.

Carson, A. (1986) *Eros the Bittersweet: An Essay*. Princeton.

Carter, J. G. (1910) *Quintilian's Didactic Metaphors*. Diss. New York.

Cassin, B. (1990) 'Bonnes et mauvaises rhétoriques: De platon à Perelman', in Meyer and Lempereur 1990: 17–37.

Champlin, E. (1980) *Fronto and Antonine Rome*. Cambridge, Mass.

Chassignet, M. (ed.) (1986) *Caton: Les Origines*. Paris.

Chierchia, G. (1992) 'Anaphora and Dynamic Binding', *Linguistics and Philosophy* 15: 111–83.

Chomsky, N. (1991) 'Some Notes on Economy of Derivation and Representation', in Freidin 1991: 417–54.

Christes, J. (1979) *Sklaven und Freigelassene als grammatiker und Philologen im antiken Rom.* Wiesbaden.

Chroust, A. H. (1973) *Aristotle: New Light on His Life and on Some of His Lost Works.* 2 vols. Notre Dame.

Citroni, M. (1989) 'Marziale e la Letteratura per i Saturnali (poetica dell' intrattenimento e cronologia della pubblicazione dei libri)', *Illinois Classical Studies* 14: 201–26.

Clarke, M. L. (1953) *Rhetoric at Rome: A Historical Survey.* London.

Clay, J. Strauss, Mitsis, P. and Schiesaro, A. (eds) (1994) *Mega Nepios: The Addressee in Didactic Epic.* Pisa.

Cloud, J. D. (1989) 'Satirists and the Law', in Braund 1989a: 49–67.

Coarelli, F. (1968) 'Il tempio di Bellona', *Bullettino della Commissione Archeologica Comunale in Roma* 80: 37–72.

Coffey, M. (1986) 'Notes on the History of Augustan and Early Imperial Tragedy', in Betts *et al.* 1986: 46–52.

Coffey, M. and Mayer, R. (ed.) (1990) *Seneca: Phaedra.* Cambridge.

Conte, G. B. (tr. C. Segal *et al.*) (1986) *The Rhetoric of Imitation: Genre and Poetic Memory in Virgil and Other Latin Poets.* Ithaca, NY.

—— (tr. G. W. Most) (1994) *Genres and Readers: Lucretius, Love Elegy, Pliny's Encyclopedia.* Baltimore.

Corbeill, A. (1990) *Political Humor in the Late Roman Republic: Romans Defining Themselves.* Diss. Berkeley.

—— (1996) *Controlling Laughter: Political Humor in the Late Roman Republic.* Princeton.

Cornell, T. J. (1986) 'The Formation of the Historical Tradition of Early Rome', in Moxon *et al.* 1986: 67–86.

Cousin, J. (1975) 'Quintilien et le théâtre', *Actes du IXᵉ Congrès Association Guillaume Budé*: 459–67. Paris.

Cova, P. V. (1989) *Il poeta Vario.* Milan.

Cox, A. (1969) 'Didactic Poetry', in Higginbotham 1969: 24–161.

Craig, C. P. (1993) *Form As Argument in Cicero's Speeches: A Study of Dilemma.* Atlanta.

Cresswell, M. J. (1973) *Logics and Languages.* London.

Crook, J. A. (1995) *Legal Advocacy in the Roman World.* London.

Currie, H. MacL. (1981) 'Ovid and the Roman Stage', *Aufstieg und Niedergang der römischen Welt* 2.31.4: 2701–42.

D'Alton, J. F. (1931) *Roman Literary Theory and Criticism.* New York.

Daviault, A. (1980) *Comoedia Togata: Fragments.* Paris.

David, J.-M. (1992) *Le Patronat judiciaire au dernier siècle de la république romaine.* Rome.

De Decker, J. (1913) *Juvenalis Declamans.* Ghent.

Deroux, C. (ed.) (1992) *Studies in Latin Literature and Roman History* 6. Brussels.

Dihle, A. (1977) 'Der Beginn des Attizismus', *Antike und Abendland* 23: 162–77.

—— (tr. M. Malzahn) (1994) *Greek and Latin Literature of the Roman Empire: From Augustus to Justinian.* London.

Dilts, M. R. (ed.) (1983) *Scholia Demosthenica* 1. Leipzig.

—— (ed.) (1992) *Scholia in Aeschinem.* Stuttgart/Leipzig.

BIBLIOGRAPHY

Dominik, W. J. (1994) *The Mythic Voice of Statius: Power and Politics in the Thebaid.* Leiden.

Dorey, T. A. (ed.) (1966) *The Latin Historians.* London.

Douglas, A. E. (1956) 'Cicero, Quintilian, and the Canon of Ten Attic Orators', *Mnemosyne* 9: 30–40.

—— (1957) 'A Ciceronian Contribution to Rhetorical Theory', *Eranos* 55: 18–26.

—— (1966) *M. Tulli Ciceronis Brutus.* Oxford.

duBois, P. (1982) *History, Rhetorical Description and the Epic from Homer to Spenser.* Cambridge.

Duckworth, G. E. (1994) *The Nature of Roman Comedy: A Study in Popular Entertainment.* 2nd edn. Princeton.

Dumont, J.-C. (1975) 'Cicéron et le théâtre', *Actes du IXe Congrès Association Guillaume Budé*: 424–9. Paris.

Dupont, F. (1985) *L'Acteur-roi, ou le théâtre dans la Rome antique.* Paris.

Eden, P. T. (1984) *Seneca Apocolocyntosis.* Cambridge.

Edwards, C. (1993) *The Politics of Immorality in Ancient Rome.* Cambridge.

—— (forthcoming) 'Unspeakable Professions: Public Performance and Prostitution', in Hallett and Skinner (forthcoming).

Eilberg-Schwartz, H. and Doniger, W. (eds) (1995) *Off with Her Head! The Denial of Women's Identity in Myth, Religion, and Culture.* Berkeley.

Elderkin, G. W. (1906) *Aspects of the Speech in the Later Greek Epic.* Diss. Johns Hopkins.

Eliot, T.S. (1930) *The Sacred Wood.* New York.

Fairweather, J. (1981) *Seneca the Elder.* Cambridge.

Fantham, E. (1972) *Comparative Studies in Republican Latin Imagery.* Toronto.

—— (1975) 'Sex, Status, and Survival in Hellenistic Athens: A Study of Women in New Comedy', *Phoenix* 29: 44–74.

—— (1978) 'Imitation and Decline: Rhetorical Theory and Practice in the First Century After Christ', *Classical Philology* 73: 102–16.

—— (ed.) (1982) *Seneca's Troades: A Literary Introduction with Text, Translation and Commentary.* Princeton.

—— (1989a) 'Latin Criticism of the Early Empire', in Kennedy 1989: 275–96.

—— (1989b) 'Mime: The Missing Link in Roman Literary History', *Classical World* 82: 153–63.

—— (1995) 'The Concept of Nature and Human Nature in Quintilian's Psychology and Theory of Instruction', *Rhetorica* 13: 125–36.

Finnegan, R. (1977) *Oral Poetry: Its Nature, Significance, and Social Context.* Cambridge.

Fitzgerald, W. (1988) 'Power and Impotence in Horace's *Epodes*', *Ramus* 17: 176–91.

—— (1992) 'Catullus and the Reader: The Erotics of Poetry', *Arethusa* 25: 419–43.

—— (1995) *Catullan Provocations: Lyric Poetry and the Drama of Position.* Berkeley.

Foulon, A. and Reydellet, M. (eds) (1992) *Au miroir de la culture antique. Mélanges offerts au Président René Marache.* Rennes.

250

Fraenkel, E. (ed.) (1962) *Aeschylus: Agamemnon*. Oxford.

Frank, M. (ed.) (1995) *Seneca's Phoenissae*. Leiden.

Fuss, D. (ed.) (1991) *Inside/Out: Lesbian Theories, Gay Theories*. New York.

Freidin, R. (ed.) (1991) *Principles and Parameters in Comparative Grammar*. London.

Garton, C. (1972) *Personal Aspects of the Roman Theatre*. Toronto.

Geffcken, K. (1973) *Comedy in the Pro Caelio, with an Appendix on the In Clodium et Curionem*. Leiden.

Gelzer, M. (1964) *Kleine Schriften* 3. Wiesbaden.

Gelzer, T. (1970) 'Quintilians Urteil über Seneca: Eine rhetorische Analyse', *Museum Helveticum* 27: 212–23.

Gilmore, D. D. (1990) *Manhood in the Making*. New Haven.

Gleason, K. (1994) 'Porticus Pompeiana: A New Perspective on the First Public Park of Ancient Rome', *Journal of Garden History* 14: 13–27.

Gleason, M. W. (1995) *Making Men: Sophists and Self-Presentation in Ancient Rome*. Princeton.

Goldberg, S. M. (1983) 'Terence, Cato, and the Rhetorical Prologue', *Classical Philology* 78: 198–211.

—— (1986) *Understanding Terence*. Princeton.

Golden, M. and Toohey, P. (eds) (1997) *Inventing Ancient Culture: Historicism, Periodization, and the Ancient World*. London.

Goody, Jack and Watt, I. (eds) (1963) 'The Consequences of Literacy', *Comparative Studies in Society and History* 5: 304–45. = Goody, J. (ed.) (1968) *Literacy in Traditional Societies*: 27–68. Cambridge.

Goodyear, F. R. D. (1987) 'Rhetoric and Scholarship: Fronto', in Kenney 1987: 676–8.

Gotoff, H. C. (1993) 'Oratory: The Art of Illusion', *Harvard Studies in Classical Philology* 95: 289–313.

Gowers, E. (1994) *The Loaded Table*. Oxford.

Grant, M. (tr.) (1969) *Selected Political Speeches of Cicero*. Harmondsworth.

—— (1994) *The Antonines*. London.

Grant, M. and Kitzinger, R. (eds) (1988) *Civilizations of the Ancient Mediterranean: Greece and Rome*. New York.

Greenblatt, S. (1980) *Renaissance Self-Fashioning*. Chicago.

Greenidge, A. H. J. (1901) *Roman Public Life*. New York.

Griffin, J. (1976) 'Augustan Poetry and the Life of Luxury', *Journal of Roman Studies* 66: 87–104.

Grilli, A. (ed.) (1962) *M. Tulli Ciceronis Hortensius*. Milan.

Grimal, P. (1992) 'La Philosophie de M. Cornelius Fronto', in Foulon and Reydellet 1992: 251–7.

Grimaldi, W. M. A. (1980) *Aristotle, Rhetoric I: A Commentary*. New York.

Gross, N. P. (1985) *Amatory Persuasion in Antiquity: Studies in Theory and Practice*. Newark, NJ.

Grossberg, L., Nelson, C. and Treichler, P. (eds) (1992) *Cultural Studies*. New York.

Gruen, E. S. (1990) *Studies in Greek Culture and Roman Policy*. Leiden.

—— (1992) *Culture and National Identity in Republican Rome*. Ithaca, NY.

Gunderson, E. (1996) *Contested Subjects: Oratorical Theory and the Body*. Diss. Berkeley.

—— (forthcoming) 'Discovering the Body in Roman Oratory', in *Gender and History*.

Güngerich, R. (1951) 'Der *Dialogus* des Tacitus und Quintilians *Institutio Oratoria*', *Classical Philology* 46: 159–64.

Habinek, T. N. (1994) 'Ideology for an Empire in the Prefaces to Cicero's Dialogues', *Ramus* 23: 55–67.

Habinek, T. N. and Schiesaro, A. (eds) (forthcoming) *The Roman Cultural Revolution*. Cambridge.

Haines, C. R. (ed. and tr.) (1920) *The Correspondence of Marcus Cornelius Fronto*. 2 vols. London.

Hallett, J. P. (1989) 'Women as "Same" and "Other" in the Classical Roman Elite', *Helios* 16: 59–78.

Hallett, J. P. and Skinner, M. B. (eds) (forthcoming) *Roman Sexualities*. Princeton.

Halliwell, S. (1994) 'Rhetoric and Philosophy', in Worthington 1994a: 222–43.

Halm, K. (ed.) (1868–9) *M. Fabi Quintiliani Institutionis Oratoriae Libri Duodecim*. 2 vols. Leipzig.

Hanson, J. A. (1959) *Roman Theater–Temples*. Princeton.

Harding, P. (1994) 'Rhetoric and Comedy', in Worthington 1994a: 196–221.

Harris, W. V. (1989) *Ancient Literacy*. Cambridge, Mass.

Hartmann, P. (1891) *De Canone Decem Oratorum*. Diss. Göttingen.

Havelock, E. A. (1963) *Preface to Plato*. Oxford.

—— (1982) *The Literate Revolution in Greece and its Cultural Consequences*. Princeton.

—— (1986) *The Muse Learns to Write: Reflections on Orality and Literacy from Antiquity to the Present*. New Haven.

Hawkes, T. (1972) *Metaphor*. London.

Heldmann, K. (1980) 'Dekadenz und literarischer Forschritt bei Quintilian und bei Tacitus', *Poetica* 12: 1–23.

—— (1982) *Antike Theorien über Entwicklung und Verfall der Redekunst*. Munich.

Henderson, C. (1955) 'Cato's Pine Cones and Seneca's Plums', *Transactions of the American Philological Association* 86: 256–67.

Henderson, J. (1987) 'Lucan/The Word at War', *Ramus* 16: 122–64.

—— (1994) 'On Getting Rid of Kings: Horace, *Satire* 1.7', *Classical Quarterly* 44: 146–70.

Hendrickson, G. L. (1926) 'Cicero's Correspondence with Brutus and Calvus on Oratorical Style', *American Journal of Philology* 47: 234–58.

Herzfeld, M. (1985) *The Poetics of Manhood: Contest and Identity in a Cretan Mountain Village*. Princeton.

Hewitt, N., O'Barr, J. and Rosebaugh, N. (eds) (1996) *Talking Gender: Public Images, Personal Journeys, and Political Critiques*. Chapel Hill.

Higginbotham, J. (ed.) (1969) *Greek and Latin Literature: A Comparative Study*. London.

Highet, G. (1972) *The Speeches in Vergil's Aeneid*. Princeton.

Hinds, S. (1987a) *The Metamorphosis of Persephone: Ovid and the Self-Conscious Muse*. Cambridge.

—— (1987b) 'Generalising about Ovid', *Ramus* 16: 4–31.

Holdsworth, C. and Wiseman, T. P. (eds) (1986) *The Inheritance of Historiography: 350–900*. Exeter.

Hollis, A.S. (1973) 'The *Ars Amatoria* and *Remedia Amoris*', in Binns 1973: 84–115.

—— (1977) *Ovid, Ars Amatoria: Book I*. Oxford.

Hopkinson, N. (1988) *A Hellenistic Anthology*. Cambridge.

Hubbell, H. (ed. and tr.) (1949) *Cicero: De Inventione, De Optimo Genere Oratorum, Topica*. London.

Hughes, J. J. (1987) *Comedic Borrowing in Selected Orations of Cicero*. Diss. Iowa.

—— (1992a) 'A "Paraklausithyron" in Cicero's *Second Philippic*', in Deroux 1992: 215–27.

—— (1992b) 'Piso's Eyebrows', *Mnemosyne* 45: 234–7.

Izenour, G. (1992) *Roofed Theaters of Classical Antiquity*. New Haven.

Jacoby, F. (ed.) (1923–) *Die Fragmente der griechischen Historiker*. Leiden.

Jal, P. (ed. and trans.) (1967) *Florus: Oeuvres* 2. Paris.

Johnson, W. R. (1994) 'Information and Form: Homer, Achilles, and Statius', in Oberhelman *et al.* 1994: 25–39.

Jones, A. H. M. (1972) *The Criminal Courts of the Roman Republic and Principate*. Oxford.

Jordan, H. (1860) *M. Catonis Praeter Librum de Re Rustica Quae Exstant*. Leipzig.

Joshel, S. R. (1992) 'The Body Female and the Body Politic: Livy's Lucretia and Verginia', in Richlin 1992b: 112–30.

Kallendorf, C. (1989) *In Praise of Aeneas: Virgil and Epideictic Rhetoric in the Early Italian Renaissance*. Hanover.

Kaster, R. A. (ed. and tr.) (1995) *C. Suetonius Tranquillus: De Grammaticis et Rhetoribus*. Oxford.

Kellum, B. (forthcoming) 'Concealing/Revealing: Gender and the Play of Meaning in Augustan Rome', in Habinek and Schiesaro (forthcoming).

Kennedy, D. (1993) *The Arts of Love: Five Studies in the Discourse of Roman Love Elegy*. Cambridge.

Kennedy, G. A. (1963) *The Art of Persuasion in Greece*. Princeton.

—— (1969) *Quintilian*. New York.

—— (1972) *The Art of Rhetoric in the Roman World: 300 B.C.–A.D. 300*. Princeton.

—— (1987) *Classical Rhetoric and its Christian and Secular Tradition from Ancient to Modern Times*. Chapel Hill.

—— (ed.) (1989) *Cambridge History of Literary Criticism* 1. Cambridge.

—— (1994) *A New History of Classical Rhetoric*. Princeton.

Kenney, E. J. (1961) *P. Ovidi Nasonis Amores, Medicamina Faciei Femineae, Ars Amatoria, Remedia Amoris*. Oxford.

—— (1963) 'Juvenal: Satirist or Rhetorician?', *Latomus* 22: 704–20.

—— (1987) *Cambridge History of Classical Literature* 2: *Latin Literature* Cambridge.

King, K. L. (ed.) (forthcoming) *Women and Goddess Traditions*. Minneapolis.

Kirby, J. T. (1990a) 'The "Great Triangle" in Early Greek Rhetoric and Poetics', *Rhetorica* 8: 213–28.

—— (1990b) *The Rhetoric of Cicero's Pro Cluentio*. Amsterdam.

—— (1992) 'Rhetoric and Poetics in Hesiod', *Ramus* 21: 34–60.

Koestenbaum, W. (1991) 'The Queen's Throat: (Homo)sexuality and the Art of Singing', in Fuss 1991: 205–34.

Köhnken, A. (1973) 'Das Problem der Ironie bei Tacitus', *Museum Helveticum* 30: 32–50.

Kowalski, G. (1947) 'De Phrynes Pectore Nudato', *Eos* 42: 50–62.

Kröhnert, O. (1897) *Canonesne Poetarum Scriptorum Artificum Per Antiquitatem Fuerunt?* Diss. Königsberg.

Kühnert, F. (1964) 'Quintilians Stellung zu der Beredsamkeit seiner Zeit', *Listy Filologické* 87: 33–50.

Labate, M. (1984) *L'arte de farsi amore: Modelli culturali e progetto didascalico nell'elegia ovidiana.* Pisa.

Lakoff, G. (1987) *Women, Fire, and Dangerous Things: What Categories Reveal About the Mind.* Chicago.

Lakoff, G. and Johnson, M. (1980) *Metaphors We Live By.* Chicago.

Laureys, M. (1991) 'Quintilian's Judgement of Seneca and the Scope and Purpose of *Inst.*, 10,1', *Antike und Abendland* 37: 100–25.

Leach, E. W. (1988) *The Rhetoric of Space: Literary and Artistic Representations of Landscape in Republican and Augustan Rome.* Princeton.

Leeman, A. D. (1963) *Orationis Ratio: The Stylistic Theories and Practice of the Roman Orators, Historians and Philosophers.* Amsterdam.

—— (1975) 'The Structure of Cicero's *De Oratore* I', in Michel and Verdière 1975: 140–9.

Leeman, A. D., Pinkster, H. *et al.* (1981–9) *De Oratore Libri III.* 3 vols (to date). Heidelberg.

Lefèvre, E. (1985) 'Die philosophische Bedeutung der Seneca-Tragödie am Beispiel des "Thyestes"', *Aufstieg und Niedergang der römischen Welt* 2.32.2: 1263–83.

Leo, F. (1878) *De Senecae Tragoediis Observationes Criticae.* Berlin.

—— (1898) Review of A. Gudeman, *Taciti Dialogus de Oratoribus* (Boston, Mass. 1894), *Göttingische Gelehrte Anzeigen* 160: 169–88. = *Ausgewählte Kleine Schriften* 2 (1960): 277–98. Rome.

Lindsay, W. M. (1903) *Nonius Marcellus: De Compendiosa Doctrina.* Leipzig.

Lipscomb, H. C. (1909) *Aspects of the Speech in the Later Roman Epic.* Diss. Johns Hopkins.

Lloyd, G. E. R. (ed.) (1978) *Hippocratic Writings.* London.

Lord, A. B. (1960) *The Singer of Tales.* Cambridge, Mass.

Lowe, J. C. B. (1985) 'Cooks in Plautus', *Classical Antiquity* 4: 72–102.

Luce, T. J. (ed.) (1982) *Ancient Writers: Greece and Rome* 2. New York.

—— (1993) 'Reading and Response in the *Dialogus*', in Luce and Woodman 1993: 11–38.

Luce, T. J. and Woodman, A. J. (eds) (1993) *Tacitus and the Tacitean Tradition.* Princeton.

MacKendrick, P. (1989) *The Philosophical Books of Cicero.* New York.

McKeon, R. (1987) 'The Uses of Rhetoric in a Technological Age', in Backman 1987: 1–24.

MacMullen, R. (1982) 'Roman Attitudes to Greek Love', *Historia* 31: 484–502.

Malcovati, H. (ed.) (1975) *Oratorum Romanorum Fragmenta Liberae Rei Publicae*. 4th edn. Turin.

Masters, J. (1992) *Poetry and Civil War in Lucan's Bellum Civile*. Cambridge.

Matthiessen, K. (1970) 'Der *Dialogus* des Tacitus und Cassius Dio 67,12', *L'Antiquité Classique* 39: 168–77.

May, J. M. (1988) *Trials of Character: The Eloquence of Ciceronian Ethos*. Chapel Hill.

Mayor, J. E. B. (1872) *Thirteen Satires of Juvenal* 1. London.

Mellor, R. (1988) 'Roman Historiography and Biography', in Grant and Kitzinger 1988: 1541–62.

Mette-Dittmann, A. (1991) *Die Ehegesetze des Augustus*. Stuttgart.

Meyer, M. and Lempereur, A. (eds) (1990) *Figures et conflits rhétoriques*. Brussels.

Michel, A. (1960) *Rhétorique et philosophie chez Cicéron*. Paris.

—— (1962) *Le Dialogue des orateurs de Tacite et la philosophie de Cicéron*. Paris.

Michel, A. and Verdière, R. (eds) (1975) *Ciceroniana: Hommages à Kazimierz Kumaniecki*. Leiden.

Millar, F. (1977) *The Emperor in the Roman World*. London.

—— (1986) 'Politics, Persuasion and the People Before the Social War (150–90 B.C.)', *Journal of Roman Studies* 76: 1–11.

Miller, J. F. (1994) 'Apostrophe, Aside, and the Didactic Addressee: Poetic Strategies in *Ars Amatoria* III', in Clay *et al.* 1994: 231–42.

Mommsen, T. (1874) 'Die Chronologie der Briefe Frontonis', *Hermes* 8: 198–217.

Montefusco, L. Calboli (1986) *La dottrina degli 'status' nella retorica greca e romana*. Hildesheim.

—— (ed.) (1993) *Papers on Rhetoric* 1. Bologna.

Moore, T. J. (1991) '*Palliata Togata*: Plautus, *Curculio* 462–86', *American Journal of Philology* 112: 343–62.

Morford, M. P. O. (1967) *The Poet Lucan: Studies in Rhetorical Epic*. Oxford.

Moxon, I. S., Smart, J. D. and Woodman, A. J. (eds) (1986) *Past Perspectives: Studies in Greek and Roman Historical Writing*. Cambridge.

Müller, C. F. W. (1890) *M. Tullii Ciceronis Opera* 4.3. Leipzig.

Murgia, C. (1980) 'The Date of Tacitus' *Dialogus*', *Harvard Studies in Classical Philology* 85: 99–125.

Myerowitz, M. (1985) *Ovid's Games of Love*. Detroit.

Narducci, E. (ed. and trans.) (1995a) *Cicerone: Bruto*. Milan.

—— (1995b) *Processi ai politici nella Roma antica*. Rome.

Nauck, A. (1964) *Tragicorum Graecorum Fragmenta. Supplementum Adiecit B. Snell*. Hildesheim.

Nicolet, C. (1980) *The World of the Citizen in Republican Rome*. Berkeley.

—— (1991) *Space, Geography, and Politics in the Early Roman Empire*. Ann Arbor.

Norden, E. (1915) *Die Antike Kunstprosa* 1. 3rd edn. Leipzig/Berlin.

Novara, A. (1986) 'Cultura: Cicéron et l'origine de la métaphore latine', *Bulletin de l' Association Guillaume Budé*: 51–66.

Oberhelman, S. M., Kelly, V. and Golsan, R. J. (eds) (1994) *Epic and Epoch: Essays on the Interpretation and History of a Genre*. Lubbock.

Ofenloch, E. (ed.) (1907) *Caecilii Calactini Fragmenta*. Leipzig.

Oliensis, E. (forthcoming) 'Horace, Maecenas, and the Erotics of Patronage', in Hallett and Skinner (forthcoming).

Ortner, S. B. and Whitehead, H. (eds) (1981) *Sexual Meanings*. Cambridge.

O'Sullivan, N. (1992) *Alcidamas, Aristophanes and the Beginnings of Greek Stylistic Theory*. Stuttgart.

Parker, H. N. (1992) 'Love's Body Anatomized: The Ancient Erotic Handbooks and the Rhetoric of Sexuality' in Richlin 1992b: 90–111.

Parks, E. P. (1945) *The Roman Rhetorical Schools as a Preparation for the Courts under the Early Empire*. Baltimore.

Pepe, L. (1958) 'Catone Maggiore e la scuola di Frontone', *Giornale Italiano di Filologia* 11: 12–25.

Peter, H. (1914) *Historicorum Romanorum Reliquae* 1. 2nd edn. Leipzig.

Peterson, W. (ed.) (1892) *M. Fabi Quintiliani Institutionis Oratoriae Liber Decimus*. Oxford.

Pfeiffer, R. (1968) *History of Classical Scholarship: From the Beginnings to the End of the Hellenistic Age*. Oxford.

Pickard-Cambridge, A. (1968) *The Dramatic Festivals of Athens*. Oxford.

Platnauer, M. (ed.) (1968) *Fifty Years (and Twelve) of Classical Scholarship*. Oxford.

Pöhlmann, E. (1973) 'Charakteristika des römischen Lehrgedichts', *Aufstieg und Niedergang der römischen Welt* 1.3: 813–901.

Porter, J. I. (ed.) (forthcoming) *Constructing the Ancient Body*. Ann Arbor.

Quinn, K. (1979) *Texts and Contexts: The Roman Writers and Their Audience*. London.

Radin, M. (1911) 'Literary References in Cicero's Orations', *Classical Journal* 6: 209–17.

Ramage, E. S. (1973) *Urbanitas: Ancient Sophistication and Refinement*. Norman.

Raschke, W. J. (1987) '*Arma Pro Amico*: Lucilian Satire at the Crisis of the Roman Republic', *Hermes* 115: 299–318.

—— (1990) 'The Virtue of Lucilius', *Latomus* 49: 352–69.

Rawson, E. (1985) *Intellectual Life in the Late Roman Republic*. London.

Reverdin, O. and Grange, B. (eds) (1982) *Éloquence et Rhétorique chez Cicéron*. Geneva.

Reynolds, L.D. (ed.) (1983a) *Texts and Transmission*. Oxford.

—— (1983b) 'Fronto', in Reynolds 1983a: 173–4.

Richardson, L. Jr (1987) 'A Note on the Architecture of the *Theatrum Pompei*', *American Journal of Archaeology* 91: 123–6.

Richlin, A. (1992a) *The Garden of Priapus: Sexuality and Aggression in Roman Humor*. 2nd edn. New York.

—— (ed.) (1992b) *Pornography and Representation in Greece and Rome*. London.

—— (1992c) 'Reading Ovid's Rapes', in Richlin 1992b: 158–79.

—— (1992d) 'Roman Oratory, Pornography, and the Silencing of Anita Hill', *Southern California Law Review* 65: 1321–32.

—— (1993) 'Not before Homosexuality: The Materiality of the *Cinaedus* and the Roman Law against Love between Men', *Journal of the History of Sexuality* 3.4: 523–73.

—— (1995) 'Making Up a Woman: The Face of Roman Gender', in Eilberg-Schwartz and Doniger 1995: 185–213.

—— (1996) 'How Putting the Man in Roman Put the Roman in Romance', in Hewitt *et al.* 1996: 14–35.

—— (1997) 'Towards a History of Body History', in Golden and Toohey.

—— (forthcoming a) 'Cicero's Head', in Porter (forthcoming).

—— (forthcoming b) 'Carrying Water in a Sieve: Class and the Body in Roman Women's Religion', in King (forthcoming).

Robb, K. (1994) *Literacy and Paideia in Ancient Greece.* Oxford.

Roberts, W. Rhys (1901) *Dionysius of Halicarnassus: The Three Literary Letters.* Cambridge.

Rorty, R. (1980) *Philosophy and the Mirror of Nature.* Princeton.

Rose, G. (1993) *Feminism and Geography: The Limits of Geographical Knowledge.* Minneapolis.

Rosenmeyer, T. G. (1989) *Senecan Drama and Stoic Cosmology.* Berkeley.

Ross, D. O. Jr (1987) *Virgil's Elements: Physics and Poetry in the Georgics.* Princeton.

Rowe, G. (1966) 'The Portrait of Aeschines in the Oration *On The Crown*', *Transactions of the American Philological Association* 97: 397–406.

—— (1968) 'Demosthenes' *First Philippic*: The Satiric Mode', *Transactions of the American Philological Association* 99: 361–74.

Rudd, N. (1987) *Horace: Satires and Epistles. Persius: Satires.* Harmondsworth.

Russell, D. A. (ed.) (1964) *'Longinus': On the Sublime.* Oxford.

—— (1981) *Criticism in Antiquity.* London.

—— (1983) *Greek Declamation.* Cambridge.

—— (1990) *Antonine Literature.* Oxford.

Russell, D. A. and Wilson, N. G. (eds) (1981) *Menander Rhetor.* Oxford.

Said, E. W. (1979) *Orientalism.* New York.

Santoro L'hoir, F. (1992) *The Rhetoric of Gender Terms.* Leiden.

Schaefler, J. (1884) 'Ciceros Verhältniss zur altrömischen Komödie', *Blätter für das bayerische Gymnasialschulwesen* 20: 285–97.

Schiavone, A. (1987) *Giuristi e nobili nella Roma repubblicana: Il secolo della rivoluzione scientifica nel pensiero giuridico antico.* Bari.

Scott, I. G. (1927) *The Grand Style in the Satires of Juvenal.* Northampton, Mass.

Seel, O. (1977) *Quintilian: Oder die Kunst des Redens und Schweigens.* Stuttgart.

Sharrock, A. (1994) *Seduction and Repetition in Ovid's Ars Amatoria II.* Oxford.

Sinclair, P. (1993) 'The *Sententia* in *Rhetorica ad Herennium*: A Study in the Sociology of Rhetoric', *American Journal of Philology* 114: 561–80.

Skinner, M. B. (1993) '*Ego mulier*: The Construction of Male Sexuality in Catullus 63', *Helios* 20: 107–30.

Skutsch, O. (ed.) (1985) *The Annals of Quintus Ennius*. Oxford.

Slater, N. W. (1985) *Plautus in Performance*. Princeton.

Smith, R. M. (1995) 'A New Look at the Canon of the Ten Attic Orators', *Mnemosyne* 48: 66–79.

Solmsen, F. (1941) 'The Aristotelian Tradition in Ancient Rhetoric', *American Journal of Philology* 62: 35–50, 169–90.

Spain, D. (1992) *Gendered Spaces*. Chapel Hill.

Stambaugh, J. E. (1988) *The Ancient Roman City*. Baltimore.

Stroh, W. (1975) *Taxis und Taktik*. Stuttgart.

Suss, W. (1910) *Ethos: Studien zur alteren griechischen Rhetorik*. Leipzig.

Sussman, L. A. (1984) 'The Elder Seneca and Declamation Since 1900: A Bibliography', *Aufstieg und Niedergang der römischen Welt* 32.1: 557–77.

—— (1994) 'Antony as a *Miles Gloriosus* in Cicero's *Second Philippic*', *Scholia* 3: 53–80.

—— (forthcoming) 'Antony the *Meretrix Audax*: Cicero's Novel Invective in *Philippic* 2.44–46', *Eranos*.

Sutton, D. F. (1984) 'Cicero on Minor Dramatic Forms', *Symbolae Osloenses* 59: 29–36.

—— (1986) *Seneca on the Stage*. Leiden.

Tarrant, R. J. (1978) 'Senecan Drama and its Antecedents', *Harvard Studies in Classical Philology* 82: 213–63.

—— (ed.) (1985) *Seneca's Thyestes: Edited with Introduction and Commentary*. Atlanta.

Thomas, R. (1989) *Oral Tradition and Written Record in Classical Athens*. Cambridge.

—— (1992) *Literacy and Orality in Ancient Greece*. Cambridge.

Thomas, R. F. (1982) *Lands and Peoples in Roman Poetry: The Ethnographical Tradition*. Cambridge.

Thomason, R. H. (ed.) (1974) *Formal Philosophy: Selected Papers of Richard Montague*. New Haven.

Toohey, P. (1992) 'Love, Lovesickness, and Melancholy', *Illinois Classical Studies* 17: 265–86.

—— (1994) 'Epic and Rhetoric', in Worthington 1994a: 153–75.

Trillitzsch, W. (1971) *Seneca im literarischen Urteil der Antike* 1: *Darstellung und Sammlung der Zeugnisse*. Amsterdam.

Untersteiner, M. (1949) *I sofisti*. Turin.

Usener, H. and Radermacher, L. (eds) (1899–1929) *Dionysii Halicarnasei Opuscula*. Leipzig.

Usher, S. (1965) 'Individual Characterization in Lysias', *Eranos* 63: 99–119.

Vasaly, A. (1985) 'The Masks of Rhetoric: Cicero's *Pro Roscio Amerino*', *Rhetorica* 3: 1–20.

—— (1993) *Representations: Images of the World in Ciceronian Oratory*. Berkeley.

Veeser, H. A. (ed.) (1989) *The New Historicism*. Berkeley.

Vickers, B. (ed.) (1982) *Rhetoric Revalued*. Binghamton.

—— (1988) *In Defence of Rhetoric*. Oxford.

Wack, M. F. (1990) *Lovesickness in the Middle Ages: The 'Viaticum' and its Commentaries*. Philadelphia.

Walbank, F. W. (1972) *Polybius*. Berkeley.

Walsh, G. B. (1984) *The Varieties Of Enchantment: Early Greek Views of the Nature and Function of Poetry*. Chapel Hill.

—— (1988) Review of Carson (1986), *Classical Philology* 83: 369–73.

Walsh, P. G. (1962) *Livy: His Historical Aims and Methods*. Cambridge.

Warmington, E. H. (ed. and tr.) (1937) *Remains of Old Latin* 2. London.

—— (ed. and tr.) (1938) *Remains of Old Latin* 3. London.

Watson, P. (1982) 'Ovid and *Cultus*: Ars Amatoria 3.113–28', *Transactions of the American Philological Association* 112: 237–44.

—— (1983) 'Mythological Exempla in Ovid's *Ars Amatoria*', *Classical Philology* 78: 117–26.

Wehrli, F. (ed.) (1967–9) *Die Schule des Aristoteles*. 2nd edn. Basel.

White, H. (1987) *The Content of the Form: Narrative Discourse and Historical Representation*. Baltimore.

Wilamowitz-Moellendorff, U. von (1900a) 'Asianismus und Attizismus', *Hermes* 35: 1–52. = *Kleine Schriften* 3 (1969): 223–77.

—— (1900b) *Die Textgeschichte der griechischen Lyriker*. Berlin.

Wilkins, A. S. (ed.) (1888–92) *M. Tulli Ciceronis De Oratore*. 2nd edn. 3 vols. Oxford.

Williams, C. (forthcoming) *Homosexuality and the Roman Man: A Study in the Cultural Construction of Masculinity*. Oxford.

Williams, G. (1978) *Change and Decline: Roman Literature in the Early Empire*. Berkeley.

—— (1980) *Figures of Thought in Roman Poetry*. New Haven.

Williams, H. L. H. (1951) 'Political Speeches in Athens', *Classical Quarterly* 1: 68–73.

Winkler, J. J. (1990) *The Constraints of Desire: The Anthropology of Sex and Gender in Ancient Greece*. New York.

Winterbottom, M. (1970) *M. Fabi Quintiliani Institutionis Oratoriae Libri Decem*. Oxford.

—— (1974) *The Elder Seneca: Declamations* 1. London.

—— (1980) *Roman Declamation: Extracts with Commentary*. Bristol.

—— (1982) 'Schoolroom and Courtroom', in Vickers 1982: 59–69.

Wiseman, T. P. (1979) *Clio's Cosmetics*. Leicester.

—— (1981) 'Practice and Theory in Roman Historiography', *History* 66: 375–93. = Wiseman, T. P. 1987: 244–62.

—— (1986) 'Introduction: Classical Historiography,' in Holdsworth and Wiseman 1986: 1–6.

—— (1987) *Roman Studies: Literary and Historical Studies*. Liverpool.

—— (1994) *Historiography and Imagination: Eight Essays on Roman Culture*. Exeter.

Wofford, S. L. (1992) *The Choice of Achilles: The Ideology of Figure in the Epic*. Stanford.

Women and Geography Study Group of the IBG. (1984) *Geography and Gender*. London.

Woodman, A. J. (1988) *Rhetoric in Classical Historiography: Four Studies*. London.

259

Wooten, C. (1975) 'Le Développement du style asiatique pendant l'époque hellénistique', *Revue des Études Grecques* 88: 94–104.

Worthington, I. (ed.) (1994a) *Persuasion: Greek Rhetoric in Action*. London.

—— (1994b) 'The Canon of the Ten Attic Orators', in Worthington 1994a: 244–63.

Wright, F. W. (1931) *Cicero and the Theater*. Northampton.

Wyke, M. (1987) 'The Elegiac Woman at Rome', *Proceedings of the Cambridge Philological Society* 33: 153–78.

—— (1995) 'Taking the Woman's Part: Engendering Roman Love Elegy', in Boyle 1995: 110–28.

Zanker, P. (tr. A. Shapiro) (1990) *The Power of Images in the Age of Augustus*. Ann Arbor.

Zillinger, W. (1912) *Cicero und die altrömischen Dichter*. Würzburg.

Zumthor, P. (tr. K. Murphy-Judy) (1990) *Oral Poetry: An Introduction*. Minneapolis.

Zwierlein, O. (1966) *Die Rezitationsdramen Senecas*. Meisenheim am Glan.

General index

This selective index mainly contains the more common names and topics mentioned in the text, although there are a few references to the notes. It does not include the names of modern scholars and ancient works: full details of modern works referred to in the text and in the notes to chapters 1–14 may be found in the bibliography on pp. 246–60; an index of the main passages discussed from ancient works appears on pp. 267–8.

Atticism (Attic/Atticist style) 7–8,
17, 35–46, 59, 84–7, 106–7, 236;
see also Atticist–Asianist
controversy
Atticist–Asianist controversy 17,
44, 46, 84–7, 91–2, 106–7
Augustus (Octavian) 40–1, 95, 115,
167–9
Aurelius, Marcus 235, 238–43

Ballio 190, 196
Brutus, Marcus 17, 38, 106–7, 161–2
Bulbus 192, 195

Caecilius of Calacte 8, 34, 40–6
Caecilius Statius 189, 191
Caelius Rufus, Marcus 92–3, 120,
221
Caesar Strabo, Iulius 83, 168, 187,
194
Caesar, Julius 17, 65, 114–15, 121,
168
Calvus, Gaius Licinius 17, 106–7
canon 7, 57, 60, 65; canon of ten
Attic orators 8, 32–46
Carian rhetoricians 85, 104–5
Carneades 38, 231
Catiline 169; Catilinarian crisis 114
Cato (the elder) 6, 9, 11, 17, 82, 94,
112, 115–17, 151, 154, 184, 217,
223, 231–2, 236, 238, 242–4
Cato (the younger) 62, 148
Catulus, Quintus Lutatius 212,
214, 218, 222–3, 225
Cestius Pius 96–7, 174
Cethegus, Marcus Cornelius 3, 17
Chaerea, Fannius 190, 193, 196
Cicero, Marcus Tullius *passim*;
style of 17, 19–30, 51–2, 54, 57,
64, 106–7
classicicism (classical style) 7, 43,
57, 64, 66
Claudius 121, 163, 169
Clodius, Publius 18, 21–2, 27,
29–30, 117, 121
Cluentius Habitus, Aulus 120,
190–1
Coelius Antipater 11, 222–3
cognitio 121–2

color/colores 152–3, 172–4, 177
Columella 101, 242
comedy 85; and rhetoric 10,
182–96; *see also* Roman New
Comedy
comoediae palliatae 183, 185, 187
comoediae togatae 184–5
conjunction 19, 23–6, 28–9; *see also*
parallelism
consolatio 154–5, 216
contestation: in satire 147–64
controversia 72, 83, 97, 104, 148,
235
Crassus, Lucius Licinius 7, 10, 17,
72–5, 78, 169, 187, 188, 193–4,
214, 222
Crassus, Marcus 92–3
Curiatius Maternus: *see* Maternus
culture: and oratory 7–9, 11, 71–88,
132, 136, 139

declamation 10, 15, 61, 81, 95, 96,
170–4, 179; in satire 147–64
Demetrius of Phalerum 37, 84
Demosthenes 17, 33–4, 42–3, 45,
73, 87, 100, 104, 112, 124, 186,
236
didactic poetry 10, 204–6; and
persuasion 198–9, 202–5, 209
dialectic: and rhetoric 5
Dio of Prusa 33–4, 38–9
Dionysius of Halicarnassus 33–4,
37–43, 45–6
disjunction 19, 23–8, 30; *see also*
parallelism
Domitian 62, 163, 224

elegy 56, 208; as persuasion
199–200, 209
elocutio 46, 50, 200–2, 244; *see also*
lexis, style
enargeia 98, 150, 195
Ennius 3, 52, 73, 162, 169, 223
Ephorus 36, 38
epic 56, 131–44; didactic 204, 206;
differences between Greek and
Roman 131–8; Hellenistic 134;
imperial Greek 133–4; literary
132–5, 138, 143; oral 132–5, 138,

Index locorum

The following is a list of the main passages discussed from ancient works. Passages cited as additional illustration are not included.